FROM DAWN
TILL DUSK

*This book is dedicated to the memory of **Peter Harris** (1943–2007), my brother-in-law, who, with his many highly skilled colleagues, at all levels, was involved in the many programmes made in the Midlands which have given countless hours of entertainment to the people of the whole Region in the Heart of England.*

To them all we owe a debt of gratitude. (See page 210).

FROM DAWN TILL DUSK

A History of Independent Television in the Midlands

JOHN W PETTINGER

FOREWORD BY ALTON DOUGLAS

BREWIN BOOKS

First published by
Brewin Books Ltd, 56 Alcester Road,
Studley, Warwickshire B80 7LG in 2007
www.brewinbooks.com

ISBN: 978-1-85858-418-8 (Paperback)
ISBN: 978-1-85858-408-9 (Hardback)

The moral right of the author has been asserted.

A Cataloguing in Publication Record
for this title is available from the British Library.

Typeset in Bembo
Printed in Great Britain by
Cromwell Press Ltd.

CONTENTS

ACKNOWLEDGEMENTS

This book could not have been written without the work of all those people who have spent much of their lives at whatever level in the production and transmission of programmes; for the millions of viewers across the Midlands and beyond. They are the people who have through their many skills and talents provided the viewers with the enormous mass of programmes that have entertained them, educated them, made them laugh and hopefully made them think from time to time.

They are the people who have always been behind the many thousands of artistes and celebrities who have been the faces on our screens.

There are many pictures in the book and I have endeavoured to get permission to use them, in particular I thank my work colleagues Keith Horton, Roger Quiney, Roy Davis and Steve Smith for jogging my memory and permission to use their pictures. Pete Simpkin, presenter and broadcaster for WM Radio, who trained in broadcasting at ATV, provided a number of valuable historical photographs of early ATV facilities at Foley Street in London. It has been difficult to establish copyright ownership of some of the pictures originally used in the press releases and company newsletters of the previous owners of the Midlands franchise, consequently ITV-plc is unable to speak for its predecessors but confirm that they do not raise any objection in principle to their use. I am sure that many of these pictures will have been taken by the professional photographers, in particular Willoughby "Gus" Gullachsen and Des Gershon, employed by ITV's predecessors throughout the years.

Gus's recent book **Shooting Through Life** captures some of the highlights of his work in the Midlands and is, as the Stratford-upon-Avon Herald has said, "A remarkable collection of celebrity portraits". Des is now Principal of the Gershon Picture Library, www.digitalrailroad.net/desgershon

FOREWORD BY ALTON DOUGLAS

It started, as so many things do, with a phone call. Would I write the foreword for this very important book?

Scratch my head time. What can I add? Maybe I could fill in some of the cracks? The problem with John's work is that it is so meticulously crafted, so carefully constructed, that there don't appear to be any helpful gaps! Then I thought, why don't I do exactly what every reader of the book will do – get personal. So, I've concentrated on some of the characters and programmes mentioned and added my own reminiscences from my days as a studio warm-up comic, actor and at times, general rent-a-face personality.

PAT ASTLEY (continuity announcer). He became a dear friend when we worked together as voiceover artistes for commercial radio. Being a great giggler, my bad impression of his idol, Al Jolson, used to reduce him into a state of near hysteria. In his back garden flew The Union Flag on top of a massive flagpole "…..and that doesn't come down 'till the lads get back from The Gulf." He was working, when he died, on a model of an SAS raid on a German fuel depot that he'd been involved in during the Second World War. Incidentally, his dad, Harry Wellesley, was a Scottish variety comic and his son, Gordon, was a presenter on Radio WM.

SHAW TAYLOR (presenter). He booked me, in his capacity as an agent, to appear in cabaret in Sardinia. The audience was so totally out of it that the next day, at breakfast, a fellow said to me, "You should have been here last night; you'd have enjoyed the comedian."

GODFREY WINN (broadcaster/journalist). My mother corresponded with him for a number of years. Knowing that she had terrible problems he recommended her to a friend of his who was an absent healer. She derived great comfort both physically and emotionally from their relationship.

"THE GOLDEN SHOT." I'd been the warm-up comic for the programme for several years when Norman Vaughan was taken ill in 1973 and I had to suddenly take over and compere the show live with only a couple of hours preparation. Despite a degree of critical acclaim, I've never been sure whether it helped my career or not!

"NEW FACES." I resigned after the first series because I couldn't stand the sight of my fellow artistes being "shredded" in public. One of the panellists was Arthur Askey who sent me my one and only celebrity fan letter after seeing my warm-up. It started a lengthy correspondence with him that lasted until shortly before his death. He used to sign-off his notes with the phrase, "Remember, it's the legs that go first." The irony was that, shortly before his demise, poor old Arthur had both his legs amputated.

"BOON." I appeared in the first ever episode. Years later, when Michael Elphick and I were guest speakers at a dinner, he remembered that I'd delivered the last line, after a fight scene, with a thick Birmingham accent and the words, "I'd have given you a hand, Mr Boon."

"CENTRAL NEWS." I deliberately used one of the all-time bad gags at the end of an interview when I said, "I'm just off to appear in cabaret in Felixtowe." "Where's Felixtowe?" "At the end of his foot."

Well, I could go on but you'll be relieved to know that I'm not going to – and for one good reason – I'm holding you up from reading from dawn till dusk, "From Dawn till Dusk", this fascinating history of Independent Television in the Midlands. Thanks John for cleaning the screen and giving shape and order to our memories.

Alton Douglas

Alton Douglas is the author of over three dozen books on the Midlands and two children's books of nonsense verse; all the titles, including his biography, "The Original Alton Douglas", are published by Brewin Books Ltd.

INTRODUCTION

Television has played a part in all of our lives; everyone feels some nostalgia for the television programmes they watched when they were very young. Television has shaped our individual lives and the nation's habits both at home and in the shops in many ways; the history of television is our history.

National television became available after World War II; with only a single channel and hence no choice for viewers; the whole country watched the same programmes, those that the British Broadcasting Corporation, in its paternal wisdom, decided to present to us. As viewers we either accepted what we were given or switched off; these were the only choices available to us. We could of course listen to the radio, again with a limited choice, or read a book or talk amongst ourselves!

It was not until the middle 1950s that the people of Britain were given another choice with the arrival of Independent Commercial Television. To us in the Midlands this meant the addition of Associated Television during the week and ABC Television at weekends.

The early part of the book details how the ITV Network came into being, how the contractors were selected and allocated regions, and various technical matters are discussed to show how the various contractors fitted together on the Network.

How ATV and ABC, the two Midlands contractors came together to find a site for a joint studio centre at Aston, the essential equipment required to operate a television station, through to them actually going on air for the very first time are related.

This is followed by a nostalgic look back over the many programmes, both from within their studios and from their outside broadcast facilities, produced by both ABC and ATV within the Midlands region, about the region and involving the people of the Midlands. Following this is a further nostalgic look at the many programmes ATV produced for the whole ITV Network and for the rest of the world.

Their output was to be very different to that of the BBC, commercial television was regulated by the Independent Television Authority who directed that its output should not only contain programmes broadcast nationally, like the BBC, but that it should, as a considerable portion of its output, contain programmes that related to the area or region each individual television company was serving. Those programmes were to be made in the region and had to reflect the various aspects of the region in relation to all its facets; culture, sport, religion, etc.

Considering the meagre resources available to the original companies, who were starting a new way of broadcasting in this country, of which the only experience to date was in the USA, they learnt fast and gave their viewers a real choice. They soon became an important part of the local scene; in the Midlands, both ATV and ABC were to be found wherever anything of importance was happening, they made it their business to make sure the viewers knew that they were in touch with local events. They used announcers or as ABC called them, 'station hosts', in vision to connect with the viewers. The independent contractors realised how important their viewing audience were, the more viewers they could attract the more advertisers would want to do business with them, hence larger profits, which of course was what they were in business for. Each contractor looked after its own patch or region in its own way, but all put the viewer at the top of their priorities. Their output was so successful that the BBC were not long in following their lead, and began producing their own regional programmes.

For those interested in the technology involved in producing programmes and broadcasting them some detail is presented to show how initially Alpha Television (working for both ATV and ABC), and later ATV, developed their technical facilities, resulting in the building of state of the art, world class studio centre in the centre of Birmingham.

As time went on pressure groups, politicians and the press began to criticise the original companies for not being regional enough, they complained that their particular part of the region or their football club was being neglected and not given sufficient coverage.

By the time ABC Television had been dismissed from the Midlands, leaving ATV alone to serve the region seven days a week, a powerful lobby of politicians and the press were criticising the company for not effectively reflecting the East Midlands, and for retaining its large and successful network programme production facilities in London. Unfortunately ATV were a little slow in responding, but eventually they promised to transfer its London operation to the East Midlands and to build a large programme making facility in Nottingham. They were too late; the ITA had already decided that this was what was going to happen when licences to transmit were renewed. But further they clipped ATV's wings considerably by insisting that they were to own only 51% of the new franchise holding company, Central Independent Television. The ITA had hoped that the remaining 49% of the company would be taken up by local Midlands companies. Unfortunately there was little interest locally and the remaining shares were bought up by large city institutions.

But ATV, having changed its name to reflect its new position to Central Independent Television, was true to its word and built not only a sub-region studio to serve the East Midlands but also, at the time, the largest television production facility in Europe in the City of Nottingham. Further they opened another sub-region studio at Abingdon near Oxford to serve the South Midlands.

Mrs Thatcher's Broadcasting Act of 1990 saw major changes to the industry, in future licences were to be awarded to the highest bidder. At the same time as ATV were being forced to change, Thames Television in London was sacked by the ITA and replaced by Carlton Television, a decision that has been considered by many to have resulted in the quality of television in the London region being degraded to its lowest yet. But that was not the end of the story; Carlton began to buy out the shares in Central, and eventually made a bid to take over the company.

There follows another section of nostalgia, the many programmes made in the Midlands, at Nottingham, in Birmingham and out on location throughout the region, which made a considerable impact upon the ITV Network as a whole are reviewed.

From this point on things changed at a pace, first Carlton closed the extensive programme making facilities in Birmingham, and moved most of its programme production to Nottingham.

Later, having merged with Granada Television that new company closed the Studio complex in Nottingham, and ceased transmission from Birmingham. At that point all that remained in the Midlands region was regional news making facilities in Birmingham, Nottingham and Oxford. Later the single small studio at Birmingham was physically divided into two halves, one half serving the East Midlands and the other the West.

So after all these years the viewers of the Midlands Region have had their regional programming torn away, reduced to much less than its much criticised predecessor ATV provided some fifty years ago. No programmes are made in the region; it has no transmission facilities and only minor News reporting capabilities. Only a few region programmes remain, made by independent producers.

Has it all gone forever, are the Midlands to become the lost region, and are the Midlanders to be deprived of programmes that reflect their lives and diverse culture? It seems that fashionable programme makers can only see life within the M25 and make programmes with a Cockney accent; but they are still forced by legislation to produce some programmes outside the M25, and have chosen to move as far away as they dare to the North and North-East. Can Ofcom (the new 'soft-touch regulator), be seen to accept and tolerate this situation? Where are the strict controls exercised by its predecessors? Perhaps more importantly where are those who criticised ATV for failing to reflect the East Midlands, at this time ITV does very little representing of any part of the region? ITV has become a national broadcaster generally feeding the same programmes (with little exceptions) to the whole country, just as the BBC did until the mid-1950s.

Fortunately for the viewer whilst ITV was frantically reducing its regional output, other sources of television have been developing, there are now many more choices for the viewer, but unfortunately very little that reflects the culture, sport, religion, etc. of the Midlands. Birmingham gets scant mention, let alone Nottingham, Leicester, Oxford, Worcester and the rest of the Midlands. There is no longer even a soap that reflects the Midlands life. Soaps now seem to be only made either in London or in Yorkshire and the North-East, with of course the old chestnut of Coronation Street from Manchester. Although there are glimmers of light, experiments are taking place in 'local television', viewable on broadband or via satellite which cover local communities.

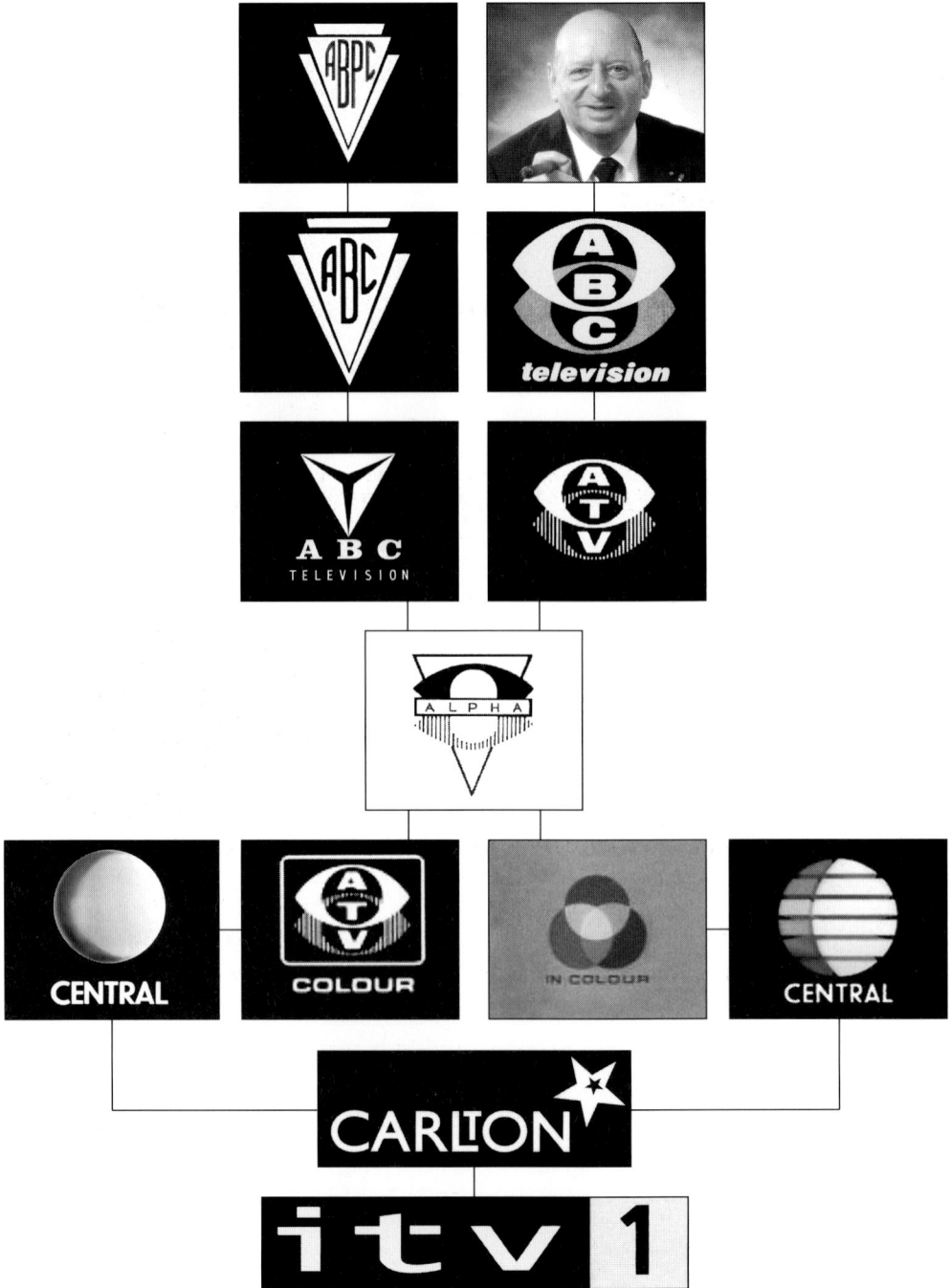

1. TELEVISION IN THE UK – THE BEGINNINGS

EARLY TELEVISION SYSTEMS

Television is the process of the breaking-down of an image into small parts for transmission by an electro-magnetic carrier wave and subsequent re-assembly of the parts on a receiver screen.

In 1926 the Scottish electrical engineer John Logie Baird demonstrated the first television set to the Royal Institute, in London. Two years later in 1928 colour television was demonstrated at the Bell Laboratories in the USA. Also in that year the BBC broadcast the first television programme, and in 1929 it adopted Baird's system. The same year saw the first regular US television broadcasts. In 1932 the BBC was persuaded to take over the test transmissions on the crude 30-line Baird system. But it soon became apparent that the time was right for a high definition public television service to be developed. The BBC was empowered by the Government to start testing two systems. Baird's improved 240-line mechanical system was tested alongside a new all electronic system on 405-lines, devised by EMI engineers.

Top: Baird commemorative plaque.
Bottom: Original Baird television apparatus (1925).

Britain led the world in television despite the fact that in its early days the upper levels at the BBC disliked it and were distinctly cold about its future. Much of the pioneering work was done by companies such as Marconi and EMI. Eventually the Corporation launched its first public television service, transmitted from Alexandra Palace in North London on 2nd November 1936; it covered an area, described by the *Ideal Home* magazine, as:

a ring including Cambridge, Colchester, Whitstable, Tunbridge Wells, Horsham, Reading, Aylesbury, Wolverton and Bedford, although regular 'freak' reception could be had as far away as Brighton and Coventry. Broadcasts, on a single channel, lasted for two hours every day, there being no service on Sundays.

This was one of the services that the BBC was expressly instructed to encourage in its Royal Charter, and one that, for technical reasons, was killed by the out-break of war in 1939. The service was shut down on 2nd September 1939 for the duration of the war. This was a bitter blow; for Britain, and in particular the BBC along with the Baird, EMI and Marconi Companies. Britain had

Baird 30-line mirror drum scanner, made by B.J. Lynes, and used by BBC at Broadcasting House.

been well ahead of all other countries in television technology; however, the war gave an impetus to technical advance in the field of electronics, which was to be of immense value when television broadcasting commenced in 1946.

GOVERNMENT INVOLVEMENT BEFORE COMMERCIAL TELEVISION

The United Kingdom Government has always played an important regulatory role in the development of broadcasting policy, which in turn has had direct implications for the production of television programmes. The only significant structural changes that have occurred within the broadcasting system have come from a report of a Government Committee, followed by an Act of Parliament. Regulation was obviously necessary, because given an inch programme producers were always inclined to take a mile.

- **Report of the Television Committee 1934/5** (Cmnd 4793)
  Selsdon Committee – January 1935.
  This Report recommended that both the Baird, electro mechanical system
  and the Marconi-EMI all electronic system should continue to be developed.
  It also said that the BBC should be the television broadcasting
  authority regardless of which technology was eventually to be adopted.
  The cost of the service should be borne out of a Licence Fee, levied upon
  those who possessed receiving equipment, with the Treasury making
  a contribution from its share of the revenue.

- **Broadcasting Committee 1935** (Cmnd 5091)
  Ullswater Committee — February 1936.
  The BBC Charter was extended for 10 years and the Licence Fee was to remain at 10 shillings (50 pence).
- **Report of the Television Committee 1943**
  Hawkey Committee — March 1945.
  Although not reporting until after the World War II this Committee was set up in 1943:
  'to prepare plans for the re-instalment and development of the television service after the War.... to the larger centres of population within a reasonable period.'
  It recommended the revival of the service which had existed up to the start of the War (1939). It was to operate initially in the London area on the 405-line system; and that a high-definition 1000-line system should be developed, for use in cinemas. The Committee saw that television would open up considerable possibilities in bringing exciting and memorable events to the viewer as they happened.
- **Broadcasting Policy** (Cmnd 6852)
  White Paper — 2nd July 1946.
  On 7th June 1946 the BBC resumed television broadcasting, a monopoly it enjoyed until Associated-Rediffusion and ATV commenced independent television ten years later.
- **Report of the Broadcasting Committee 1949** (Cmnd 8116)
  Beveridge Report — 18th January 1951.
  This Committee considered the possibility of introducing commercial television, but in the end decided in favour of continuing the BBC Monopoly against advertising or 'sponsorship.'
  But the Committee produced a 'Minority Report' by Selwyn Lloyd, who proposed a very different situation. The setting up of a British Broadcasting Commission to control BBC Radio, a British Television Corporation, one or two other National commercial broadcasters each for radio and television and a potentially large number of local radio stations. How similar this is to what we have today!
- **Memorandum on the Report of the Broadcasting Committee 1949** (Cmnd 8291)
  White Paper — 10th July 1951.
  The Labour Government of the day endorsed the Beveridge Report and in so doing rejected the minority report by Selwyn Lloyd.

- **Memorandum on the Report of the Broadcasting Committee 1949**
(Cmnd 8550)
White Paper – 15th May 1952.
But in October 1951 the political climate changed, a Conservative Government was elected and it published its own plans.
It proposed a break of the BBC monopoly, if only for television. It said,
'In the expanding field of television, provision should be made to permit some form of competition when resources made it feasible. Any new services would make use of the higher transmission frequencies.

- **Broadcasting Policy** (Cmnd 9005)
White Paper – 13th November 1953.
The Conservative Government then proposed a Public Corporation which would control the standards of programmes made by privately financed companies. These companies would be permitted to sell advertising time, but 'sponsorship of programmes' would not be permitted. This new Corporation would also own and operate the network of transmitters, whose use would be leased to the programme companies in return for fees which would finance the transmitter network.
This announced the introduction of commercial independent television to the Nation.

2. SETTING OUT THE FRAMEWORK OF INDEPENDENT TELEVISION

By the early 1950s, the only television service in the United Kingdom was that operated as a monopoly by the BBC, and financed by an annual Television Licence Fee, introduced in 1946, payable by each householder which had installed one or more television receivers. In contrast to the previous Labour Government the newly elected Conservative Government, elected in 1951 wanted to create a commercial television service to give viewers a wider choice of programming; but this was a controversial subject. The only other examples of commercial television that existed at that time were to be found in the USA, and it was widely considered that as an example of commercial television it was 'vulgar' and dominated by intrusive commercials.

INDEPENDENT TELEVISION AUTHORITY

The Government's solution to the problem was to create the Independent Television Authority, to supervise the creation of Independent Television, the first commercial television network in the United Kingdom. The Authority was empowered to determine the location, construction, building and operating the transmitters to be used

The original Authority, 1954: Left to right – J. Alban Davies; Dr. T. Honeyman; Diana Reader Harris; Sir Ronald Matthews; Sir Kenneth Clark; Sir Robert Fraser; Dilys Powell; Sir Henry Hinchcliffe.

by the ITV Network, as well as closely regulating the new independent channel in the interests of 'good taste', it would determine the franchise areas and award franchises to independent programme companies for each region on fixed terms only.

Towards the end of Parliamentary business in the summer of 1954 a Bill was passed and the Independent Television Authority was created, for a period of ten years, its life was later extended for another twelve years to 1976. It was the Television Act 1954 which permitted the creation of the first independent television network in the United Kingdom.

The Conservative Government had set a number of guidelines to which the Authority had to adhere:

■ Programmes were to be of high quality.
■ A proportion of feature films and 'telefilms' were to be British in origin.
■ The amount of advertising should not be so great as to detract from the value of the programmes; commercials being clearly distinguishable from programmes.

The reference to feature films and 'telefilms' indicates that at that time the majority of pre-recorded material available for transmission was only available on film, 35mm and 16mm. Video tape recorders were only in their early development stages. The purpose was to limit the amount of material broadcast which was sourced in the USA.

With remarkable speed the Authority set about its task; they had some difficult decisions to make. The Act, which had been described as being 'all spirit and few letters', had made it clear that there must be more than one company, but it was left to the Authority to determine what structure should be established. Should the new television network be divided in terms of programme responsibility, with a drama company, a light entertainment company, a current affairs company, and so on: or alternatively to divide it by the days of the week, or even by the hours of the day? By October 1954 the Authority had made its decision, the new ITV Network was to be divided on a regional basis. Each Regional company would produce the whole range of programmes to be transmitted within its region. But it was also possible for other Regions to purchase programmes produced by others.

With regards to advertising the ITA directed that six minutes in every hour or 10 per cent of programme time could be taken up by advertising, and that it would have to come only in what it called 'natural breaks.' They also directed that there should be no connection between the actual programme and the advertisements; it also made it clear that no advertisement would be allowed which in their words, *"will lead children to believe that if they did not own a certain product they will be inferior to other children."*

In organising independent television, the Authority adopted what it called the 'plural' system. It did so because it wanted to realise the benefits of a decentralised form of organisation: that is, to encourage the development of a service which would tend to portray a variety, a diversity, of character and attitude, rather than concentrate on those of London and the Home Counties as the BBC had been inclined to do. The Authority in effect divided the United Kingdom into thirteen areas.

Fourteen companies were to operate in the ITA's thirteen areas, obtaining their revenue from the sale of advertising time and paying a rental to the ITA and later a levy (introduced by Television Act of 1964), based on net advertisement revenue, to the Exchequer.

The ITV companies were contracted by the ITA to provide a local television service for their particular region, and were to produce such programmes as a local news bulletin and documentaries. Each company also was to produce programming that would be shown over the whole ITV network, with the four largest regions, who were known as the 'Big Four' (London weekday, London weekends, North and Midlands) producing the bulk of the network output. Each regional service was to have its own on-screen identity to distinguish it from other regions.

When the franchises were advertised throughout the country groups of people joined together and formed companies to bid for the franchises to operate television stations in the regions defined by the Authority.

The ITA duly considered the applications for the franchises. With an initial number of 98 applicants, the Authority demanded that applicants wishing to be considered for a franchise had to be able to back itself up with £3 million capital investment. The number of applicants immediately fell to 28. The ITA then awarded franchises to applicant companies, selecting them on the basis of their financial strength, the proposals for the service they offered, and on any connections between the applicants and the areas.

The physics of broadcasting on VHF (very high frequencies) meant that the majority of the country's population could be covered by a relatively small number of transmitters. The technical requirements of the new network were decided to be monochrome on a 405-line VHF system.

The Independent Television Authority
invites applications from those interested in becoming
PROGRAMME CONTRACTORS
in accordance with the provisions of the Television Act.

Applicants should give a broad picture of the types of
programmes they would provide, their proposals for
network or local broadcasting of their programmes,
some indication of their financial resources, and the
length of contract they would desire.

All applicants will be treated in the strictest confidence.

Advert Times Newspaper – Wednesday 25th August 1954.

Contracts to run an ITV regional service were not permanent, the ITA were to review the contracts every few years, and it was not guaranteed that the original holder of the licence would be granted an extension, they could be refused and then a new company would take over instead.

THE AWARD OF CONTRACTS
Initially the Independent Television Authority selected several companies from amongst the applicants to provide programmes in the London, Midlands and Northern main regions beginning in 1955. It was decided that the franchise holders of these three regions (The Big Four), covering the major part of the country and population would be responsible for providing the largest proportion of network programmes, besides producing programmes specifically for their own region. The companies selected to serve the smaller regions would then only be responsible for producing mainly local programmes for their region.

Associated Newspapers and BET's Rediffusion formed a company called **Associated–Rediffusion**, the group had experience in commercial radio and in electronics was selected for London weekdays franchise.

The Associated Broadcasting Development Company led by Norman Collins was selected for London weekends and for the Midlands weekdays.

Granada Theatres developed **Granada Television Network** under the leadership of the Bernstein brothers, who had initially been against the idea of commercial television, but now that it was coming into being wanted part of the action. Their group was selected for Northern weekdays.

Kemsley Newspapers joined with Maurice Winnick of Winnick Entertainment to form **Kemsley-Winnick**, which was selected for Northern and Midlands weekends.

Although this was the initial decision by the ITA, as reality began to set in things began to change.

With regards to the Midlands, the Associated Broadcasting Development Company had been formed earlier in 1952, and acted as a pressure group for the introduction of Commercial Television into Britain. The founders of this company included Norman Collins, C.O. Stanley (chairman of Pye) and Robert Renwick. The company although awarded a contract had difficulty in forming a programme production arm and had exaggerated its ability to raise sufficient finance.

One of the losers in the award of contracts was the **Independent Television Company** (ITC), the ITA having considered that it had too great a controlling interest in artistic talent and because of the involvement of agents Lew and Leslie Grade, Val Parnell, Prince Littler of Stoll Moss Theatres and others. But in the light of the difficulties being experienced by ABDC the Authority approached the ITC to ask if they were prepared to consider merging with that company.

Negotiations followed and a new company was formed on a 50/50 basis. ITC remained in existence as a programme production company and did not form part of the new company. The company called itself the **Associated Broadcasting Company** (ABC), and set about preparing to go on the air weekdays in the London region on 25th May 1955.

The retention of ITC as a separate production company was a typically shrewd move on the part of the ITC board as it meant that they could make their own programmes and then sell them initially to a company in which they owned fifty per cent, and also to the rest of the network and beyond.

With regards to the weekend contract in the Midlands and the North a further problem arose. Henry Winnick admitted to the Authority that he was not able to raise the finance to run two separate television stations, in the North and the Midlands.

Again he had exaggerated the financial position, but he hoped it would materialise if granted a contract. It was not forthcoming and Lord Kemsley's newspaper group was frightened away by the potential losses. Although Henry Winnick still believed he could gather sufficient people and talent together to run his franchise, Kenneth Clark and the Authority became convinced that the consortium was a failure. They had to find some alternative.

When the Kemsley-Winnick consortium fell apart, Kenneth Clark contacted the **Associated British Picture Corporation** to see if they would be prepared to consider taking the contract.

ABPC, with its chain of cinemas throughout the country, had not applied for a contract and in fact had opposed the idea of advertising-supported television. They reasoned that the introduction of commercial television would take cinema-goers away from their theatres and advertisers would take their adverts away also, depriving the ABPC of revenue. So ABPC were unlikely to accept. But with time running out, Kenneth Clark was offering large returns for little risk – two days a week in two regions – with a promise to pay some of the £750,000 government money if ITV should fail.

ABPC accepted it as a business opportunity with its guarantee of breaking even. Sir Philip Warter and Howard Thomas for ABPC signed the ITA contract with Sir Robert Fraser on 21st September 1955, the day before the opening of commercial television in London, and only five months before the Midlands went on air. As Howard Thomas later recalled:

Seats were found for us at the top table (at the opening spree in the Guildhall) and as I sat there surveying the Rediffusion and ATV legions assembled I began to wonder how with my staff of one (Eve Hockman), my secretary, I was going to get an organisation together, recruit programme makers and technicians, find a studio in Birmingham, equip it, and begin transmissions on 17th February 1956. Then, without pausing for breath, we would have little more than three months to set up an even larger operation in Manchester.

Immediately, as London went on-air, a major problem arose, the new North and Midlands weekend franchise holder had called itself ABC Television to match their

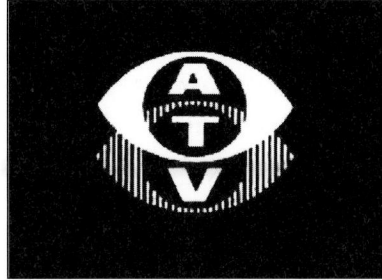

cinema chain, and were then immediately in dispute with the Associated Broadcasting Company, which also was using an on–air symbol of ABC! A lengthy and costly legal rankle was about to take place, but fortunately this was avoided when the Associated Broadcasting Company agreed to change its name to Associated Television (ATV) from 6th October 1955, having been on air as ABC since 21st September of that year.

INDEPENDENT TELEVISION NEWS

In January 1955 the ITA authorised the setting up of the Independent Television News service. This was a new company operated and owned collectively by the ITV companies, and was to provide a national news service for the whole Network.

ENGINEERING MATTERS

At the start of Independent Television the Authority had no engineer and it was not until December of 1954 that they appointed a Chief Engineer. Considerable engineering matters had to be decided; initially it had been assumed that the BBC would be invited to provide the facilities for transmission using its existing transmitter sites. The BBC had, in fact, offered to do so as soon as the ITA was set up.

But there was a problem, the BBC had transmitted on Band I and the ITA was to use Band III, a higher frequency. The BBC masts were not situated in the best places, and were physically incapable of taking the aerials required to provide the best coverage on Band III.

Although the ITA was keen to use the BBC masts where possible, it decided to design, build and install its own transmitters; to build its transmitter network and operate 32 transmitting stations to cover up to 98% of the population from scratch; additional relay stations would be built to improve and extend coverage. Transmission was to be on a 405 line system in monochrome. The first transmitters were sited at:

- Croydon, London   September 1955
- Lichfield, Midlands   February 1956
- Winter Hill, Lancashire   May 1956
- Emley Moor, Yorkshire   November 1956

These four transmitters covered approximately 60% of the population and four separate companies were appointed to provide programmes for these areas on a pattern which divided week-day contractors from week-end ones as follows.

London	Monday to Friday	Associated Rediffusion Ltd
London	Saturday and Sunday	Associated Television Ltd
Midlands	Monday to Friday	Associated Television Ltd
Midlands	Saturday and Sunday	ABC Television Ltd
North	Saturday and Sunday	ABC Television Ltd
North	Monday to Friday	Granada TV Network

The four transmitters were linked together by the already existing and comprehensive network of Post Office sound and vision circuits and repeater stations.

Once in operation the first transmitter, at Beulah Hill, Croydon, London – near to the BBC transmitter at Crystal Palace, started test transmissions from a caravan, owned by Belling and Lee, which enabled receiving aerials and sets to be installed prior to the official start of ITV in September 1955.

Between 1957 and 1962 transmitters were erected to serve the outlying areas of the other ITV regions. The first at Black Hill, Scotland went on air on 31st August 1957; the contractor appointed for the region was Scottish Television.

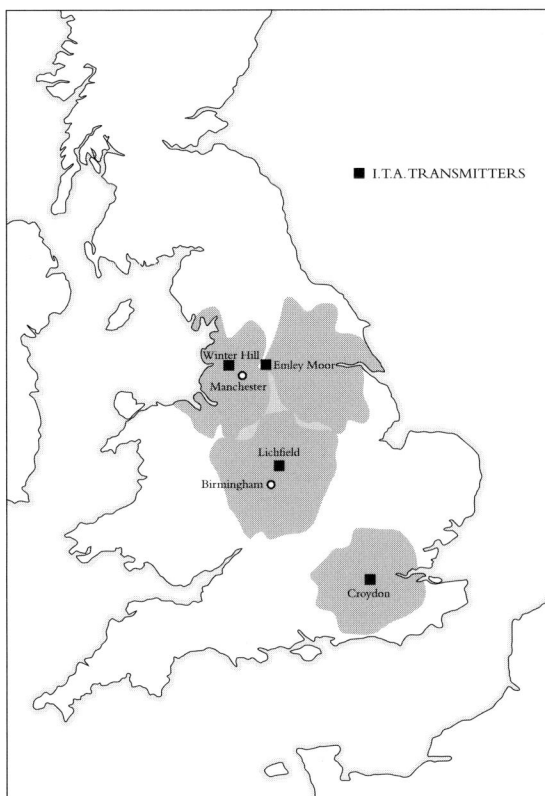

Lasky's lead again!

FIRST CLASS
BAND III CONVERTERS
ALMOST HALF - PRICE!

Famous make and one of the finest Converters made. Brand new in maker's cartons. TUNABLE OVER ALL 13 CHANNELS and incorporates own power supply for 200-250 v. A.C. mains. 2 valve cascode R.F. amplifier PCC84 and PCF80, metal rectifier. Metal case, 10in. wide, 5½in. deep, 3½in. high, smart fawn enamel finish.
Listed at £10/17/6.
LASKY'S PRICE **£5/19/6**
Post and pkg., 5/- extra.
Strictly limited number only. Send now.

Left: Coverage by the first four ITA Transmitters, winter 1956. Right: The first Set-top box.

CHANGES FOR THE VIEWER

The introduction of ITV did not just happen for the viewer, like the current change over to digital television, as with the introduction of colour television and the change to the 625-line system, the poor viewer was required to spend some money if he wished to upgrade.

Most pre-ITV television receivers were tuned at the factory to a channel in Band I to receive the BBC; if the owner moved area the set needed to be retuned by a service engineer.

When ITV started, transmitting on Band III, a higher frequency, viewers were required to buy a converter (the first 'set-top box'), which converted the Band III signal down to the BBC Band I channel. Some manufacturers produced their own custom converters for their existing sets, but a universal type was also available which

13

was not tied to any particular make of set. New television receivers from that time had a built-in tuner with a 13 channel selector knob on the front panel.

But this was not the end of the expense for the viewer; besides buying either a new receiver or converter, he also had to purchase and install another aerial for Band III reception. This often pointed in a different direction to the BBC aerial – depending upon the locations of the relative transmitters.

Today's viewers are faced with similar decisions on expense with the current change-over to digital television.

LATER FRANCHISES

There were three applicants for the franchise covering Central Scotland, which was awarded to Scottish Television (STV) in 1956.

Then there were ten applicants for the franchise to cover South Wales and the West of England that was each side of the Severn Estuary, this was awarded in 1956 to Television West and Wales (TWW).

Thirteen companies applied for the South of England franchise and it was awarded to Southern Television a year later in 1957.

Another eleven applied for the North Eastern England franchise, which went to Tyne Tees Television in 1957.

Two franchises were awarded the following year, 1958. The East of England went to Anglia Television, from eight applicants; and from only four applicants Ulster Television won the Northern Ireland franchise.

1959 saw the South West franchise go to Westward Television from a massive fifteen applicants. Plymouth was obviously very attractive.

Channel Television, one of only two applicants, was chosen for the Channel Islands franchise; and Border Television, also one of two applicants, was awarded the franchise covering the English-Scottish Border and the Isle of Man; and Grampian Television was awarded the franchise for the North East Scotland, from seven applicants. All three were awarded in 1960.

In 1961, Wales Television Association, Teledu Cymru (Wales West and North Television, WWN), was granted the franchise for West and North Wales. This company failed in 1964 due to the late commissioning of two of its three transmitters. It meant that it never reached half of its projected income. On its failure the two franchises covering Wales were merged and TWW served the whole of the Country.

The following table summarises the final disposition of the franchises:

Area	Population Coverage up to boundary of 'fringe' area	Week-day/ Week-end Franchise	Company
London	12,290,000	Week-day	Associated Rediffusion Ltd
London		Week-end	Associated Television Ltd
Midlands	7,450,000	Week-day	Associated Television Ltd
Midlands		Week-end	ABC Television Ltd
North of England	12,150,000	Week-day	Granada Television Network Ltd
North of England		Week-end	ABC Television Ltd
East Anglia	2,490,000	Whole week	Anglia Television Ltd
North-East England	2,680,000	Whole week	Tyne Tees Ltd
Southern and South-East England	4,070,000	Whole week	Southern Television Ltd
South-West England	1,541,000	Whole week	Westward Television Ltd
South Wales and West of England	3,240,000	Whole week	TWW Ltd
West and North Wales★	1,000,000	Whole week	Wales Television Association
Central Scotland	3,820,000	Whole week	Scottish Television Ltd
The Borders	5,13,8000	Whole week	Border Television Ltd
North-East Scotland	872,000	Whole week	Grampian Television Ltd
Northern Ireland	1,070,000	Whole week	Ulster Television Ltd
The Channel Islands	Not known	Whole week	Channel Television Ltd

★ *Provisional*

(Source: A short version of the Report of the Pilkington Committee – HMSO 1962).

3. THE TELEVISION NETWORK

Although the BBC and ITA were individually responsible for providing and operating their television stations, the links between studios and transmitters and between stations in each region were provided by the Post Office.

The development of the General Post Office (GPO) television network commenced in 1937, the year after the start of the television service, when a cable of the balanced pair type was laid between various points of interest in London.

The first inter-city television link was provided in 1949 between London and Birmingham. By 1961 this had grown to a national network covering the whole of Britain and Northern Ireland, with a connection to Lille in France forming the British Post Office component of the Eurovision chain. It included 2,500 miles of cable and 2,200 miles of radio links used for the distribution of vision signals. Corresponding networks had been set-up for the associated sound and control lines, which were an essential part of the circuits provided for the broadcasting authorities.

The main Post Office inter-city circuits were routed between Network Switching Centres (NSCs), of which there were about twelve covering the country.

Between the NSCs were provided a number of vision and sound channels in each direction; these could be interconnected to provide tandem connections between selected points. The vision channels had to have a 3 Mc/s bandwidth to carry a 405 line signal with minimum distortion and the sound channels 10 kc/s. The inter-city channels were rented by either the BBC or the ITA. Radiating from each centre were a number of circuits to and from the local studios and broadcast transmitting stations, each link being rented by the appropriate authority.

With the introduction of ITV, with its family of individual stations up and down the network, and the necessity to switch programme material to and from them constantly, the operation of the network by the GPO was to change. With only the BBC to consider switching of signals on the network had been very leisurely and not very frequent.

The GPO had to quickly develop a new system and new operating procedures and to train new staff. It was not their responsibility to switch the actual programmes; they had to do the manual routing switches, strictly to a time schedule to provide the circuits to be used by the contractors. It was the responsibility of the contractor's staff to fit in with the switching.

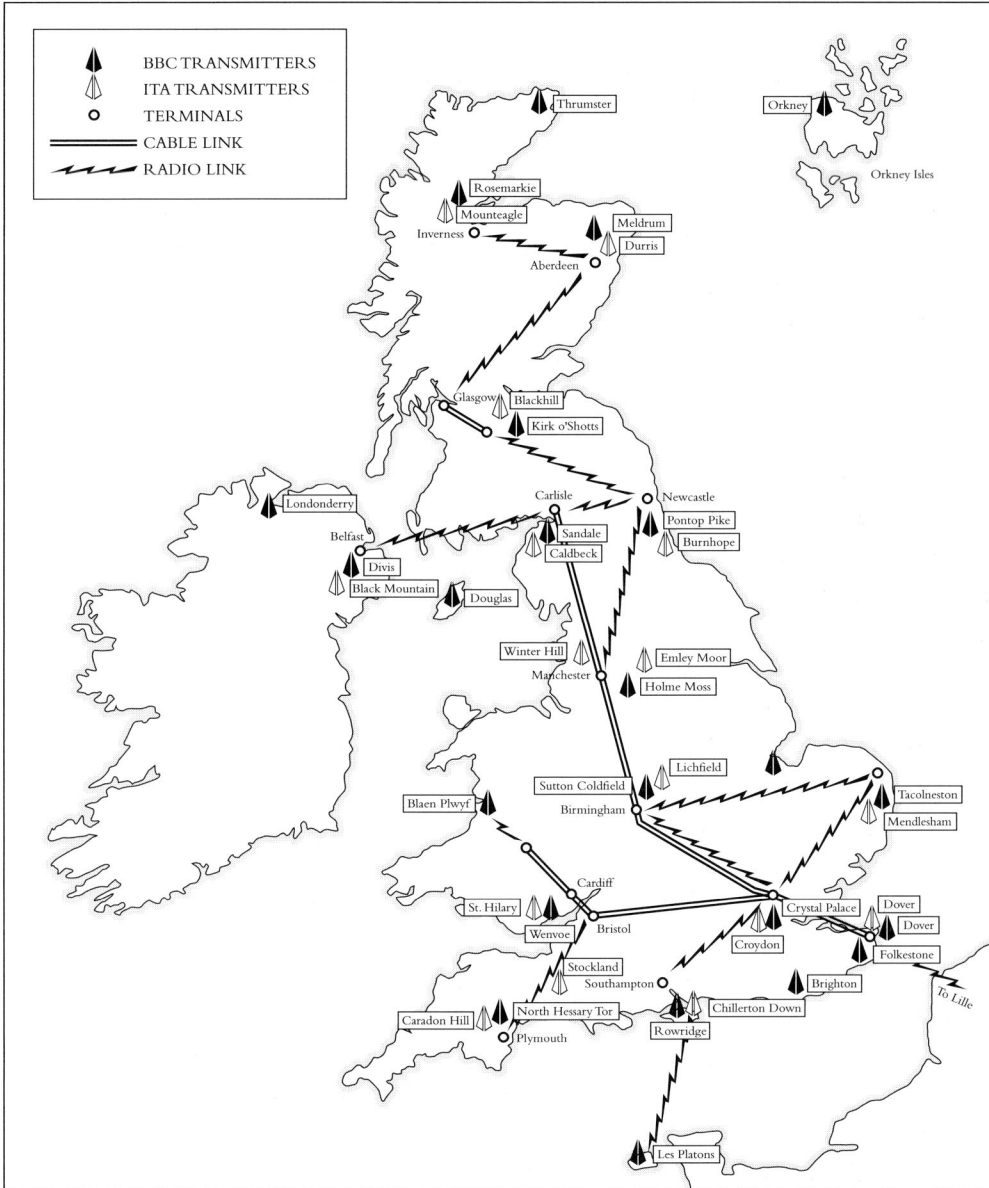

The radio and cable links in the UK television network −1961. Where a station relies on the reception of a nearby transmitter for its programmes (radio re-broadcast) no link is shown. The links between the terminal points and the transmitters are a combination of radio and cable. (Source: Wireless World June 1961).

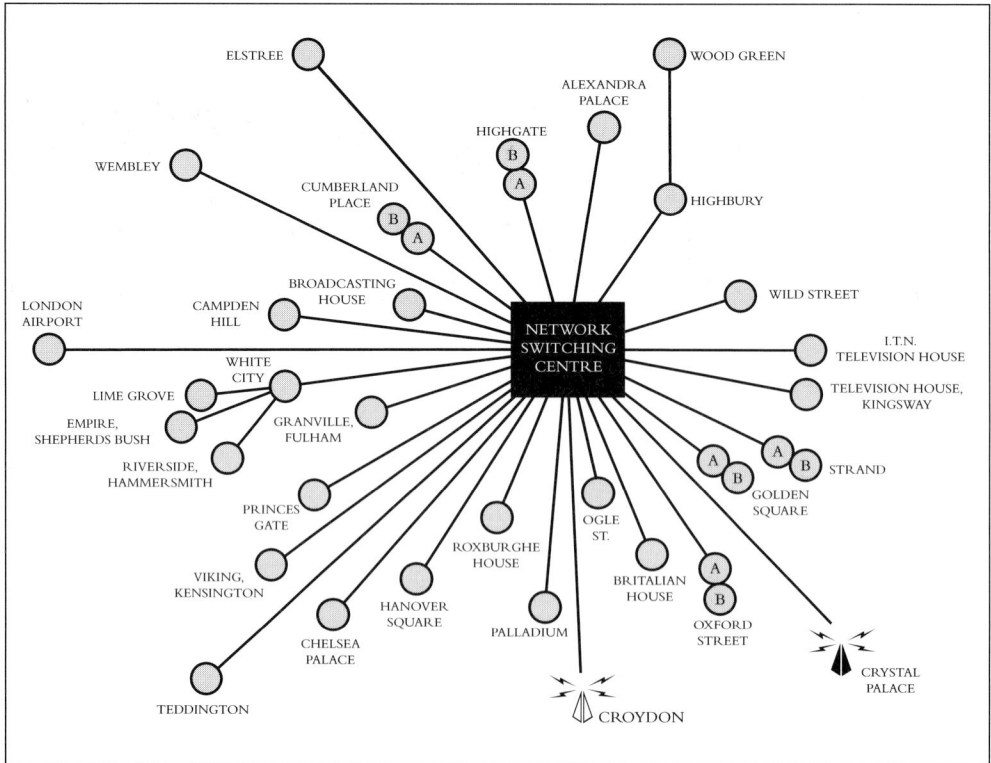

Permanent cable links from the London Switching Centre to the television transmitters, studios and centres of entertainment in the London Area – 1961.
(Source: Wireless World, June 1961).

LONDON SWITCHING CENTRE

The London Television Control Centre was situated at the Museum Telephone Exchange off the Tottenham Court Road. Two balanced pair cables which provided ten vision circuits linked the Centre to the Master Control Room of Associated Rediffusion and Independent Television News at Kingsway; and a further eight vision circuits linked it to Associated Television's Master Control at Foley Street. A one-way cable fed the transmitter at Croydon, and another took the output from ABC's Wardour Street facilities into Museum. A number of London theatres and studios were also linked by sound and vision circuits, as were a number of strategic high ground sites around the London area, which were used as insertion points for outside broadcast links.

BIRMINGHAM SWITCHING CENTRE

Here the Post Office Switching Centre was situated at Anchor Exchange at Telephone House. This was linked by a two-way radio circuit to the London Switching Centre. The transmitter at Lichfield was also linked by a two-way radio link. The Master Control Room at Alpha Television at Aston was served by five cable circuits. Then there was a two-way vision link, with amplifiers every six miles, to the Manchester Switching Centre.

Combined vision and sound control position at the London Switching Centre at The Museum Telephone Exchange off Tottenham Court Road. (Courtesy: Pete Simpkin).

MANCHESTER SWITCHING CENTRE

The Control Centre at Manchester was situated at Telephone House, being fed by the two-way vision link from Birmingham. It was linked to the Granada Master Control Room at Quay Street with five cable circuits, and the ABC Master Control Room at the Capitol Cinema at Didsbury also with five cable circuits. There were two-way radio links to feed the transmitters at Winter Hill and Emley Moor.

LINES TESTING

With so many cable and radio links connecting the studio centres, transmitters, etc. it was essential that they performed to the highest standard. To ensure this the programme centres carried out constant checks on the various circuits throughout the network. To assist in this function a vision test waveform was developed which was similar to the transient nature of the television waveform. This was the Sine-squared Pulse and Bar waveform which was transmitted over the circuits and examined for distortion either by comparison for routine tests or by photographic analysis for full acceptance tests.

STUDIO CENTRES

Although the Independent Television Authority was responsible for providing the transmitters for each area, and the General Post Office was responsible for the interconnections between the transmitters and the studio facilities of each of the new

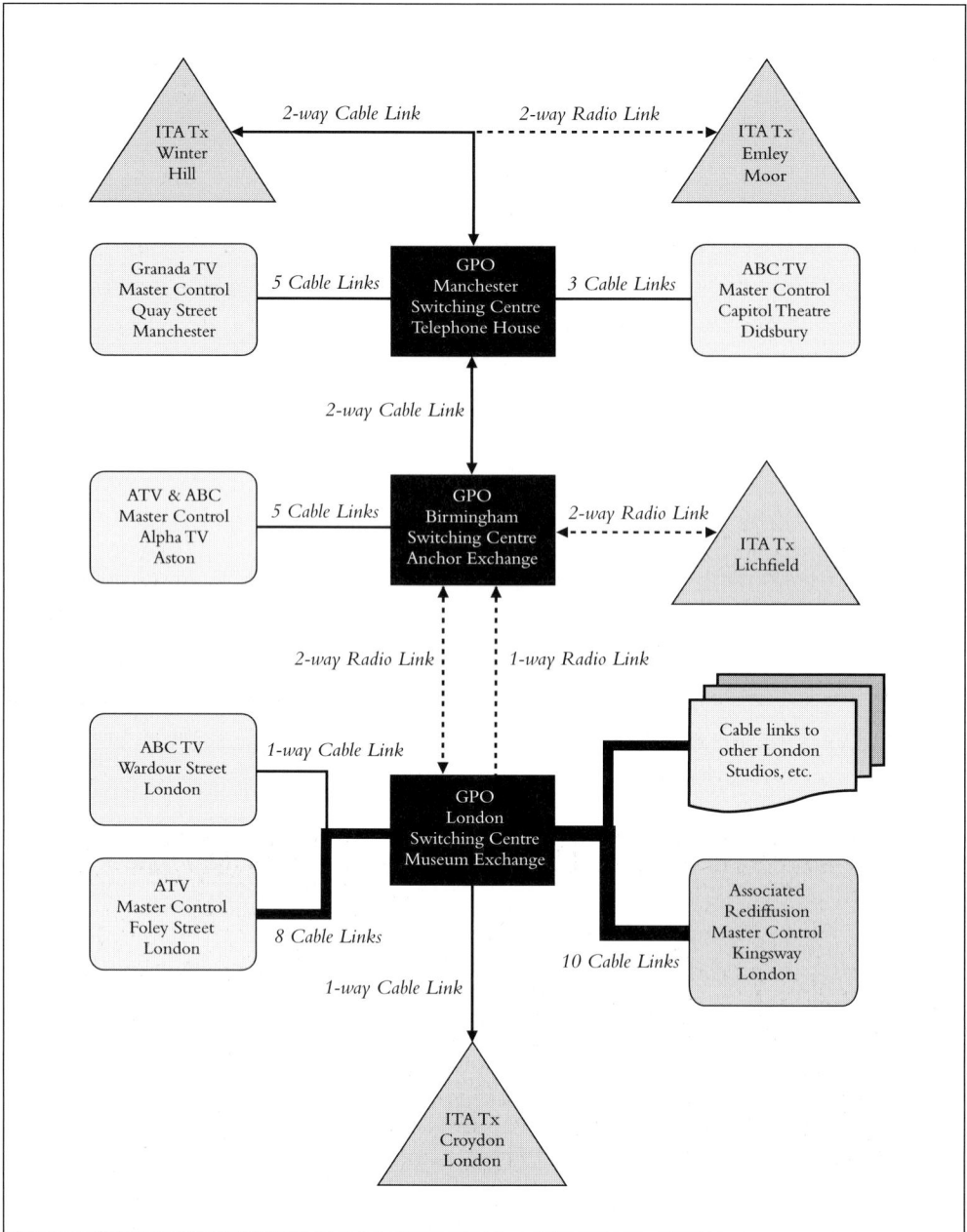

*Simplified diagram of the links between the Switching Centres,
Studios and Transmitters – 1956.*

television companies; it was the responsibility of each company to provide their own studio centres, technical facilities, staff etc. From the issuing of the franchises there was very little time. As Howard Thomas of ABC recalled in an article in the 'Television Annual for 1958':

All of the contractors had to build or acquire studios, persuade manufacturers to allocate equipment earmarked for export. Then they had to recruit staff, some from the BBC, some from films, some from Fleet Street, and electronic engineers from industry. And there was no income apart from the capital the contractors raised to go into business. Facing the contractors was an essential order of events. First they had to spend at least as much as the BBC to provide programmes more attractive than the BBC; then they had to encourage viewers by the million either to convert their receivers and aerials to receive the ITA or buy new receivers; and finally, having won this audience, they had to 'sell' the audience to advertisers in sufficient numbers to justify manufacturers spending money to reach this public.

ATV LONDON PRESENTATION FACILITIES

ATV had to equip studio centres in both London and Birmingham. As first to go on-air they concentrated on London initially. They established transmission facilities in Foley Street. They started out as tenants of Associated Rediffusion in the Kingsway, before moving into Cumberland Place in 1958. Technical Facilities in London were situated at Foley Street and at Ogle Street, actually next door to each other, midway between the BBC in Upper Regent Street and the Post Office Tower. The Master Control Room

Master Control Room, Foley Street. (Courtesy: Pete Simpkin).

and Telecine was in Foley Street and later VTR (Video Tape Recording) was in Ogle Street. Master Control was typically very small, some 15 feet square, on two levels. On the lower level were, on the left the sound desk and the vision desk on the right, both operated by Assistant Transmission Controllers. Above them and to the rear, on the right was the Transmission Controller (described below), and to his left the Master Control Engineer responsible for ensuring technical quality of transmission was of the highest level, prior to being fed to the Post Office Network and the ITA Transmitter at Croydon.

Master Control Room, Foley Street on-air.
Left to right Arthur Burbage, Mike Cobb,
Raymond Joss and Ken Pitts.

ATV London ATCs, later Transmission Controllers in Birmingham, were Maggie Dunn, John Ives, Peter Laws, Andy Martin, Jean Prince; Malcolm Neal and Mike Lloyd, who became a Programme Director, directing many well known programmes including **The Golden Shot**.

The Transmission Controllers and Assistant Transmission Controllers were responsible for transmission output according to the pre-arranged Daily Routine Sheet. They were the final link to the viewers and had total responsibility for the company's output, in particular the commercial output, the most important source of income and covered by strict ITA regulations. Any marred commercials had to be re-inserted as soon as possible. It was the TC's duty to 'roll' Telecine machines so that their output was transmitted on time, to the second – cueing was done verbally over a talk-back system.

ATV London (Rediffusion on weekdays) was known as 'The Nominated Contractor', which meant that the London Transmission Controller was also in control of the whole ITV Network. Other Companies on the Network would expect programmes they wished to transmit to appear on time from various sources on the Network, to the second. Although this was always the aim, often for a number of reasons, human error, programme over or under running and unforeseen circumstances the aim was not always achieved. In order to pre-warn companies on the Network of any deviation from the expected norm, the Nominated Contractor's

Top: Control Rooms, Foley Street. (Courtesy: Pete Simpkin). Bottom Left: Presentation Studio, Foley Street. (Courtesy: Pete Simpkin). Bottom Right: An EMI Telecine, Foley Street. (Courtesy: Pete Simpkin).

TC would contact them via a facility called 'The Red Phone', an open high quality telephone system which could only be rung by the Nominated Contractor or ITN. All the TCs on the Network could communicate together via this system, similar to a conference call. So should a particular programme be delayed for say one minute TCs on the Network could take appropriate action such as having their announcer 'ad-lib' for that time, hence avoiding the 'dreaded' one minute of 'black screen and silence', accepted on the Network as a cardinal sin.

In Foley Street the Presentation Announcer's Studio was situated on the floor above Master Control. London 'in-vision' announcers were Arthur Adair, John Braban, Peter Cockburn, Robert Gladwell, Dick Graham, Jim Lloyd, Trevor Lucas, Shaw Taylor and Norman Tozer.

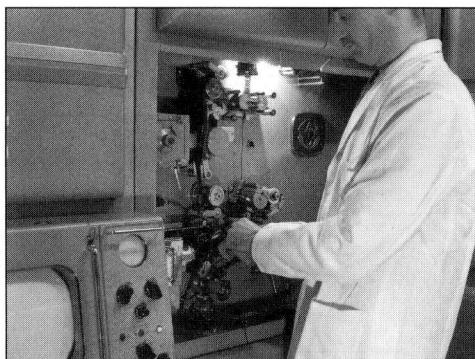

Top Left: Peter Short loads a feature film. (Courtesy: Pete Simpkin). Top Right: VTR Room. (Courtesy: Pete Simpkin). Bottom: Pye Telecine. (Courtesy: Pete Simpkin).

There was also a small Promotion Studio, used by, amongst others, **Police Five**, which was produced by an ATC with a cameraman and soundman who were on duty from the main ATV Elstree Studios.

There were a total of six Telecine machines in Foley Street, two EMI flying spot machines, used to transmit 35mm films such as **The Saint** and **Danger Man**; one Rank Cintel flying spot machine, used to transmit 16mm film series such as **Bonanza**; and two Pye vidicon machines, one of which was used exclusively for the transmission of film commercials on 35mm film.

At Ogle Street there were four Ampex 1000 2 inch Video Tape Recorders and a very small control room to the rear. These machines were introduced in 1959 and had rotating heads, transverse scanning, and FM encoding, which allowed broadcast quality pictures at 15 inches per second on 90 minute reels. Early VTR tapes were notoriously variable in quality and had to be checked prior to use for 'drop outs' (caused by missing oxide on the tape), which showed up as white lines on the picture. Checked tapes were classified according to the number of 'drop outs', only the best were used to record programmes, too many and the tape was returned to the manufacturer to be replaced. Later equipment was developed that was able to mask the effects of 'drop outs.'

ATV London also had a mobile VTR with a single camera attached called 'Monoculus', which was used for recording at Outside Broadcasts and on programmes in the 60s, such as **Honey Lane**, similar to the present BBC's **Eastenders**.

Ampex 1000 2 inch Video Tape Recorder as installed at Ogle Street.

PROGRAMME PRODUCTION – ELSTREE

Elstree Studios located in Borehamwood in Hertfordshire, is world renowned and occupies an important place in the British film industry.

At the start of the twentieth century cinema was an exciting new technology and art form. Early cinematographers came to this part of Hertfordshire before the First World War and set up premises near the village of Elstree. A number of separate companies worked alongside each other and the area became a British Hollywood in microcosm.

John East of Neptune Films bought a field there for his studio in 1914, where he produced several full-length films including **Harbour Lights** and Britain's first cartoon films. His studios were eventually leased to a company called Ideal Films and a number of specialised documentaries pioneering time-lapse photography were made there.

Sound techniques were developed by Ludwig Blattner at Elstree during the 1930s.

Six film studios were built in Clarendon Road, Borehamwood; now the home of the BBC's **EastEnders** set. These studios were later sold to the British National Film

Company which produced a series of Anne Ziegler and Webster Booth musicals, comedies featuring the Crazy Gang and famous films such as the thriller **Gaslight**, **Edge of the World** and **One of Our Aircraft is Missing**. Douglas Fairbanks Jnr. leased the studios in the 1950s and made 160 films there for American television.

It was then that the studios were sold to ATV for use as their television programme production unit. It remained with ATV for twenty-two years and produced most of the company's main programmes to be shown on the ITV Network.

ATV Elstree Television Studio, in Clarendon Road, was considered the finest production house in the world, where between the 1960s and 1970s a large selection of the most popular programmes seen on British and American television were produced. Household names ranging from The Beatles to Bing Crosby, The Muppets to Morecambe and Wise performed before the cameras there. American television companies used to come over to ATV Elstree to make their shows because the studio, its facilities and technicians were considered to be the best production venue.

In 1961 **The Jo Stafford Show**, a joint British–American production was made there; this was followed by the successful **Tony Hancock** series. Music shows hosted by Tony Bennett and Tom Jones, **Emergency Ward 10** (British television's first ever medical soap) and many popular dramas followed.

During 1973 a Marty Feldman comedy made there won the first of two Golden Rose of Montreux awards for ATV; the second was for the Jim Henson Company's **Muppet Show** also produced there. That Company's **Sesame Street** wonderful characters appeared for the first time on television in **The Julie Andrews Hour**.

Bing Crosby made his final performance, singing with David Bowie in his **Merry Olde Christmas Show**.

ABC Television also used the studios, producing such shows as **The Avengers**.

ATV Elstree and its long run of magnificent programmes came to an end whilst it was still at the height of success. Following considerable political pressure from the East Midlands, who complained that ATV was not representing that area sufficiently well, the Independent Broadcasting Authority forced its closure by insisting that ATV built a large scale studio base in the East Midlands. Elstree was closed and many of its staff transferred to Nottingham.

THE MIDLANDS STUDIO CENTRE – BIRMINGHAM

Partly due to the very short notice ABC were given to prepare for transmission in 1956 and despite their initial disagreement over names, ABC and ATV came together to share studies and technical facilities in Birmingham. As late-comers ABC recognised that the engineers they wanted had either already transferred nervously into ITV, or signed new contracts with the BBC. But as ATV and ABC were no longer in competition for contracts, and at a time when every penny had to be considered – television was not yet, nor for many years would be 'a licence to print money' – they soon realised that there would be many advantages if the two operated on a joint basis. They set about looking for a single site out of which they could both operate over the seven days of the week.

The site chosen was the recently closed Astoria Cinema. It was relatively close (approximately 1 mile) to the centre of the City of Birmingham. Aston was the home of the Aston Villa football club, the HP Sauce factory and the ancient Aston Hall. In the past Birmingham was in fact a suburb of Aston Manor. It was at the heart of the country with its developing communication links with the rest of the country, the M1 motorway already connected London directly to the Midlands, although it would be a few more years before the M6 was built to link Birmingham to Manchester, and still more years before the rest of the Midlands Motorway Network made it the important centre it is today.

A BIT OF HISTORY – THE NEW THEATRE ROYAL ASTON

The Astoria Cinema had already a long history of involvement in the entertainment industry.

As far back as 23rd September 1892 an agreement was signed between George and Robert Hall to erect a theatre on a site in Aston Road North, Aston Manor. The theatre was opened on Monday 7th August 1893 having cost £6,500 to build. A year later it was sold to Charles Barnard in 1894, who carried out extensive refurbishment. The General Manager was E. Hewston and the acting manager F. Whittles.

A further refurbishment took place in 1912, after nineteen years, at a cost of £7,000; its seating capacity was then 2,000. Then, as the technology of cinematography developed, it was closed as a theatre in 1926 to be reopened on 12th December 1927 as the Astoria Cinema, with a seating capacity of 1,194.

It was as a popular cinema that it remained in operation until 26th November 1955, when it finally closed.

It closed just in time to take advantage of yet another advance in technology; it was converted into the latest in entertainment, a television theatre or studio. By the time it closed as a television theatre in 1970 it had served the public in the field of entertainment, virtually uninterrupted for some 78 years. Even then, it continued until recently as the home of BRMB a local Radio Station.

ALPHA TELEVISION SERVICES (BIRMINGHAM) LTD

Having chosen their site the two companies formed a new company, Alpha Television Services (Birmingham) Ltd, which was to establish and operate for them the full range of technical equipment, facilities and staff to make programmes, convert films into television pictures (Telecine), receive programme material from other companies and to pass the station's output into the communications network to be fed to the transmitter and to other companies.

It was also to become dear to the hearts of Midlands viewers as the station where both companies regarded them as their most important asset and involved them as closely as possible in many of their programmes.

At the Alpha Studios each company provided their own Transmission Controllers and Continuity Announcers, and each had its own style of presentation and station identity.

The conversion of the Astoria Cinema at Aston involved an entirely new interior, leaving only the audience seating in the circle. The conversion was carried out under the direction of architects Satchwell and Roberts. The area that had been the stalls and beyond became Studio 1.

Alpha Television Services (Birmingham) Ltd was run by General Manager, Frank Beale, who had left the BBC with Keith Rogers (Peter Dimmock's right hand man) in 1955, one month before Bill Ward, who had been with the BBC since 1936. Tom Stirrop was Company Secretary, Dave Whittle was the Chief Engineer with Gerry Kaye as his deputy. They selected and employed over the coming years a team of Engineers, Cameramen, Sound Engineers, Lighting Directors and Technicians, Scenes and Propertymen, Make-up and Wardrobe Experts, Carpenters, Electricians, House

Left: Alpha General Manager – Frank Beale. Right: Alpha Chief Engineer – David Whittle talking with Stanley Broughton, Head of Vision Control.

Maintenance men, Floor Managers, Catering Staff, Scenic Designers, Security Staff, Administrators and Office Staff; all were of the highest possible quality, to rival any other such team in the country. In fact in those early years the staff of Alpha Television was considered throughout the Network as being the best and they were constantly being 'poached' as other companies started up. Alpha Studios, justifiably, became known as 'a centre of professional skill', working seven days a week for two separate Companies with different presentation styles and identities gave the staff extra experience, flexibility and adaptability, not possessed by any other company on the Network.

ABC, of course, also had to provide facilities in Manchester, similar to Birmingham, they chose and converted the old Capitol Cinema at Didsbury in Manchester. This was split into two studios and had a small presentation studio. In London they took over the old Pathe studio in Wardour Street, which they used for simple magazine programmes and for interviews. Initially the company found it difficult to encourage artists to travel to Manchester to take part in their productions, and took over and adapted Warner Brothers film studios at Teddington in March 1959 as their London based production centre.

For both ABC and ATV, having studios and production facilities in London was essential as the first franchise holders were charged not only with providing a regional service but also had to produce a quota of high quality programmes to be transmitted over the entire network. London was the obvious choice for locating these production facilities as artists were not used to having to travel the country to take part in television. The BBC had always been able to accommodate them in London and the resulting programmes would be shown throughout the country from London; ITV were compelled to follow suit.

PRESENTATION REQUIREMENTS

The start of Independent Television in this country in 1955 was rather too sudden for the engineers who had to plan and make provision for the studios and communication networks between the centres.

Until that time the BBC monopoly, with its policy for broadcasting on a national rather than a regional basis, meant that there was only one presentation centre feeding all the transmitters throughout the country with identical programmes. Linking and presentation itself were therefore, simple and leisurely. There was no particular reason why a programme should not over or under run by a few minutes. Any changes made to scheduling were not a problem as all the transmitters throughout the country were fed from a single presentation centre.

Independent television was obviously going to be very different from this. Firstly, broadcasting was to be on a regional basis and secondly, one thing that was bound to be important was time. If you sell it, you must be accurate about it. Furthermore, as the different regions would often want to share the same programme the start and finish of that programme should not be vague. British television broadcasting had no experience of this type of operation. It is not surprising; therefore, that many of the new Programme Contractors looked for guidance in the planning of their presentation facilities to the USA, where similar operations were already in existence. Commercial television was already a fact of life there, with regional broadcasting, insertion of commercials and even time delay across the country.

ORIGINAL FACILITIES AT ALPHA

In the Midlands, where Alpha Television in Birmingham provided facilities for the two programme companies operating in the region, an American 'dummy studio' technique was adopted. This consisted of a studio type of control room with vision and sound mixers but no studio floor apart from a small announcer's booth to go with them. The inputs to the mixers in such a system were other studios, remote sources, Outside Broadcasts, films (from Telecine equipment), caption scanners, station clock, etc. The output from theses mixers was fed to the local transmitter.

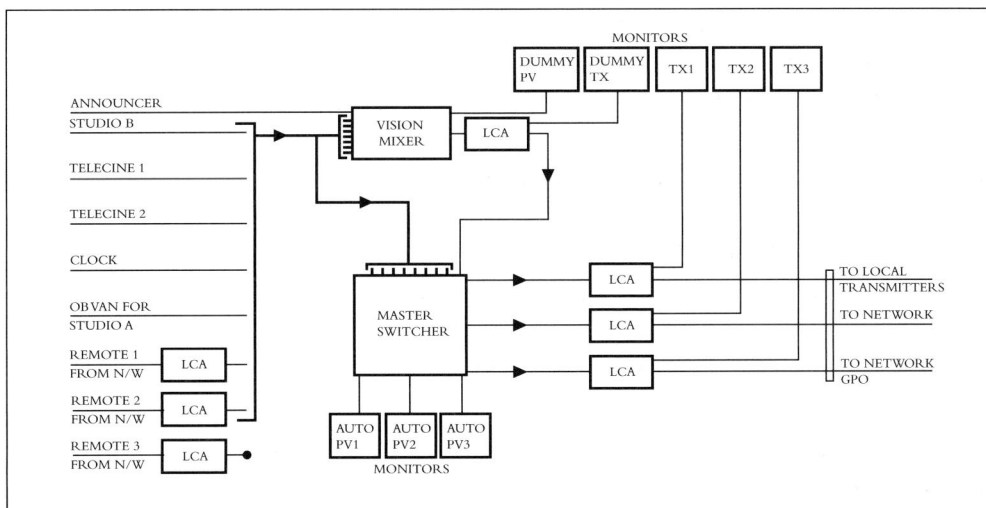

The original presentation facilities at Alpha Television.
(Source: Sound and Vision Broadcasting Summer 1962).

At Alpha, the sources available to the mixers were one studio, the control room of which was initially an OB van, a further studio, two Telecine machines, a caption scanner, three incoming lines from the rest of the network, and an announcer's studio in sound only.

These sources were fed into the vision and sound mixers and also into a master switching matrix, having eight inputs and three outputs for both sound and vision. The eighth input to the master matrix was fed from the output of the sound and vision mixers. The three outputs were routed one to the local transmitter, and the other two to the network.

The concept of 'clean' feeds and 'dirty' feeds was used from a very early stage. A 'clean' feed being one with gaps in it for commercials and a 'dirty' feed one with commercials already inserted. Since all commercials were inserted at the local centres of the programme companies throughout the country, programmes fed out to the network were 'clean' to ensure that one company's commercials were not by accident transmitted in another contractors region.

The outputs of the presentation or dummy mixer were 'dirty' and were therefore only to be fed to the local transmitter. This was the transmission output of the station. They were fed via the first transmission bank of the master switcher and, in fact, this bank remained switched to position 8 for most of the time. 'Clean' feeds; either

The Presentation Suite at Aston − on the right is the window of the Presentation or Announcer's Studio.

locally originated or otherwise, were fed directly to the network by the second and third banks of the switcher.

All this took place in the Presentation Suite, which was the 'heart' of the television station. Whatever was being produced within the station, programmes from a studio, films produced from Telecine, incoming programmes from other parts of the network, or outside broadcasts were mixed together by presentation staff, under the direction of the Transmission Controller, along with the all important commercials, also on film. It has been described as being similar to a railway goods marshalling yard where trucks carrying a variety of products and goods are shunted from different places to be connected together to produce a train.

The Presentation Suite was part of what was to be called the Central Area of the Studios, its purpose then was to provide those central facilities, available to the studios for the making of programmes. It provided feeds of both 16mm and 35mm Telecine machines, with both optical sound and separate and combined magnetic sound, caption scanners and 35mm slides into the studios.

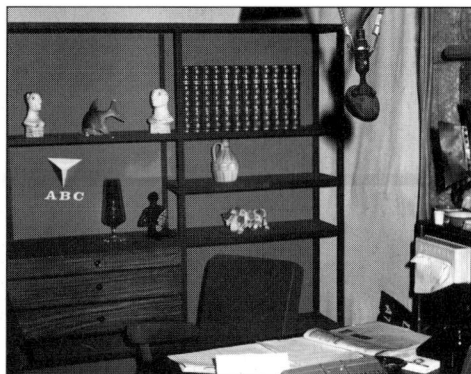

Left: An earlier picture of the Presentation Suite 'on air' – note absence of tape deck adjacent to the sound desk. Operating the Suite are, right to left: Transmission Controller Lou Rivers, Vision Mixer Graham Wormald, on the Master Switcher John Pettinger, and the Central Area Supervisor Dave Simmons; on the Sound Desk to the rear, is Clive Dear.
Right: Interior of the Announcer's Studio – set up for operation at the weekend when ABC Television were transmitting.

The Transmission Controller was seated to the right of the centre desk with the vision mixer to his left and the master switcher to his left. The sound mixing desk was to the rear, with its tape and grams desks. In front of the central desk can be seen the operational bank of monitors, sound patch panels and the all important clock.

Beyond the monitors were racks of equipment and the door at the far end of the corridor led to the Telecine Area.

To the rear of the Presentation Suite stairs led down to the basement of the old Theatre, where the Lines Department was situated. This was the television station's link with the outside world; sound, vision and telephone links from here to the Post Office put Alpha in communication with the Network.

All incoming and outgoing lines both sound and vision were terminated in these racks, and were patched by 'u-link' or cord to destinations according to requirements. Outside Broadcasts also entered the station here, and were treated as being just another source.

The transmission output of the station also passed through the lines racks of equipment on its way to the transmitter.

Telephone engineering control lines connected the lines engineers to the engineers of the Post Office, ITA Transmitter and the other Television Stations as well as those at Outside Broadcasts. Similar control lines permitted production staff in studios and at Outside Broadcast sites to talk to one another.

The technical quality of these communications was very high and they were being tested regularly.

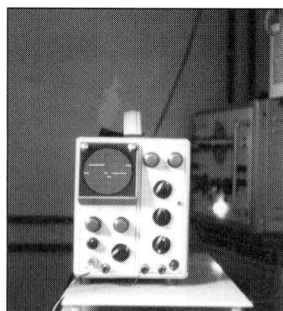

Top Left: The Announcer's view of his all important clock, monitors and remotely controlled camera – above the clock. Standby and 'on air' lights can be seen either side of the clock.
Top Right: Pulse and Bar waveform on the oscilloscope was used to monitor and test the technical quality of the various lines throughout the network.
Bottom: The Lines Department was the domain of Joe Ryder (kneeling) and Geoff Arrowsmith, both ex-Post Office Engineers. Joe had been involved in the development of Radar during the Second World War.

4. INDEPENDENT TELEVISION GOES ON THE AIR

After a gigantic joint effort between architects, builders, equipment manufacturers, installation engineers and managers; studios, control rooms, sound and vision communications, scenery construction workshops, in fact everything, every detail of television stations were constructed ready for the momentous first transmission to an eagerly awaiting British public.

LONDON

As would be expected the London area was the first to receive the new Independent Television output. ATV jointly with Associated Rediffusion were the first Independent Television Companies to go on air.

On the occasion the Editorial of the first issue of the TV Times commented that:

Television is at last given the real freedom of the air. The event is comparable with the abolition of the law that kept motor-cars chugging behind a man with a red flag.

Now it's the 'go' signal, the green light for television too – with no brake on enterprise or imagination.

So far, television in this country has been a monopoly restricted by limited finance, and often, or so it has seemed, restricted by a lofty attitude towards the wishes of viewers by those in control.

That situation undergoes a great and dramatic change. Viewers will no longer have to accept what is deemed best for them. They will be able to pick and choose.

And the new Independent Television planners aim at giving viewers what viewers want – at the time viewers want it.

Standards will be raised by this new competitive spirit – with new opportunities for artists, for writers and producers and for technicians. Famous showmen like Jack Hylton and Val Parnell will present on the television screen, as they now do on the stage, the highest-paid stars of this and other countries....

So, following almost 10 years of campaigning, much argument and political wrangling, studio building, engineering and production team recruiting and training, at 7.15pm on 22nd September 1955 Independent Television was launched in London.

The Halle Orchestra, conducted by Sir John Barbirolli, played Elgar's 'Cockaigne', to be followed by Leslie Mitchell (one of the first BBC Presenters) who announced that, *"This is London. This is channel 9 on Band III, which brings you programmes by Associated Rediffusion, every week from Monday to Friday."*

The evening production on that night was a joint production by Associated Rediffusion and Associated Television Ltd. The Times listed the evening's programmes:

COMMERCIAL TELEVISION

This evening commercial television begins, and the following is the first programme.

- 7.15pm   *Preparations for* **Opening Ceremony at Guildhall**.
- 7.45pm   **Inaugural speeches** *by Sir Seymour Howard, the Lord Mayor, Charles Hill the Postmaster General, and the Chairman of Independent Television Authority, Sir Kenneth Clark.*
- 8.00pm   **Variety** *– with Shirley Abicair, Elizabeth Allen, Daphene Batchelor, Billy Cotton, Reg Dixon, Lucille Graham, Hughie Green, John Hanson, Sheila Mathews, Michael Miles, Bessie Rofers, Shirley Norman, Leslie Randall, Derek Roy, Joy Shelton, Harry Secombe, Leslie Welch, Kip Van Nash, Theda Sisters and the George Carden Dancers.*
- 8.40pm   **Drama** *– introduced by Robert Morley – Excerpts from:* **"The Importance of Being Earnest"** *by Oscar Wilde, with Dame Edith Evans, Margaret Leighton and Sir John Gielgud:* **"Baker's Dozen"** *by Saki, with Pamela Brown, Alec Guinness and Faith Brook:* **"Private Lives"** *by Noel Coward, with Kay Hammond and John Clements.*
- 9.10pm   **Professional Boxing**. *Jack Solomons presents: Terence Murphy v. Lew Lazar, in a 12-round contest for the Southern Area Middleweight Championship, from the Shoreditch Town Hall.*
- 10.00pm   **News and Newsreel**
- 10.15pm   **Gala Night at the Mayfair**, *from the Mayfair Hotel, London. Leslie Mitchell introduces some of the guests.*
- 10.30pm   **Star Cabaret**, *with music by Billy Ternant and his Orchestra.*
- 10.50pm   **Preview** *– forthcoming programmes.*
- 11.00pm   **Epilogue**. *The National Anthem and close-down.*

The all important advertisers on that night were charged a premium rate of £1,500 a minute for the honour of screening their products on the first night. There were 23 slots available throughout the evening and as the demand was so high, lots were drawn to determine whose would be first to appear. Gibbs SR toothpaste was

```
┌─────────────────────────────────────────┐
│                                           │
│         THE CEREMONY AT                   │
│           GUILDHALL                       │
│              7.15                         │
│         THE GUESTS ARRIVE                 │
│      Commentator: John Connell            │
│                                           │
│              7.30                         │
│        THE HALLE ORCHESTRA                │
│     Conductor: Sir John Barbirolli        │
│   Overture, "Cockaigne" (In London Town)  │
│         by Sir Edward Elgar               │
│                                           │
│         The National Anthem               │
│                                           │
│              7.45                         │
│       INAUGURAL SPEECHES                  │
│                by                         │
│    The Rt. Hon. The Lord Mayor of London, │
│         Sir Seymour Howard                │
│       The Postmaster - General,           │
│     Dr. the Rt. Hon. Charles Hill, M. P.  │
│  The Chairman of the Independent Television│
│      Authority, Sir Kenneth Clark         │
│                                           │
└─────────────────────────────────────────┘
```

drawn and has gone down in history as being the first advertisement to be broadcast on British Independent Television. Other commercials shown on that night were:

- Brillo
- Cadbury's Drinking Chocolate
- Dunlop Tyres
- Ford
- Lux
- Shredded Wheat
- Surf
- Woman Magazine

Even on that first night not everything went as the advertisers would have wished and the uncertainties of 'live' television were soon apparent. During the Boxing that evening, 15 second commercials were being inserted during the between-round breaks. During one particular break there was a cut away from a boxer sitting in his corner taking a drink from a bottle, to a 15 second beer advertisement, which then cut back to the boxer as he spat out his mouthwash into a bucket. Not quite the effect the advertiser wished to achieve!

The next day, Friday 23rd September 1955, was the first full day of the new ITA Service and its Schedule for the day was:

- 10.45am   **"Sixpenny Corner"** (a serial)
- 11.00am   **Hands About the House**
- 11.45am   **Book Review**
- 12.00am   **News**
- 12.10pm   **Friday's Man**
- 12.15pm   **Programme for children under five**
- 12.30pm   **Time**
- 5.00pm   **Forthcoming Programmes**
- 7.00pm   **News and Weather**
- 7.15pm   **For the Motorist**
- 7.20pm   **Take Your Pick**
- 8.30pm   **"The Big Escape"** by James Moner
- 9.00pm   **Reg Dixon's Half Hour**
- 9.30pm   **Round the World with Orson Welles**
- 10.00pm   **News and Newsreel**
- 10.15pm   **Visitor of the Day**
- 10.20pm   **Out of Town**
- 10.50pm   **And So To Bed**
- 11.00pm   **Epilogue**

Note that programmes did not start until 10.45am and that they ceased between 12.30pm and 7.00pm with only a short preview of forthcoming programmes, the station closed down after the Epilogue with the playing of the National Anthem. The periods in the mornings and afternoons between on-air times were filled by the Transmitter Test Card and background music.

Associated Television's first morning 'on-air' was on Saturday 24th September 1955. They went on as Associated Broadcasting Company, ABC! Associated British Picture Corporation was horrified, as their cinema chain was called ABC Cinemas and they wished to protect that name.

It could be argued that as Associated British Picture Corporation had initially not intended to be a part of Independent Television, that Lew Grade was justified in using the name of Associated Broadcasting Company. Matters were made worse when it was realised that, Sir Philip Warter had signed a contract with the Independent Television Authority for ABPC to replace the failed bid by Kemsley-Winnick Television as contractor in the Midlands and North, only a few days before London went on-air!

ABPC intended to call its television arm Associated British Corporation. Both companies then wished to use the letters ABC on their station logos. ABPC went to the Courts, seeking and obtaining an injunction that prevented Associated Broadcasting from using the name 'ABC.' Following a month of argument, with their fourth weekend 'on-air' fast approaching and with their company losing money, Prince Littler and Lew Grade gave up the fight and agreed to change the name of the company to Associated Television Ltd.

This is what the company had to offer its viewers in the morning and afternoon on that important first day:

- 9.30am **Week-End** – An informal magazine for the family
- 10.30am **Testing** – A service for the convenience of the public and dealers to help with adjustment of sets. Continuous background music played while a test card and interesting pictures are screened. Time signals will be given at every hour throughout the day
- 3.00pm **ABC Music Shop** – The rendezvous of popular recording stars from both sides of the Atlantic – with Gerry Wilmot
- 3.30pm **My Hero** – staring Robert Cummings – Tramp for a Day
- 4.00pm **Home With Joy Shelton** – Informal, entertaining – a wide variety of items of interest to the housewife
- 4.20pm **ABC Club** – Young People's Club
- 4.30pm **Tales of Hans Anderson** – Emperor's New Clothes
- 5.00pm **Michaela and Armand Denis** – A special series of films in Africa
- 5.15pm **Do It Yourself** – New Bathrooms for Old – W.P. Matthew
- 5.30pm **Sport** – Football Results! News! Opinion! – Howard Peters
- 6.00pm **Close-down** till 7.00

Early television receivers needed to be tuned in correctly and so the Test Card was important for both viewers and set retailers. Before the day's programmes commenced a simple test card was transmitted, to allow 'the man of the house' to display his expertise in making those important final 'tweaks.' During the remainder of television's close-down time (of which there was quite a lot) a more detailed test card for retailers and set and aerial installers to use for optimum set-up was transmitted from the transmitters.

If nothing else the display of the test card on sets in the retailer's window proved that they were working!

The period between 6.00pm and 7.00pm was called the 'Toddlers Truce', with both ITV and BBC TV off the air, so that the children could be put to bed. The 'truce' period lasted until 16th February 1957 when the BBC took to the air with *Six-Five Special!*

On that first day ATV returned for the evening's programmes at 7.00pm:

- 7.00pm   **News**
- 7.10pm   **Strange Experiences**
- 7.15pm   **Around the Town** – People are Funny
- 7.45pm   **Colonel March of Scotland Yard** – serial
- 8.15pm   **Saturday Showtime** with Harry Secombe, Norman Vaughan and the Tiller Girls
- 9.00pm   **TV Playhouse** – Mid Level by Berkley Mather
- 10.00pm   **The ITN News and Newsreel**
- 10.15pm   **The Jack Jackson Show**
- 11.00pm   **Epilogue and Closedown**

THE MIDLANDS GOES ON-AIR

On 17th February 1956, four months after the London region went on-air; Alpha Television Studios hit the 'on-air' button and radiated a new set of television waves to the aerials of its Midlands viewers. This followed a huge amount of work in preparing the old Astoria Cinema, setting up new equipment, and rehearsals.

OPENING NIGHT IN THE MIDLANDS

The service to the Midlands was launched by a great Gala Ball held at the Town Hall, Birmingham, with inaugural speeches by the regions Civic Heads and the Chairman

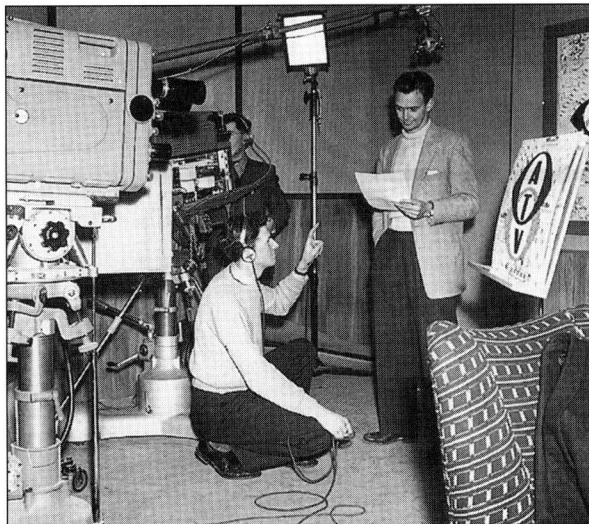

*Left: First Night rehearsals taking place at Alpha Studios whilst the original
audience seating in the circle of the old Astoria Cinema was being given a clean.
(Courtesy: Birmingham a Look Back by Alton Douglas).
Right: Rehearsals taking place for the Opening Night's programme with
Director Reg Watson standing in for the presenter Leslie Mitchell.
(Courtesy: Birmingham in the Fifties by Alton Douglas).*

of the Independent Television Authority, Sir Kenneth Clark. The opening ceremony
was relayed to the studio centre from an OB picture unit operated by Stan Broughton,
an ex-Battle of Britain Hurricane pilot and Eric Pemberton, who also served with the
RAF in Singapore; both had recently taken a plunge into the unknown by leaving the
BBC in the Midlands to join ATV.

It has been estimated that 1,500,000 viewers tuned in to the first evening of ITV
in the Midlands Region. But ATV themselves estimated that only 450,000 watched the
first programme radiated from the ITA's Midland Transmitter at Lichfield. The two new
Midlands contractors came together on Birmingham's Opening Night which was a
joint ABC/ATV production. The programmes commenced at 7.45pm. with presenter
Leslie Mitchell once again opening and welcoming viewers to the service, and
introducing the speakers at the Opening Ceremony at the Birmingham Town Hall. The
inaugural ceremony was by the Lord Mayor and civic dignitaries, and the following
evening's viewing consisted of:

- 7.45pm **Introduction** by Leslie Mitchell
- 7.55pm **News**
- 8.00pm **Variety Show** staring Bob Monkhouse, Denis Goodwin, Mr Pastry, Barbara Lyon and Tyrone Power
- 8.45pm **The Adventures of Robin Hood** – film series
- 9.15pm **Boxing** – Lightweight Contest from the Embassy, Sparkbrook.
- 10.00pm **I Love Lucy** – film series
- 10.30pm **Midlands Cabaret** with Joe Loss
- 10.50pm **Epilogue** the Bishop of Birmingham
- 11.00pm **Close Down**

Writing in 1968 Alpha's General Manager, Frank Beale, recalled the excitement and problems of that night:

There were V.I.P.s everywhere, V.I.P.s from the City of Birmingham, V.I.P.s from the original contractors, V.I.P.s from the ITA – the place just swarmed with V.I.P.s.

Joe Loss and his Orchestra supplied the music at the Town Hall and Joe was very upset to find only three cardioid microphones covering his whole band. I told him that we had brand new sound equipment in commercial television which enabled far better coverage by each mike plus a brilliant Sound Balancer and the effect was just great! What I could not tell him was that we only had three mikes and these we had borrowed.

Came the cabaret and, with the announcement in progress introducing Boyer and Revell, a lady and gentleman walked on to the 'floor show' area and sat on the two chairs already positioned for the artistes.

"Get 'em out quick," I cried to Bill Ward of ATV. "Not me," says Bill – "that's Sir Philip and Lady Warter." "I don't...... care who they are." said I. However, with controlled tact and diplomacy and with due apologies, too, most readily accepted by the Chairman and his Lady, the situation was retrieved.

That's television for you – but not how to win friends and influence the right people!

HISTORICAL CONTEXT

In those pioneering days of the mid-fifties Anthony Eden had just succeeded Winston Churchill as Prime Minister. There was trouble between Israel and the Arabs and there was the Suez crisis. Petrol, strictly rationed, went up from 4/6d to 6/- a gallon (22.5p to 30p). The Chancellor of the Exchequer, Harold Macmillan, appealed for restraint in wages, prices and dividends and the Bank rate rose to 5.5 per cent, the highest for twenty-five years.

While ITN covered the world, ATV launched the first regional news service on British television, presented by the first lady newsreader Patricia Cox. Reports in 1956 included a four day working week at the Austin Motor Works at Longbridge because of over-production, and the purchase of the Singer Motor Company by the Rootes Group.

In the sporting world, Birmingham City Football Club got to the F.A. Cup Final at Wembley where they were beaten 3–1 by Manchester City, and where Bert Trautman the Manchester City goalkeeper broke his neck. Midlander Randolph Turpin was British Light Heavyweight Boxing Champion.

5. THE WORK OF A TELEVISION STATION

In those early days the functions of a Television Station could be shown on a fairly simple diagram. The output from the Station was its transmission, which was intended to be a smooth flow of Programmes interspersed with Commercials and Promotions for forthcoming Programmes with a particular style chosen to reflect the image the particular company was attempting to put over to its viewers.

STYLE

Presentation is the manner in which programmes are linked one to another. Different companies had different ideas as to how presentation should be achieved. Except for the commercials there was no money to be made from the intervals between programmes and in early years little attention was paid to it. That is until the ITA expressed dissatisfaction with ABC's presentation style. This was a body blow to ABC; they hired a skilled presentation manager and re-launched their on-air identity, and they began to put money into presentation.

The identity of the station became important, the presentation style was what was impressed upon the minds of its viewers, and it was what made it different from ATV or Granada. ABC took the challenge very seriously, it would never again be criticised for poor presentation.

Since then all companies have recognised the importance of presentation style and huge amounts of money have been poured into it in order to impress the viewer, to impress its identity on the minds of the viewer.

Both Midlands companies used a regular team of friendly presentation announcers who became almost a part of everyone's family. They were so familiar that they would be recognised anywhere; they were everywhere, they opened fetes and shops across the region and appeared wherever anything of importance was happening in the region. Both ATV and ABC wanted to be noticed and made sure that the viewers knew that it was they who brought the important matters in their lives to their attention on screen.

Each time an announcer appeared on screen the company logo was also seen in the background or as a badge on a blazer, scarf or tie. Clothes were very important and announcers dressed differently between day time and evening. ABC called their team 'station hosts' and when viewers sat down to watch a programme they were made to feel they were doing so with their station host. Every effort was made to sell the company image, each programme produced its collectable 'stickers', there were television annuals, viewers were encouraged to feel a part of the company.

Other than News Readers the only comparable use of presenters nowadays is with the people who read the weather forecasts – but here their use is inappropriate and confusing in that they distract the viewer from the pictorial message, the weather-chart. They do not sell 'the message' or the TV station, just themselves, but they are the last vestige of the television station's own personalities presenting a friendly face to the viewer.

LIVE TRANSMISSION

It is sometimes forgotten that when independent television started the whole of transmission was 'live', in the sense that it was actually happening at the same time as it was transmitted and viewed on the television sets in people's homes. There was no second chance, if something went wrong then everyone saw or heard it, from actors forgetting their lines, films breaking, scenery falling over, props not working, whatever, the whole audience was aware of it. This added to the excitement of those working in the business, everyone had to fully understand their job and know immediately what had to be done if something went wrong. Today most programmes are pre-recorded, sometimes after a number of 'takes' and editing to ensure that everything is right and that nothing can go wrong on transmission.

Programmes themselves could come from a number of sources, the Station's own Studios, other contractors on the Network, Outside Broadcasts, from film, either 35mm or 16mm. Film itself could be either a Feature Film fed directly to transmission or as inserts, film, slides or captions fed into a Studio Programme.

Commercials were also on film, or occasionally on slides injected into transmission during the 'natural breaks' within or between programmes.

PLANNING, SCHEDULING AND CONTROL

The smooth output of transmission content had to be planned in great detail. There were people who decided which types of programme were to be made, what film series and feature films to purchase from distributors both locally and abroad, which programmes to purchase from other contractors up and down the Network. Decisions had to be made as when to schedule various programmes within the year, month, week day and time of day. Each day the programme schedule had to be planned to the second, and a Daily Routine Sheet had to be prepared so that each second was accounted for. A never ending round of decision making as every second of permitted transmission hours had to be filled. Viewers have never been tolerant of even a few seconds of blank screen or silence. Every second had to be filled with something!

Then each day the Daily Routine Sheet had to be followed, vision and sound mixers in the Master Control Room had to be instructed which source was next and cued when to 'take' it. Someone had to decide what course of action to take whenever anything went wrong. These people had to be very special, as the whole of a Station's programme output, and commercial revenue was in their hands. They could damage a company's reputation by 'clipping' the ends of programmes, putting parts of feature films out in the wrong order, and could save a company countless thousands of pounds by re-inserting lost or marred commercials, they could save viewers from foul mouthed remarks or inappropriate behaviour by guests and artists appearing on shows, by cutting them off.

These functions were carried out by the station's Presentation Department.

PRESENTATION DEPARTMENT

Writing in 1958 Sheila Langham-Thompson of ATV, described Presentation as being made up of three sections – Film Traffic, Promotion and Transmission Control, pointing out that their work was closely woven in with other departments such as Film Department, Operations, Lines and Engineering.

John Terry was then head of the Presentation Department, Barbara Swindells managed the Film Traffic, keeping track of every ATV film to be transmitted by each of the programme contractors on the network.

When the Sales Make-up, spot lists and film running times were finalised, it was Margaret Steller's job to co-ordinate the mass of data into the 'Daily Routine Sheet', Margaret assisted by Barbara Fountain, had to work out to the last second the exact moment at which the live programmes, films, commercials, slides, announcements and the dulcet tones of the ATV chimes would go out on air; and specify by a code of abbreviations such as HE, MC, PRES, ANN, SOF 35, BM'C the point of origin of each item, specifying whether it was live or filmed. Once completed the sheets were always subject to alteration, even whilst on air.

Once the Routine Sheet was issued, the Assistant Transmission Controllers (ATC) would get to work, viewing films, choosing trailers, recording music and announcements to tape, arranging promotion spots and checking Routine Sheets prior to printing. On a week day basis the packing of the 'Birmingham Box' had to be carried out. This was a cross between an ordinary cardboard box and a picnic hamper, which held all the material to be used on transmission in Birmingham the following day, routine sheets, slides, films, trailers, amendments to amendments, etc.

At that time the ATCs appeared to have been Tony White an electronic engineer, Roger Tucker who had a degree in Social Studies, John Crowest an actor, David Scott another actor, Duggie Fairburn, and Jack Clegg who had psychic powers. In charge of the many slides and captions, standby films and telescriptions is Marj Young, from Melbourne Australia.

The Transmission Controllers were at that time, Chris Philip and John Marten in London and Lou Rivers and Tony Parker in Birmingham. Through their hands passed the films and slides that represent almost the entire advertising revenue of ATV. They were the people who, using the Daily Routine Sheet switched from one set of mysterious abbreviations to another whilst murmuring such incantations as " Standby Telecine One, Roll One – fade grams – ask the OB to stand by, Change slide – cue OB." It was they who decided whether to fade or not to fade, to allow an over-run or to cut, to re-transmit a commercial, or to 'stay with' a networked programme which was over-running. And if they did, simultaneously they had to work out the technicalities of re-routing and timings for the programmes to follow!

The Birmingham Studios used by ATV during the week, Sheila pointed out were run by Alpha Television Services, but ATV had a small Presentation Department, which coped with the five days transmission each week.

TRANSMISSION CONTROLLERS

Transmission Controllers were in sole charge of the final output of the television station and directly responsible to the Head of Presentation for the correct presentation of each day's programmes as scheduled on the Daily Routine Sheet for the day. In a 'dummy studio' set-up, his function although similar to the Director in a studio, carried far greater responsibility as he had to be completely familiar with:

- The ITA rules and regulations regarding Programme hours, commercial distribution and transmission in general.
- News Flash procedure.
- Obituary procedure.
- Network switching.
- Commercial segment times.

The duties and responsibilities of the Transmission Controller covered three main areas of the days transmission for which he was to oversee:

- Before Transmission.
- During Transmission.
- After Transmission.

The following is reproduced from the ATV Presentation Department Operations Manual, produced by Leslie Lugg, the Head of Presentation in July 1970.

Before Transmission

1. *He must check the Daily File, to ensure that all the information that it contains regarding the day's transmission is shown on the Routine Sheet. He should, with the aid of the scripts and synopsis familiarise himself with the cast and story line of all programmes, so that should an actor die, or an event occur that parallels the story line, he is in a position to save not only his own company, but other Contractors embarrassment.*

2. *He must check the Routine Sheet for errors or point of impractical presentation, paying particular attention to the fact that all times add up correctly. It is his responsibility to ensure that all members of the Master Control Room staff are quite clear as to their own particular functions as far as the Routine Sheet is concerned. He should also check his Routine Sheet against the Daily Programme Schedules and against TV Times Billings.*

3. *The Transmission Controller must ensure that either he or an ATC (Assistant Transmission Controller) has seen every foot of film that he is scheduled to transmit, including commercials which must be checked for 'clashing products and story lines.'*

4. *He must check with both the Telecine and VTR Supervisors that they hold all material required for the day's transmission.*

5. *He must make certain that he has every slide, both promotion and commercial, together with the relevant scripts. These he must check against the Routine Sheet both for accuracy and in conjunction with the Duty Announcer for correct timing, and ensure that the information they contain is correct in all details.*

6. *It is the Transmission Controller's responsibility to ensure that the Announcer has been supplied by the Promotion Department with ample standby material in the form of promotion for future programmes.*

7. *The Transmission Controller is responsible for ensuring that all members of Master Control, Production and Telecine Staffs are fully aware of any last minute alterations that may have been made to the Routine Sheet after its issue.*

8. *Should any special discs be required, he should ensure that the operator has them available, and that timings (where necessary) have been checked. He must also ensure that a standby disc is available in the case of a breakdown and that the operator is fully versed in the procedure to be adopted.*

9. *The Transmission Controller may request an ATC to carry out some of the above duties, but as the ultimate responsibility for errors lies with the Transmission Controller, he must ensure that any duties designated to another, are correctly carried out.*

During Transmission

1. *The Transmission Controller must satisfy himself that the Senior Engineer has checked sound and vision from every source due to provide programme material at a reasonable period before the source is due on the air, and that he is aware of all programmes that are to be networked.*

2. *He must be prepared to cue every item that is transmitted and each technical operation that is involved except live or taped programmes, in which case he must give a start time.*

3. *He should notify Production Assistants of the cues he will give (if any) and what cues he expects from them, as well as checking the agreed in and out time of their programme and details of commercial breaks.*

4. *In the event of a breakdown, the Transmission Controller must put out a suitable announcement and ascertain the cause and likely duration of the failure. From this information the Controller must decide what procedure should be adopted in order to continue providing the viewer with entertainment. If the programme that has broken down, was being networked, and the Controller decides to use a standby, he must offer it to the network, and depending on whether some or all of the network accept the standby, he must rearrange the programme start times accordingly.*

5. *In the event of a live programme over-running, he must decide whether any or all of the over-run can be taken, bearing in mind switch times, and commercial segments. He must then arrange with the network the new start times for programmes.*

6. *In carrying out his duties, the Controller must at all times adhere to the regulations laid down by the ITA, and the company regarding to transmission of programme material and commercials.*

After Transmission

1. *The Transmission Controller must originate an Irregularity Report, on which the errors and their causes are detailed.*

2. *He must pass to the Film Department, a report on faults or damage to commercial films originated by Telecine.*

3. *He must return to the Presentation Office the Daily File containing:*

   a. His own amended Routine Sheet.

   b. The Irregularity Report.

   c. Film Rehearsal Sheets.

   d. Programme-as-Recorded Forms.

   e. Music Copyright Return. This must show details of all music played by Presentation, e.g. breakdown or standby music, ATV March and National Anthem, and music used for promotion spots.

   f. The Announcer's copy of the Continuity Script showing all amendments and additional promotion announcements which have been made.

   g. The Daily Programme Schedule.

The Preservation of Good Taste

It is difficult to define the responsibility of the Transmission Controller when he is called upon to exercise good taste on the policy of the company. He is nevertheless still responsible for preserving the decorum, and responsibility rests on him alone as he is the final link between the company and the Viewer. Should he suddenly be faced, during transmission, with a programme of doubtful taste, and there is not time to refer the matter to higher authority, the Transmission Controller must act on his own initiative and fade the programme, making a suitable breakdown apology. (This should be of temporary nature). He should then inform the producer of the action he has taken and state that he will only restore the programme when good taste is re-established.

Although programmes were timed to the second, quite often, through breakdowns, human error, or unforeseen overrunning or under running of programmes caused very complicated repercussions for the Transmission Controller, particularly so if the programme was being networked. Any changes to timing had to be notified to the stations on the network taking the programme and those who may not but who would join the network at a later time. All stations had to be able to join the network at the same time.

All such communication to the network was through an open high grade telephone line, called the Red Phone. This could only be rung by the Transmission Controller in London or by ITN, as described earlier.

6. TELEVISION SOURCES

STUDIOS

Atelevision studio is an enclosed area of floor space within a specially constructed room used for the setting up of the particular requirements of a television programme. They obviously vary in size from the small presentation announcer's booth to a much larger area into which many different 'sets' can be constructed for the many scenes of a drama, for instance, can be acted out.

Whatever takes place within a studio needs to be conveyed to the audience in the outside world. Unlike a theatre stage where the complete audience is seated in rows in front of the only place where the action takes place; in the case of a television studio the audience is dispersed across a wide area with each member or small groups viewing a selection of the action on a television set. There may of course be a small audience within the studio itself, but that, it might be considered, is a part of the action taking place.

The means by which the action is conveyed from the studio floor out into the wide world is by means of television cameras for vision and microphones for sound. In the case of a presentation announcer a static camera and microphone are all that are required because the action is arranged to come from a single point.

In the case of a large drama production, with a number of different 'sets', a number of moveable cameras and microphones are required to move within each set and from one set to another as well as producing different shots of actors and different angles within the set. Unlike the theatre stage with the audience being able to see everything that is taking place, the output of a television studio can be much more selective; including close–ups not available to a theatre audience. All the cameras within a particular set will be active and producing different shots of the scene according to a predetermined order or script and a programme director within a nearby control room able to view all camera outputs side by side instructs vision and sound mixers to change from one camera shot to another as he directs. The director will also have access to, as other switchable sources the outputs of telecine machines, caption and slide scanners, other studio and outside broadcast outputs, as required. He will also have the use of an adjacent sound control room providing sound effects, taped or disc audio inserts, and a lighting control room with apparatus for altering under computer control the lighting within each of the sets on the studio floor.

Initially at Alpha Television there was a single studio in the heart of the original cinema with its original circle seating for audiences. The control room for this studio was the equipment 'de-gutted' out of an outside broadcast control van. Besides inputs from the few cameras on the floor the only other inputs were from telecine, for film inserts and outside broadcast material patched to it by the Lines Department in the basement.

FILM – TELECINE

In the early days of Independent Television broadcasting programme material was either live or on film. There was virtually no video tape recording. Early recordings were on film, called telerecordings – an elaborate method made when a live show was transmitted and fed to a specially adapted large, high grade flat television screen; a film camera was aimed at the screen, shooting at a frame rate in synchronisation with the television frame rate. Picture quality was inevitably of poor quality and the process was very expensive.

Even live programmes from studios would have film inserts and slides, fed in on transmission from telecine as another picture source, and of course 'end' captions, usually from a camera pointing at a caption stand on the studio floor.

Consequently the conversion of film material to television pictures was extremely important. The device used to transfer film into video is called telecine. The history of telecine is only as old as broadcast television; early applications were to broadcast motion picture film live on air.

Telecine at Alpha involved the combination of a synchronised motion picture projector with a television camera called photoconductive.

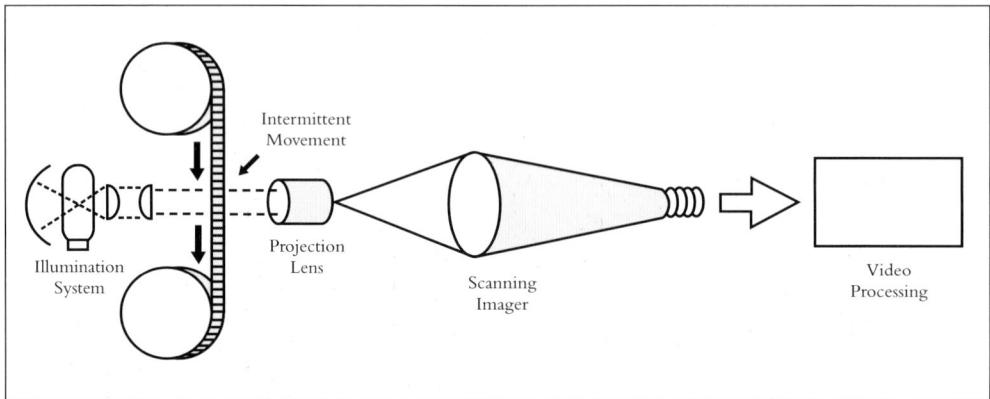

Photoconductive Telecine – simplified.

The standard 405 line photoconductive (vidicon) telecine installation at Alpha Studios consisted of a combination of two film projectors and one slide projector arranged around a camera and optical unit mounted on a cubicle, housing a camera control unit. The optical unit contained an arrangement of semi-mirrors so that when any one of the three projectors was illuminated its output, through lenses, would fall onto the front of the camera tube. A schematic diagram of the arrangement is shown overleaf.

In the picture below, the Control Console is on the left. To the left of the camera is a standard Philips PF7 projector mechanism with a special Pye lamp housing replacing the Philips lamp house. To the right of the camera housing is a cabinet housing a 16mm projector, and to the front of the camera is a 35mm slide projector.

In addition to local controls for the operation of the projectors and camera chain, remote operational facilities were provided on a control console which could be situated some distance away. This contained a picture monitor, waveform monitor, and an audio amplifying unit.

Monitoring and peak programme metering of the main audio signal was achieved by means of the audio amplifying unit, which also incorporated a talkback

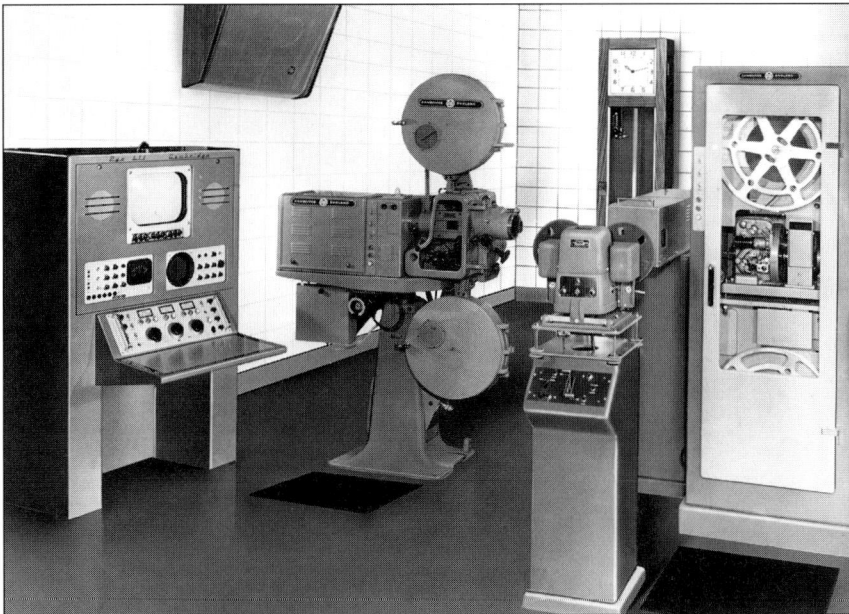

Pye Multiplexed Photoconductive (vidicon) Telecine as installed at Alpha Studios.

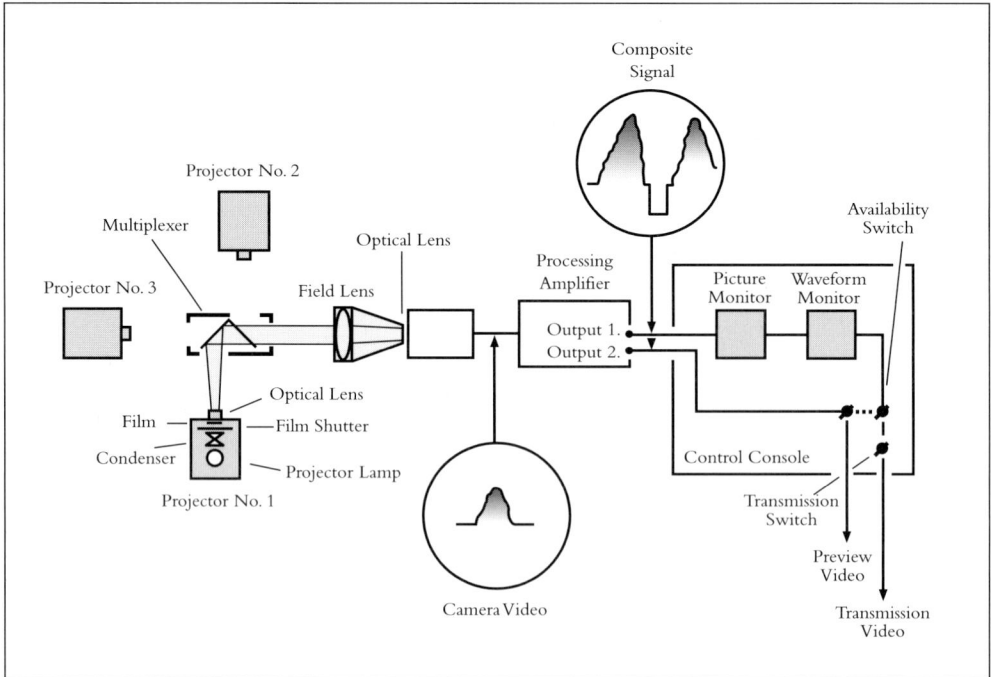

Staticon Telecine Equipment, Schematic Diagram of Video System.

amplifier for inter-communication purposes and a loudspeaker amplifier for monitoring the sound.

The 35mm projector driven by a motor gave a picture speed of 25 frames per second to coincide with the television scanning system. The lamp house contained a 750 watt 110 volt picture lamp, which was cooled by a blower and considerably under run to increase lamp life to some hundreds of hours (60 to 70 watts). An infrared filter reduced radiation on film, enabling still frames to be shown.

The lamp produced a beam of light which passed through the film via a standard shutter. The film mechanism being intermittent, i.e. 'pull down a frame and stop'; ensured that the film was only exposed to light when stationary. The image of the film frame was focused onto the light sensitive target or face of a photo conductive pick-up tube via an optical arrangement consisting of a semi-transparent mirror and a field lens. The image on the target was scanned by an electron beam producing an electronic video signal at the output of the camera tube. The signal was processed and external blanking pulses inserted, i.e. made ready to fit into the television system.

OVERALL DESCRIPTION OF THE TELECINE AUDIO SYSTEM
OPTICAL SOUND TRACK

The modulated sound track on the film moved in the path of and scanned by a narrow beam of light. The beam being formed by passing the light produced by a pre-focused exciter lamp through a condenser lens and glass rod (collimator), the later arrangement intensified the beam and produced uniformity of illumination. A microscope lens on the other side of the film projected an enlarged image of the sound track onto a white screen via a mirror. In the middle of the screen was a narrow scanning slit. The light rays passing through this slit being concentrated by another condenser which threw an image of the sound track onto a photo-cell.

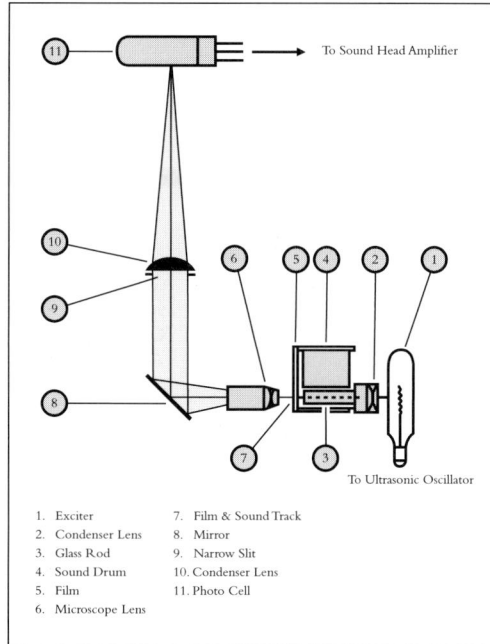

To Sound Head Amplifier

To Ultrasonic Oscillator

1. Exciter	7. Film & Sound Track
2. Condenser Lens	8. Mirror
3. Glass Rod	9. Narrow Slit
4. Sound Drum	10. Condenser Lens
5. Film	11. Photo Cell
6. Microscope Lens	

Schematic of Projector Sound Head.

The lights and shades of a modulated film track produced corresponding variations in intensity of the narrow light beam focused onto the photo-cell from which variations in current output were obtained at a frequency within the audio spectrum. Thus an optical sound track was converted into an electronic audio signal.

MAGNETIC SOUND TRACK

When operating from magnetic stripe film (Commag), a magnetic head which passed in contact with the film has its output fed to a magnetic pre-amplifier whose output took the place of the output from the photo-cell to produce the audio signal.

TELECINE EQUIPMENT AT ALPHA TELEVISION STUDIOS

Beyond the telecine control panels was an alcove which housed a caption scanner into which caption cards could be slotted in front of the station clock. Each day at 1 o'clock the station clock was replaced by a special 'Lunch Box' clock which had no mechanism as it was always radiated at that time. But the station clock always had to

Above Left: View of Telecine 2. Above Right: 35mm Telecine projector.
Bottom Left: 16mm Telecine projector cabinet.
Bottom Right: Control Desks for Telecine 2 (left) and Telecine 1 (right).

be checked prior to transmission as it always had to be correct. On one occasion the author not having been working at Alpha very long noticed that the clock was wrong just prior to transmission, running to the caption scanner he moved the hands to the correct time, just as the clock went on air, an action seen by millions of viewers and earning him the nick-name of 'Fingers.'

FILM MAKE-UP

In the early days at Alpha Studios the Telecine Department were responsible for making-up the commercial reels for the day. Commercials were invariably shot on 35mm film and transported to Birmingham from London over-night. Each commercial was contained in its own film tin and it was Telecine's first job of the day to join up the commercials into the order in which they were to be run, commercial break by commercial break. Between commercials an 'optical' relating to ATV or ABC was inserted.

At the end of the day the commercial reels were broken down and the individual commercials returned to their tins to be returned to London by transport called the 'night flyer.'

DAY: Thursday	DATE 14th November 1963.			Page 11.
TIME	NET PROGRAMME	AUDIO	VIDEO	SWITCH
21.52.47+ Bk.2.05 (To be completed before 22.00)	PARK DRIVE CIGS. (00.15) 2460R/FD	SOF	35	
	LYONS REASTNIX (00.15) 62/3	SOF	35	
	ROBERTSONS SILVER SHRED (00.30) No.54	SOF	35	
	V53. CAMPBELLS SOUP (00.30) 85464	SOF	35	
	PROPAX PEAS (00.30) FXS.15% C.5224	SOF	35	
21.54.52	NET THE ALFRED HITCHCOCK HOUR II (19.14)	SOF	35	
22.14.06+ Bk.3.10	STORK MARG. (00.30) JS 232	SOF	35	
	RICHMOND SAUSAGES (00.30) RS/4	SOF	35	
	VOSENE SHAMPOO (00.45) No.79	SOF	35	
	ROWNTREES PEPPERMINT CRACKNEL (00.15) 25/15R Alan Keith	SOF	35	
	BUTLINS CAMPS (00.30) XC 72P/3A/63 J. Witty	SOF	35	
	DENTU-CREME (00.30) DC 5R R. Lorraine & G. Elliot V/O	SOF	35	
22.17.16	NET THE ALFRED HITCHCOCK HOUR III (14.18)	SOF	35	
0	"ATV Presentation + 2 secs black screen		SL	
22.31.36+ Bk.3.08	BATCHELORS SURPRISE PEAS (00.30) FXS.15% 2/62 Ralph Wightman & Marie Sutherland	SOF	35	
	FAIRY SOAP (K) (00.30) T.55303%/6	SOF	35	
	ROWNTREES LYRICS (00.15) FXS.15% LYR/15/1	SOF	35	
	BISTO (00.30) FXS.15% No.1	SOF	35	
	QUINTET HEATERS (00.15) OPL 310	SOF	35	
	BIRDS EYE FISH FINGERS (00.30) FXS.15% BIFF 25% Andrew Faulds V/O	SOF	35	
	PALMOLIVE TOILET SOAP (00.30) No.39	SOF	35	
22.34.44	Annt. (00.16)	Bn.4	Bn.4	
22.35.00	THIRTY MINUTE THEATRE I (16.25) Truth Is A Stranger VTR/ATV/1324	OC/VT	OC/VT	

Top Left: Photograph of a film editing desk in Telecine at Alpha Studios.
Bottom Left: Commercial assembly film editing desk in Telecine at Alpha Studios.
Right: Page from a Daily Routine Sheet, demonstrating the importance and frequency of Telecine output. SOF indicates that Sound is on Film and 35 that the film is 35mm.

7. OUTSIDE BROADCASTS

An Outside Broadcast is a television programme which originates away from or outside of the permanent television station. As with a studio production it has cameras, lighting and sound equipment operating into a control room with vision and sound mixers under the control of a director. The control room is built into a specially built mobile unit. The output from the unit needed to be fed into the Post Office network, insertion points were positioned at a number of locations, or fed back to the studio centre by means of mobile microwave links

Left: Early ATV OB van circa 1959 (ex NBC).
Top Right: An early Lunch Box OB. Bottom Right: OB at a Go-cart Meeting.

Top Left: ATV OB – Air Training Cadets being instructed in gliding techniques.
Top Right: ABC Outside Broadcast Scanner and crew 1957 on location for the Holiday
Town Parade programme. Bottom Left: ABC Outside Broadcast cameras mounted on a
converted Blackpool Tram, driven by David Southwood. Bottom Right: Outside Broadcast
down on The Other Man's Farm, with Ronnie Baxter on camera and floor
manager John Russell.

During the first years of television the grey and blue outside broadcast vans of ATV became a familiar part of the Midlands scene.

To the viewers the term 'outside broadcast' almost automatically meant sport; selected events from the Midlands' sporting calendar, covering horse racing, boxing, football, professional wrestling, skating, snooker and so on, were relayed from all parts of the region.

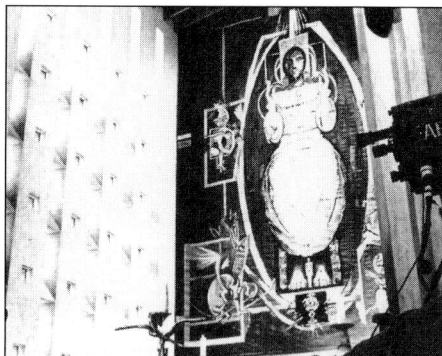

Top Left: Rigger Driver Ernie Hawksworth and Communications Engineer Frank Taylor clear a path for OB Unit 1 to get to a site near Doncaster for a Let's Go programme. The winter of February, 1960. Top Right: In May, 1962, the first Communion in Coventry Cathedral, was shown by OB cameras. Bottom Left: A first for ABC Outside Broadcasts – the first-ever live television show from the Isle of Man – August 1957. At the Palace Ballroom, Douglas. Bottom Right: This photograph was taken at a scramble meeting at York's famous Bentley Springs course.

There was an instructional programme weekly called **Seeing Sport** which brought tuition by top ranking sportsmen and women to younger viewers.

But sport was only a part of the OB activities. Television history was made in 1956, when ATV were present at the installation of a Lord Mayor in Coventry.

Other events broadcast included fashion shows, the Shropshire and West Midland Agricultural Show, the World Scout Jamboree from Sutton Park, Shrewsbury Musical and Floral Fete and the City of Birmingham Show.

ABC had a vast fleet of Outside Broadcast vehicles (until the late 1960s) the largest on the Network. It brought viewers many good programmes such as Professional Wrestling, Horse Racing, Rugby League and Motor Racing. Besides sport they brought **The Blackpool Show** and **Holiday Town Parade** to viewers' screens.

ABC Outside Broadcasts introduced its viewers to the sport of Motor Cycle Scrambling. Viewers were drawn into the excitement, the mud and the spills on Sundays.

OUTSIDE BROADCAST LINKS

Outside broadcast programmes could be fed back to the television studio either by a cable link provided by the Post Office or by the television company's own mobile microwave links.

Quite large distances could be covered by microwave links, routing the television signal around or over obstacles, hills or tall buildings in a number of 'hops.' One dish would transmit the signal from the OB site to be picked up by a receiver dish, monitored and processed, and then passed to the next transmitter dish. Finally the signal would be picked up by a final receiver disk and fed by cable into the television station.

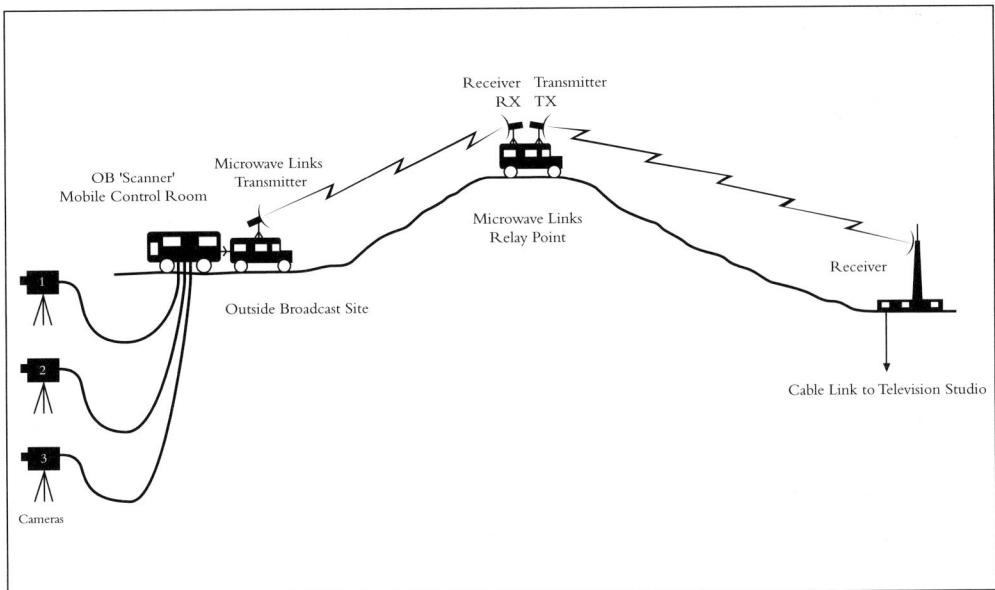

Diagram of Outside Broadcast Links.

Those who set up and operated the links were a hardy breed of men, who had to be prepared to work, often in the open, in all kinds of weather, very nice in the summer, but not so nice on a damp, cold winter's day.

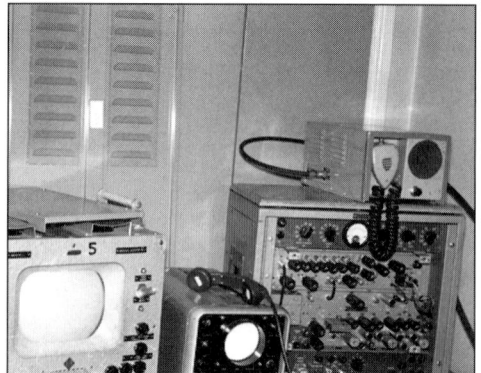

ATV Outside Broadcast Links equipment installed on the roof of the CML Building in Great Charles Street Birmingham; the tallest building in the City at that time.

8. A LACK OF COMMUNICATION WITHIN A COMMUNICATION COMPANY

A PROBLEM OF DISTANCE

A problem that often occurred for ATV in its early years was poor communication between Birmingham Studios and the Head Office in London; the problem was highlighted in 1958.

A copy of *'Focus on ATV'* the ATV House Magazine (Vol.1, No.2), July 1958, included a tongue in cheek 'Memo from Birmingham' written by Philip Dorte, Midlands Controller Associated Television Limited. This highlights a problem experienced not only by Midlands people but by the rest of the country in relation to Londoners. Londoners live in their own little restricted world daring not to look beyond what happens further afield than Watford, for fear of recognising that there is a wonderful and vibrant country out there that they cannot hope to experience being cooped up in their overcrowded, insular patch, where they convince themselves that they are at the centre of the universe and know everything and are the very best. How wrong they are!

Memorandum
From: *Mr. Philip Dorte* **ADMINISTRATION**
To: *Mr. Lawrie Higgins* **Date:** *19th May 1958*
Subject: *Article for "Focus"*

I am sorry to read in your memo to me of 10th February that Birmingham is letting you down where contributions to "Focus" are concerned. But the fact is that we're not a large unit, that we're all very busy and that most of us didn't realise that ATV had a House Magazine until, just the other day, we found an Alpha executive trying to flog copies to anyone who would buy them down at Aston.

I am flattered by your invitation to me to write an article for "Focus", and if Alpha will flog a copy to me so that I can see what it's all about I will burn some midnight oil before the end of May and try and knock something out for you — but I shall find it difficult to relate "some amusing aspect of television life in Birmingham" because, to be honest, I don't know of one. Indeed our television lives only tend to be amusing when, occasionally, some of us enter the portals of Television House in London – when, for instance, Noel Gordon, whose face and voice is so well known to every Midlands man, woman and child, is asked at Television House who she is and what she wants (this happened only a few weeks back), when a Birmingham producer who successfully handles six programmes a week up here is told at Television House that he is little more than a promising beginner or when, on a routine visit to Television House, I told the applicable official that only a handful of Birmingham staff could get down to London for the ATV Staff Party – only to be told in my turn that the party had been cancelled ages ago and that it was amazing that we had not been advised of this by our usual informant on Television House matters, viz., the lift boy at Broadcasting House, Portland Place!

No. If I do write an article for you, I shall bear in mind that it would be read by many at Television House who have never heard of Cornwall Street, who don't realise that not so long ago Birmingham was a suburb of Aston and not the other way round, who believe that an OB from Norwich ranks as a local Midlands OB and who, above everything, never come up here and find out for themselves.

I would like to give them, for instance, a "Who's Who" where Midlands ATV is concerned because they should know that there are two Watsons, Reg the producer, Derek in Sales, that Kit Plant is no longer a Transmission Controller but, albeit with the assistance of Walton Anderson, produces and often directs five news programmes and "Paper Talk" every week, "Story-teller" frequently, live commercials more frequently, odds and ends quite frequently and by the time I write the article will also have on his plate a weekly topical programme "Midlands Montage": they should realise too that we can't produce OBs because we haven't got an OB unit any more.

All London should know too that Birmingham Transmission Control is in the capable hands of Lou Rivers who is assisted by an ex-fighter pilot Tony Parker and that even the layman appreciates how good is weekday presentation from Aston compared with – but I wouldn't be so tactless as to say with what. And they should realise that the Press Office is manned by Morgan McCallum who recently joined us from a Birmingham newspaper group and that the inexplicable hobby of his secretary Jane McNeil is nursing the lion cubs in the zoo at Berlin (Germany).

I willingly admit that London Sales do know the occupants of the Sales suite here because John Williamson, the Midlands Sales Manager, often persuades Pat Henry and his stalwarts to visit Cornwall Street. And against the possibility that other London stalwarts may do the same they should know that my own efficient (and, of course, very attractive) secretaries are Mrs. Margaret Hodgson and Miss Jennifer Dowing: if they don't know this and don't make the appropriate noises before they do come up here, they will find themselves without anywhere to lay their heads should they decide to stay the night.

And there is one more thing – and it's not about our Announcers Jean Morton and Pat Astley, about our Continuity Writer Tim Emanuel, or about – no let them find out when I write the article or when they come up here, whichever is the sooner.

I will keep faith with you, I promise.
(Signed) P.H.Dorte
P.S. – On further thoughts, why not accept this as the article?
(Initialled) PHD

AND ABC TOO!

Another incident illustrating the unbelievable ignorance of some who reside in the South, occurred one Friday when Douglas Fairburn, ABC Transmission Controller (who until 1958 worked for ATV), was leaving Teddington Studios to go on duty in Birmingham for the weekend. A young lady asked him what he was doing over the weekend, when told; she was astonished, having no comprehension of what the company she worked for could possibly be doing in Birmingham and Manchester!

BIRMINGHAM/LONDON MONITORING LINK

As the London headquarters of ATV were outside of the Midlands Area, and unable to receive the output from the Lichfield transmitter, the communication problem was solved by installing a microwave link, installed by Pye Telecommunications Ltd between Alpha Studios and London.

This was the first long distance trunk television circuit in Britain, independent of the GPO to be built, installed and maintained by private enterprise. It carried high quality vision and sound and the first to use the then new 7,000 megacycle band, the highest frequency used for a television relay.

Besides programme output the link was used for other purposes. Young artists – with their eyes on the stars – would rehearse in the Birmingham Studios and top producers in London could watch their every movement on screen in London.

The link originated at Alpha Television Studios in Birmingham being fed by cable to the transmitting terminal at the CML Building in the City Centre, the signals then passing through Repeater Stations at Meriden, Cold Ashby and Barkway to the receiver terminal at Highgate and then again over cable to ATV House, London; the overall path of the link being some 135 miles.

The transmission terminal and the first two stages of the link were maintained by the author, John Pettinger prior to being employed by Alpha.

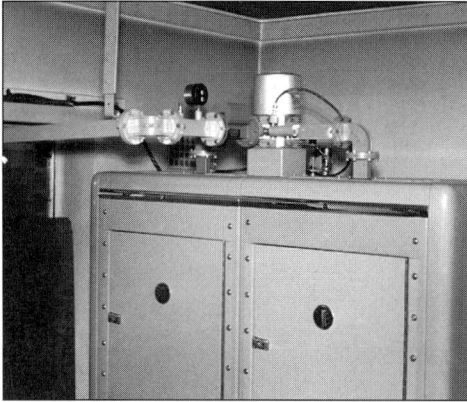

The CML Building housed the transmission terminal of a microwave link, fed by cable from the Lines Department at Alpha Studios.

The microwave equipment was fully duplicated with automatic changeover to standby equipment in the event of failure. A Pye UHF link was used on a time sharing basis for both Engineer's and Telemetry channels. On a mimic diagram the exact condition of the link was shown by the telemetry equipment, i.e. which individual units of the link were in use, whether transmission was being received in London and indicating failure in the public electricity supply at any of the terminals or repeaters.

The longest hop of approximately 52 miles was from Cold Ashby to Barkway. To achieve comparable signal to noise ratio figures a 10 ft. parabola on top of an 80 foot tower at Cold Ashby was used, beamed to an 8 x 12 foot passive reflector 200 feet up on a tower at Barkway, with the microwave transmitter and receiver aerial dishes mounted horizontally only a few feet above the ground. Normally both the dishes would have to be positioned at the top of the tower with long waveguides to feed the aerials. This was avoided by the use of the technique of 'mirroring' at the top of the tower the aerials at ground level.

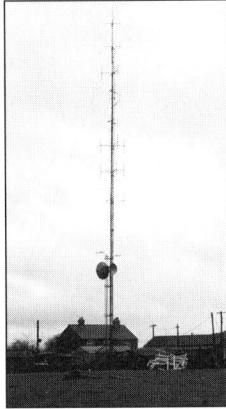

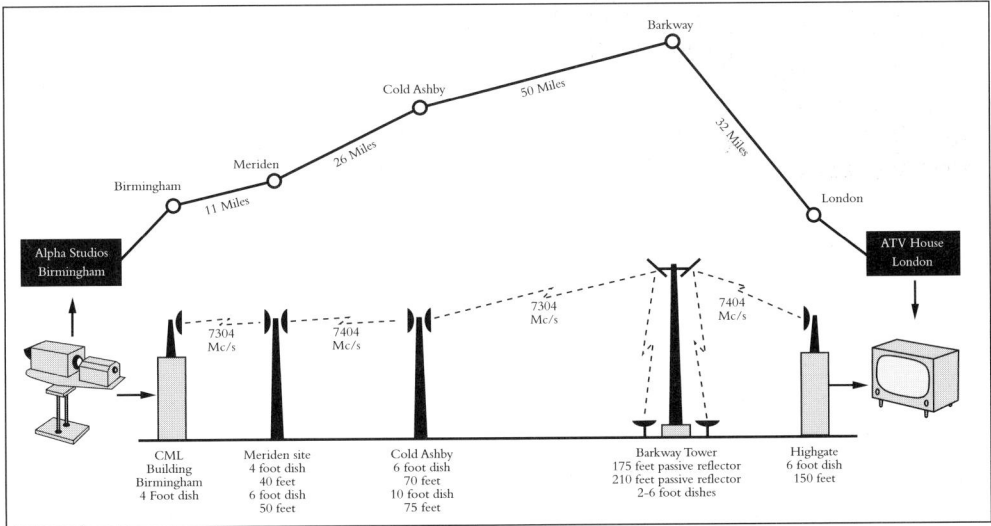

Top Left: CML Building Great Charles Street. (Courtesy: Birmingham back to the Fifties by Alton Douglas). Top Centre: Repeater Station at Meriden. Top Right: Barkway mast with passive reflector. Bottom: Diagram of the route taken by the link.
(Source: Practical Television April 1960).

9. THE FIRST FIVE YEARS IN THE MIDLANDS

During the first years of ITV Alpha Studios occupied a key position on the ITV Network. The Director-General of the Independent Television Authority, Sir Robert Fraser, when reviewing commercial television in the Midlands, stated that:

"The Alpha Television Studios have from the beginning been a centre of professional skill, of television craft. From the floors and through the controls, from the planner, the producers and the crews have come good television programmes, both bright and thoughtful, some heading for the network, some building a link between all those who live in the Midlands and between them and Independent Television."

In 1961, Philip Dorte, OBE, Midlands Controller, Associated Television Ltd. wrote in his Preface to the booklet 'Five Years at Your Fireside', stressing the regional nature of the station:

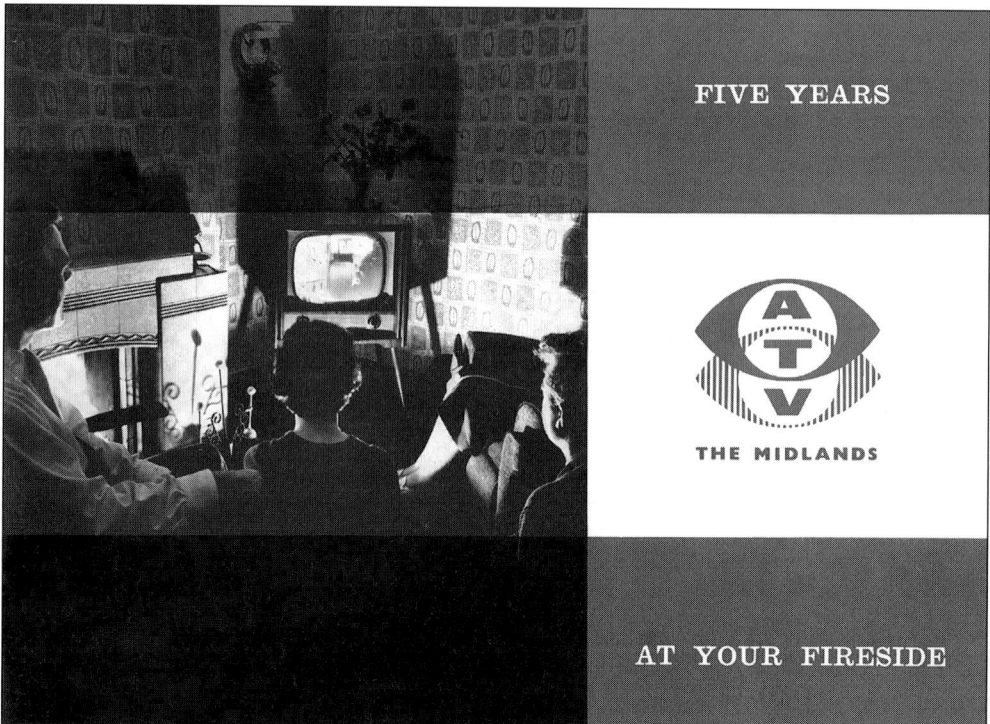

Philip Dorte OBE, Midlands Controller, Associated Television Ltd.

"Before the opening of Independent Television Authority's first Regional Transmitter at Lichfield in February, 1956, there was virtually no Regional Television Broadcasting in that all the BBC's Television Transmitters then carried the same programme wherever that programme originated.

The advent of Independent Television to the Regions changed all that, and ATV not only started local programming — we also introduced Regional Announcers (and of course the Regional Newscaster) in order to give our whole Regional Operation a more Regional flavour."

As the 1960s dawned Independent Television firmly established itself as a network as the viewers', if not always the critics', favourite. The BBC was struggling to keep up and found itself having to adapt in order to counter the competition and re-establish itself.

Independent Television had had a difficult beginning, but it had now arrived and it was clear to all that it was there to stay.

10. REGIONAL PROGRAMMES THAT BROUGHT TELEVISION TO THE PEOPLE OF THE MIDLANDS

Alpha Studios and the local programmes produced there by both ATV and ABC are remembered fondly by the people of the Midlands as they were truly regional in nature. Such programmes as:

LUNCH BOX

This became Britain's first regular mid-day television programme. It began in September 1956, and by September 1960 it had passed its 1000th performance.

It was hosted by Noel Gordon and Jerry Allen, who was also musical director. Together with the show's resident musical group, Jerry Allen on organ and his TV Trio, with drummer Lionel Rubin, bass Ken Ingerfield and on vibes Alan Graham; resident singers were, Eula Parker and Roy Edwards put on a show every week day.

It was the biggest show of its kind, and was the forerunner of many other lunchtime format shows which followed. It was transmitted for 45 minutes at 12.45 lunchtime five days a week. More a magazine show, it had guest artists, comedy, a 'memory lane' spot, viewer's letters, birthday and anniversary greetings, etc.

Initially booked by Lew Grade for six weeks, it became so popular that it ran for eight years until 1964. Besides Noel, each member of the band had their own fan club.

Roy Edwards and Eula Parker.

The first producer of Lunch Box was Reg Watson, an Australian, who before joining ATV served a ten-year apprenticeship in repertory at Brisbane as stage manager, actor and producer who was followed by Jack Barton.

Many famous international performers appeared on the show; artists like America's Liberace, Spanish dancer Antonio, Eddie Calvert, Roy Castle, The Cisco Kid, Russ Conway, Craig Douglas, Douglas Fairbanks, Jr., Dave King, Anthony Newley, Cliff Richard, Mel Torme, Dickie Valentine and David Whitfield.

The show gave many young and up-and-coming artists their first opportunity to appear on television, many of whom went on to become big stars in their own right.

The Sunday Times described it: *"This is the most folksy, matey, cuddly programme yet."*

It entertained many thousands of Midlanders who were bussed to the Alpha Studios daily from all over the Region; and when not in the studio but out 'on the road', was participated in by thousands more. Outside Broadcasts came from such places as Goodyear Park, Wolverhampton, Gloucester, Nottingham Forest football ground where 27,000 attended. Noel Gordon was to ride an elephant at a circus, there were visits to Dudley Zoo and a Swimming Pool, an 'all aboard' edition on the River Severn, there was even a version of Lunch Box on Ice.

The show often over-spent its budget, so that on occasions when it was strapped for cash the only scenery it could afford would be a single lampshade – but the show went on.

Godfrey Winn.

GODFREY WINN SPEAKING PERSONALLY

The celebrated journalist, author and broadcaster, Godfrey Winn, spoke as a Midlander (being brought up in Edgbaston), and gave advice on viewer's problems. His approach made the series very popular and attracted a huge post bag of letters to the studios each week.

Another programme hosted by Godfrey Winn was **Birthday Honours**, in which he talked to celebrities whose birthday fell during the week of the programme.

DOTTO

This was an early quiz show, voted 'the most popular show' in 1958, imported from America, in which two contestants each faced a screen which concealed, in fifty dots, the portrait of a well known personality. Contestants were asked questions in turn and on giving the correct answer a number of dots were awarded and filled in on the screen. The first contestant to successfully identify the personality was awarded £5.00 for each dot not yet filled in.

Produced by John Irwin, the first presenter was Robert Gladwell and later presenters were Jimmy Hanley and Shaw Taylor. Jerry Allen and his trio were the resident group and provided the music while the dots were joined up. The show ran from 1958 to 1960.

HIT THE LIMIT

Another series of popular early quiz shows, with a Midland flavour, involving the public. Presented by Jerry Desmond as master of ceremonies these were transmitted from works canteens throughout the region. Produced by Reg Watson they provided plenty of work for the OB Unit.

GERRY'S INN

Yet another show from Aston that featured many guest celebrities and Geraldo and his Orchestra.

CARROLL LEVIS SHOW

Midlanders with talent, and with ambition to make a career in entertainment, were given their chance on the air.

MIDLAND MONTAGE

Produced by Kit Plant, the show brought a host of personalities to Alpha each week. Leslie Dunn introduced the items with other contributions made by Pat Astley, the popular continuity announcer at Aston.

Midland Montage presenter, Leslie Dunn (left) and producer Kit Plant talking with crime fiction writer Ernest Dudley (right).

Jean Morton entertaining Commodore MacLean of Cunard.

RAINBOW ROOM

This was a cabaret style show with a Manhattan skyline, introduced by the ever popular continuity announcer and presenter Jean Morton. She entertained many distinguished visitors to her studio nightspot.

BACHELOR FLATS

Another show hosted by Noel Gordon, featured a dance team of Anne Edgar, Dickie Garver and Maggie Lee.

COVER GIRL

A very popular show involving the youngsters of the Midlands, a weekly magazine style programme introduced by Jean Morton and produced by Reg Watson. It catered for teenage tastes; each week a local new 'Cover Girl' was chosen from the young ladies who worked in the local shops, offices and factories.

Denis Detheridge, jazz expert, compared jazz music from the very popular Midlands leading 'traditional' and 'modern' groups that performed in the many, popular Midlands Jazz Clubs at the time.

Jean Morton introducing Cover Girl.

Guest stars to the show included Adam Faith, Cleo Laine, Barbara Lyon, Billy Fury, Mike Parsons, Marty Wilde, the Mudlarks and the Avons.

PAPER TALK

This was undoubtedly the most controversial Midlands series. It was originally chaired by a journalist Douglas Warth, who used 'sledgehammer' tactics calculated to rouse viewer's fury to a rare degree.

It became so popular that it achieved the longest run of any weekly series in Britain at the time.

A Birmingham headmaster, John England, became one of the subsequent chairmen. He also chaired a free-for-all forum called **Midland Affairs**.

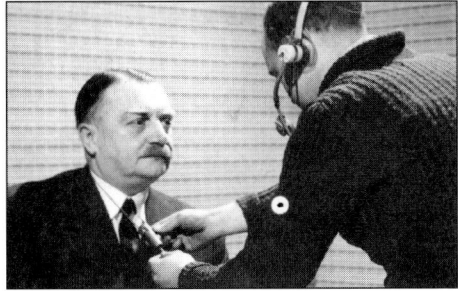

Paper Talk – Chairman, John England receives his microphone from a sound engineer.

MIDLAND PROFILE

A late night programme produced by Reg Watson, in which Midlanders who had found fame and fortune – and some who had not – told their life stories to Noel Gordon and co-presenter Birmingham journalist Ivor Jay.

General Sir Oliver Leese tells his story to Ivor Jay and Noel Gordon.

75

Left: Leslie Thomas talking turkey with one of his guests on Midland Farming.
Right: Filming sheep shearing down on the farm.

MIDLAND FARMING

The Midlands contains some of the richest agricultural land in the country, and one of ATV's most highly praised weekly programmes was **Midland Farming**. Introduced by Leslie Thomas, Regional Information Officer of the National Farmer's Union, it gave Midlands town dwellers new respect for their fellow countrymen. They marvelled at the many skills he acquired in pursuit of his occupation. Farmers welcomed the programme which kept them informed of the newest trends and techniques of good husbandry.

EDUCATION

When Associated Rediffusion, the London weekday programme company started afternoon Schools Broadcasts in September 1957, ATV readily agreed to relay them to the Midlands Schools and to share the cost of the service.

FRENCH LANGUAGE

In January, 1961, ATV introduced two morning programmes for students of French in the Midlands, Wales and the West. The first, **French from France**, was the first French language programme for schools to be produced entirely in France. It was recorded by ATV's International Mobile Unit at Chantilly.

More advanced students were catered for by **Ici La France**, a series which explored various aspects of French culture and the arts.

SCHOOL LEAVERS

ATV faced the problem of school-leavers with a series called ***Where Are You Going***. It was conducted by Mr, W. Vaughan Reynolds, editor of the Birmingham Post. It offered youngsters of school-leaving age expert advice on how to choose a career.

The series had the blessing of the then Minister of Education, Mr. Godfrey Lloyd, MP, who introduced the first programme.

STORYTELLERS

Produced by Reg Watson the ***Storytellers*** series presented fact or fiction, a good story deserving to be well told.

Evadne Price's vivid imagination and dramatic delivery sent a shiver down many Midland spines on her late-night excursions into the occult.

Professor James Webster the eminent Midlands pathologist told viewers some of his fascinating forensic experiences.

Evadne Price on set with Reg Watson.

Prof Webster and Prof Bodkin.

Another Professor, Thomas Bodkin, one time professor of Fine Arts at the Barber Institute, Birmingham, and who formerly practised at the Irish Bar, gave the viewer accounts of life on the Irish Law Circuit, which were described by critics as 'gems for the connoisseur.'

11. CHILDREN'S PROGRAMMES

POPEYE

Every Monday the ***Popeye*** cartoons were introduced by Gerald Cuff, 'The Bosun', a leading member of the Wolverhampton Repertory Theatre, who also enthralled his young 'shipmates' with fascinating facts and stories about the sea, ships and the seafaring way of life.

TINGHA AND TUCKER

This was one of the most popular of ATV's children's programmes, which stared two koala bears called Tingha and Tucker, and their friends Katie Kookaburra, Willie Wombat, Ermyntrude Emu, Porky Possum, Ossie Octopus, Kiki the Kangaroo and others with Auntie Jean Morton. The programme went out five days a week, preceding the early afternoon children's programmes.

Fred Wilby one of the early directors of the programme was often heard to say such things as, *"Cue that bear thing"*, or *"Wake that Wombat up, we are coming to it."* To us all those little creatures were very nearly real! Another director of the show, John

The Bosun with 'shipmates' on location.

Pullen, had a 'running battle' with the Graphics Department who made the various captions used on the show, and in particular those used for children's birthdays. They would often try to slip a 'rude' made-up name past him. Most could not be repeated here but to give a flavour one might suggest as an example *'Nora Legov.'* But John was very bright and aware of what was going on, I cannot recall one getting past him, but they did cause much fun on rehearsals.

The story of how the bears came to be in television in the first place has been told, but I think not quite accurately. I recall that Dave Simmons, Central Area Supervisor had twin sons, who were given the puppets as a birthday present. Dave brought them in one day, and in the spirit of innovation and fun used them during one of Jean Morton's presentation announcements. Dave crouched behind Jean and let the bears look over her shoulders, on other occasions he sat on the floor beneath her desk with his head in her lap, a puppet on each hand to whom Jean explained what was due to come next. The bears became regulars before and within children's programmes. They soon became popular and received many letters from viewers. They made appearances in **The New Adventures of Pinocchio** in 1961–2. They became so popular that it was decided to make a programme around them, **The Tingha and Tucker Club**, and to use professional puppeteers including Peter Harris, who went on to become a top director for ATV, and to direct many important shows.

Cliff Richard was a founder member of the Club and children were encouraged to join, which they did in their thousands. The Tingha and Tucker Club was a victim of its own success; thousands of letters were constantly being received each week, and 750,000 Midlands children became members. Huge crowds of children and their parents attended the Club's Annual General Meeting at Trentham Gardens. So large was their fan club that the Post Office and the company could not cope with the extra work it produced and eventually it was forced to fold in 1970, after a run of eight years.

But the programme was yet another example of how early ATV involved its viewers and encouraged them to participate. It became the children's own Midlands show. How many people now nearing middle-age will know these words?

Woomerang Boomerang, this is our song
Merrily, merrily we sing along
Woomerang Boomerang, look over there
It's Tingha and Tucker, the two little bears.

Woomerang Boomerang, this is our Sign
Your finger goes there, and your head bows like mine.
Woomerang Boomerang, please bear in mind,
Children must always be good and be kind.

Woomerang Boomerang, this is our Club,
Rub a dub, dub a dub,
Rub a dub, dub.

Woomerang Boomerang, this is our song,
Merrily, merrily we sing along,
Woomerang Boomerang, please bear in mind,
Children must always be good and be kind.

Willie Wombat went on with Jean to present a Sunday evening religious show called ***"The Tree House Family."***

The show came to an end when Lew Grade bought the **Rupert The Bear** series and decided that he did not want two shows featuring bears. All the original puppets with the exception of 'Kiki' the Kangaroo disappeared from a locked 'props' cupboard soon after the show closed, never to be seen again.

Tea time for Tingha and Tucker with Auntie Jean.

12. PRESENTATION STYLES

ATV

ATV's style revolved around a team of friendly 'in vision' presentation announcers who became part of the 'family.' The ATV Symbol invariably appeared in shot every time the announcers appeared.

The announcers were the viewer's link to ATV, they were there each weekday, not only on the screen for presentation but also contributing to programmes, and in the region, opening fetes at weekends and present when anything important was happening.

The style had such an impact that many older viewers in the Midlands will still refer to ITV as ATV.

Jean Morton and Pat Astley, perhaps the best known continuity announcers for ATV from the 1950s to early 1970, also presented *Tingha and Tucker Club* and other regional programmes.

Transmission Controller Lou Rivers discusses the script with Continuity Announcer Pat Astley.

Other well known Presentation Announcers, who were regular faces, making the link between ATV and the viewers, were:

- **Arthur Adair**   London 1955–1964.
- **Simon Bates**   Early 1970s.
- **Avril Carson**   ATV and Central.
- **Peter Cockburn**   1955–1959.
- **Patricia Cox**   Regional news presenter and continuity announcer 1960s.
- **Su Evans**   Long-serving ATV and Central, later weather presenter.

- **Derek Hobson**   Hit the big time presenting New Faces 1973–1978.
- **Margaret Hounsell**
- **Caroline Lloyd**
- **Jim Lloyd**   Former actor joined ATV 1961.
- **Trevor Lucas**   1960s, moved to the Midlands in 1968.
- **Peter Marshall**
- **Kevin Morrison**   1970s.
- **Jean Morton**
- **Joan Palmer**   A New Zealander, wife of Transmission Controller.
- **Mike Prince**   ATV and Central.
- **Michael Speake**   Ex-pirate radio DJ for Radio Scotland, worked for ATV in Telecine before moving to continuity announcing in 1970s. Had his own jazz programme on the BBC called ***Speak-Easy***.
- **Shaw Taylor**   ATV's first continuity announcer. He originally presented a show called ***Pencil and Paper***, and said that he had no intention of becoming an announcer; but when offered £30 per week and one month holiday, he became an announcer! He presented ***Police-5***, giving 25 years service.
- **Peter Tomlinson**   Long-serving announcer for ATV, one of the original four presenters of **Tiswas**, One time Managing Director of Saga Radio.
- **Norman Tozer**
- **Stewart White**   1979–1981 ATV Central to 1984.

ABC

Also had a team of regular and friendly 'in-vision' presentation announcers, whom ABC called 'station hosts', but to everyone else they were the station announcers for the weekend. They were John Benson, John Edmunds, David Hamilton and Sheila Kennedy.

ABC tried hard to impress their company image upon the viewer, their presentation simply 'oozed' ABC with its symbol exhibited at every opportunity; on blazer badges and discreetly on ties. They tried very hard to combat the presentation of ATV, but ATV could not fail to win, being there on screen for three more days a week.

Unfortunately the ABC announcers, and they were good, very good, went away at close-down on Sunday night, not to reappear until the next Saturday.

- **John Benson**   Continuity announcer for ABC in both Manchester and Birmingham. One of ITV's legendary announcers.
- **John Edmunds**   Besides announcing for ABC he was a part-time teacher.
- **David Hamilton**   Started as a scriptwriter for ATV, started announcing as a relief in both Manchester and Birmingham.
- **Sheila Kennedy**   Started with Westward Television, but made her name with ABC, she was originally an actress and dancer.

Others were **Keith Martin** and **Jill Blechley**.

13. REGIONAL NEWS

ATV REGIONAL NEWS

The first editions of ATV Midlands local news consisted of just three minutes of daily headlines by Britain's first woman newscaster, Patricia Cox. A newscaster requires a cool head and steady nerves, something Patricia Cox had in abundance. She appeared on-air (apart from holidays) every evening, Monday to Friday, introducing an up-to-date round-up of Midlands news and events.

But the bulletins grew as news stories from around the region were shot on 16mm film. The film being rushed back by dispatch rider to the film unit in Birmingham, where it was developed, processed and edited to the required length. The news stories for the next bulletin were then assembled into the order in which they were to be transmitted and rushed from the film unit to Telecine at Alpha Studios from where they were fed into the News Studio and inserted into the programme as directed.

With such a system speed was of the essence, but distance, traffic conditions, film development time and editing were all restricting factors. Distance and traffic tended to

Left: Patricia Cox introduces Local Election results.
Right: Early picture of ATV's Midlands News Studio.

restrict film items to those stories which were most local to the studios in Birmingham. Film stories from further out in the region were generally included in the weekly programme **Midlands Montage**.

This was a fact of life and only changed with the introduction of ENG (Electronic News Gathering), but this really only reduced the time scale by cutting out the film developing and processing time. Instant news was to wait for the introduction of direct satellite links into the studio.

Patricia Cox with producer Kit Plant and News Editor Bob Gillman.

ABC REGIONAL NEWS

The ITA did not specify the same level of local news coverage for the weekend contractors; but ABC, of its own accord, chose to produce a level of regional news coverage in excess of the ITA's weekend requirements. ABC being split at weekends with separate regional outputs in the North and the Midlands produced distinct News programmes for both those regions.

It was something that they did very well; overcoming the long held tradition in broadcasting that little or no news occurred at the weekend, and certainly no local news except perhaps for some sporting results.

The company's news programmes not only gave the news of the day but covered issues that were of concern in the regions; it covered stories concerning the culture, lifestyle and music of both the North and the Midlands.

ABC at Large was a seasonal (from March to October) review programme, initially transmitted on Saturday evening, but later moved to Sunday afternoons. It was introduced by David Marlowe, who was assisted by Desmond Wilcox and Tim Brinton. The format of the programme was that of a topical regional magazine, commenced with coverage of the local news, but unlike the normal news programmes there were not separate versions for each region. Following the regional news a number of film items covering various aspects of the whole ABC area would be screened. It ran from the late 1950s until 1964, when it was re-vitalised to become **ABC Weekend** and moving back to Saturday nights.

As before, this programme, preceded by local news, covered specialised issues which were discussed in the studio. It was presented by Barry Westwood, Mary

Griffiths and Gillian Reynolds. It was also seasonal, but going out over the winter; it ran from 1964 until 1968.

The National Stakes was a controversial programme, transmitted in the late evenings during the mid-1960s. It tackled controversial subjects such as divorce, capital punishment and abortion; it was noted for its strong debating style.

14. RELIGION

Religious broadcasts played an important part in ATV's service to the Midlands. The company showed its concern for the spiritual welfare of its viewers, each transmission day commenced with a **Thought for the Day**, and ended with **The Epilogue**, followed by the National Anthem.

Many church leaders such as the Bishops of Birmingham and Lichfield and the Roman Catholic Archbishop of Birmingham, took part in programmes from Alpha Studios.

Viewers readily accepted the television padre as an adjunct to their own vicar, minister or parish priest. Many letters were received which testified to their appreciation of the guidance given by ATV's panel of clergy, which included the very popular Father Pascal, Canon Charles Crowson and Father O'Mahoney.

Top Left: Father Pascal. Right: Canon Charles Crowson.
Bottom Left: Monsignor O'Mahoney.

15. ATV PROGRAMMES PRODUCED
FOR THE NETWORK

While Alpha Television produced the programmes for the Midland region, ATV Elstree Studios and ITC were busy producing quality programmes for the whole Network and for sale across the world. Some of those produced up to 1970 are recorded below. Most of these programmes have sites on the internet which are worthy of inspection as they often give much more detail about the actors and content of individual episodes than can be shown here.

ADVENTURES OF ROBIN HOOD ITC 1955/9 *Historical Adventure*

This was the first series made by Lew Grade even before ATV had a licence to broadcast. Richard Greene played Robin Hood in this series based on the legend of Robin Hood, with Robin of Loxley, the Earl of Huntington forced to rebel against the cruel Regent, Prince John and the Sheriff of Nottingham.

Exec Producer: Hannah Weinstein; Producer: Sidney Cole. 143 x 25 min B/W films.

THE CHAMPIONS ITC 1968/9 *Science Fiction*

A secret agent team, working for an International Peace Agency (Nemesis), is made up of three people having superhuman skills and powers. Following a plane crash in the Himalayas, the three were saved and healed by an old man from a reclusive Tibetan civilisation. They received finely tuned senses of hearing and sight, enhanced strength and stamina, special mental powers like telepathy; which makes them a formidable force in the interests of peace. Starring: Stuart Damon as Craig Stirling, Alexandra Bastedo as Sharon McCready and William Gaunt as Richard Barrett. Creators: Monty Berman, Dennis Spooner; Producer: Monty Berman.

DANGER MAN ATV 1960/8 *Special Agent*

The adventures of an independent spy, John Drake (Patrick McGoohan) working for NATO, covertly helping governments wherever breaches of security occur. He is competent, athletic, extremely cool and very sharp witted.

In a second series he was recast as a member of the British Secret Service, a Special Security Agent working for MI9, inspired by the Bond movies he is given an array of electronic gadgets. It was a very popular series. Patrick McGoohan was an ex-chicken farmer who became, at the time, the highest paid actor on television, earning £2,000 per week.

Creator: Ralph Smart; Exec. Producer: Ralph Smart; Producer: Sidney Cole, Aida Young. 26 x 25 min B/W films. 45 x 50 min B/W films (2 in colour).

DEADLINE MIDNIGHT ATV 1960/1 *Press Stories*
Action and adventure with the investigative reporting team of the Daily Globe, a daily fictional Fleet Street newspaper, whose News Editor is Joe Dunn (Peter Vaughan). The advisor to the programme giving it the touch of realism, was former Daily Express editor Arthur Christiansen.

Producers: Hugh Rennie, Rex Firkin. 39 x 50 min B/W films.

DEPARTMENT S ITC 1969/70 *Detective Drama*
Based in Paris, Department S, is a secret branch of Interpol, used to tackle cases that have proved difficult to solve. Flamboyant novelist Jason King (Peter Wyngard), 'action man' Stewart Sullivan (Joel Fabiani) and computer expert Annabelle Hurst (Rosemary Nichols) form a trio of special agents, whose enquiries call for lateral thinking rather than just detective work.

Creators: Monty Berman, Dennis Spooner; Producer: Monty Berman. 28 x 50 min colour films.

EMERGENCY WARD 10 ATV 1957/67 *Hospital Drama*
Britain's first twice-weekly soap opera which ran from 1957 until 1967, with very large audiences, and proved a useful training ground in television for many young actors. The action focused upon both the staff and patients of the Oxbridge General Hospital. Unlike present day hospital dramas, there were very few tragedies, with patient deaths initially limited to five per year, later falling to only two. Amongst the young stars treated at the hospital were Ian Hendry, Joanna Lumley and Albert Finney. Besides the patients, many doctors and nursing staff from the series are now well known stars. It began with the experiences of a young country girl, nurse Pat Roberts (Rosemary Miller), when adapting to the life within the city and its hospital; her room mate was Nurse Carol Young (Jill Brown) who was very popular with the male viewers. But then popular with the female viewers was surgeon Alan Dawson

(Australian Charles Tigwell), Doctor Chris Anderson (Desmond Carrington), Doctor Don Nolan (Ray Barrett), Doctor John Rennie (Richard Thorp) now known as Alan Turner in *Emmerdale*, and Doctor Richard Moone (a young John Alderton).

Emergency Ward 10 was the leader in soap operas, following its success the USA followed with the first of many successful medical/hospital series, which continue today in this country too. Lew Grade has been reported as saying that the sending of the series to the hospital mortuary was one of his few mistakes in the television business. It was revived in 1970 as *General Hospital*.

Creator: Tessa Diamond; Producers: Anthony Kearey, Rex Firkin, Hugh Rennie, John Cooper, Cecil Petty, Josephine Douglas, Pieter Rogers.

ESPIONAGE ATV 1963/4 *True Spy Stories*

Filmed throughout Europe, this was a collection of spy stories based on true events. The subjects covering all forms of international intrigue, civil war and underground resistance, were treated sombrely as their facts were taken from real events.

Exec. Producer: Herbert Hirschman; Producer: George Justin. 24 x 50 min B/W films.

FIREBALL XL5 ATV 1962/3 *Science Fiction*

Intergalactic adventures of dare-devil commander, Steve Zodiac (Paul Maxwell) and his crew of faster-than-light space craft. XL5 was one of a fleet of 'XL' vehicles of the World Space Patrol, a world space agency of the 21st century, when man has explored space extensively and made contact with alien civilisations.

Creators: Gerry and Sylvia Anderson; Producer: Gerry Anderson. 26 x 25 min B/W films.

FOUR JUST MEN ATV 1959/60 *Crime Drama*

Four former members of a wartime unit, who had fought together during the Allied invasion of Italy in 1943 are summoned to Foxgrove Manor to hear a message recorded by Colonel Bacon, their wartime commanding officer. He urges them to come together to tackle injustice and tyranny throughout the world. They are Ben Manfred MP (Jack Hawkins), Tim Collier (Dan Daley) an American reporter, Jeff Ryder (Richard Conte) a New York lawyer and Ricco Poccari an Italian hotelier. Generally each episode features only one of the four working alone. The series was based upon a novel by Edgar Wallace.

Creators: John Branson, Gerard Glaister; Producer: Gerard Glaister. 39 x 25 min B/W films.

FRAUD SQUAD ATV 1969/70 *Crime Drama*

Created by Midlands journalist Ivor Jay, a former scriptwriter for Dixon of Dock Green, the series features members of the Fraud Squad, Detective Inspector Gamble, (Patrick O'Connell) and Detective Sergeant Vicky Hicks (Joanna Van Gyseghem), one of television's first female detectives. Working together for Scotland Yard's Fraud Squad they investigate and solve crimes of fraud in all areas. Ralph Nossek played Superintendent Proud.

Creator: Ivor Jay; Producer: Nicholas Palmer. 26 x 50 min episodes.

GEORGE AND THE DRAGON ATV 1966/8 *Situation Comedy*

Chauffeur, George Russell (Sidney James) is a randy individual and enjoys a privileged position in the stately home of his employer, a retired Colonel played by John le Mesurier, at his vague and dry best. His wandering hands have already seen off 16 domestic servants, but when a new housekeeper, Miss Gabrielle Dragon (Peggy Mount) is appointed things change for him. She is a loud mouthed battleaxe, a widow using her appropriate maiden name. Battle commences!

Creators: Vince Powell, Harry Driver; Producers: Alan Tarrant, Jack Williams. 26 x 25 min episodes.

GHOST SQUAD ATV 1961/4 *Police*

Scotland Yard's Ghost Squad operates in complete secrecy, infiltrating under-world gangs, spy rings, lying low for many months at a time. They work all over the world with their lives continually on the line. Based on the activities of the world's most hush-hush crime busters, men and women out of uniform, attached to Scotland Yard's International Investigating Division. Starring: Donald Wolfit, Michael Quinn, Angela Brown, Anthony Barlow and Neil Hallett.

Producers: Connery Chappell, Anthony Kearey, Dennis Vance. 13 x 50 min film episodes in B/W. 39 x 50 min vtr episodes also in B/W; made on video tape because of an actors dispute.

HANCOCK'S HALF HOUR/HANCOCK ATV 1963 *Situation Comedy*

To many people who saw this it remains a true classic. It was one of Britain's first major comedy series. Partnered by Sidney James life's petty injustices and annoyances produced a stream of observations and criticisms to occupy the pair. Originally on radio and BBC television, Hancock produced a series himself on ATV in 1963, which was not as successful. 13 episodes.

HARPERS WEST ONE ATV 1961/3 *Department Store*

Behind the scenes of a fictional West End department store this series focuses on the various events in the lives of the staff who work there and their customers.

Creators: John Whitney, Geoffrey Bellman; Producers: Hugh Rennie, Rex Firkin, Royston Morley. A one hour series in B/W.

INTERPOL CALLING ATV 1959/60 *Police Drama*

Opening with the words: *Crime knows no frontiers. To combat the growing menace of the International criminal, the police forces of the world have opened up their national boundaries. At their Head Quarters in Paris, scientifically equipped to match the speed of the jet age, 63 nations have linked together to form the International Criminal Police Organisation – INTERPOL.*

Operating out of Interpol's Paris headquarters Inspectors Paul Duval (Charles Korvin) and Mornay (Edwin Richfield) investigate crimes throughout the world.

Producers: Anthony Perry, Connery Chappell. 39 x 25 min B/W films.

INVISIBLE MAN ATV 1958/9 *Science Fiction*

A series based on a novel by H.G.Wells. Through an accident during experimentation into light refraction Dr Peter Brady (Tim Turner) becomes invisible and is unable to reverse the process. Whilst he is researching a way of becoming visible again the UK recruits him as an intelligence agent and uses him to go where other spies could not possibly go.

Producer: Ralph Smart. 39 x 25 min B/W films.

JOE 90 ITC 1968/9 *Science Fiction*

A machine known as BIG RAT (Brain Impulse Galvanoscope, Record And Transfer) that allows the transfer of people's brain-patterns has been developed by a scientist, Prof Ian McClaine (Rupert Davies). His son, Joe (Len Jones) helps with its development and uses it regularly. Joe becomes a Most Special Agent for World Intelligence Network and through the machine is given the brain patterns of experts he sets out to solve many problems around the world.

Creators: Gerry and Sylvia Anderson; Producer: David Lane. 30 x 25 min colour films.

THE LARKINS ATV 1958/64 *Situation Comedy*

Alf Larkins, (David Kossoff) is hen-pecked by his wife, Ada (Peggy Mount). They have an unemployed son, Eddie (Shaun O'Riordan), and a daughter, Joyce (Ruth Trouncer) married to Jeff Rogers (Ronan O'Casey). Together they find themselves in a variety of farcical situations in the London suburbs, and in a later series running a country pub.

Creator: Fred Robinson; Producers: Bill Ward, Alan Tarrant.

LOVE STORY ATV 1963/69 *Romance*

A long-running collection of one-off romantic plays. Presented many notable productions, including:

The Habit of Loving by Doris Lessing, featuring Eric Portman as a despairing theatrical producer married to a naïve actress, Lana Morris.

Three Piece Suite by Edna O'Brien, a sad tale of an autumnal affair.

La Musica by Maguerite Duras, an emotional portrait of a newly-divorced woman, Vanessa Redgrave.

The Girl Opposite, a Roman Polanski script, featuring, in a serious role, Dudley Moore the popular comedian-musician.

Executive Producer: Stella Richman.

MAN IN A SUITCASE ATV 1967/8 *Private Detective*

McGill, (Richard Bradford) a discredited CIA agent after being dismissed from his post having been accused of permitting a top scientist to defect to the USSR, turns detective. As a private detective with only a suitcase and a gun he becomes a private detective and bounty hunter in the UK and Europe.

Creators: Richard Harris, Dennis Spooner; Producer: Sidney Cole. 30 x 50 min colour films.

MAN OF THE WORLD ATV 1962/3 *Photo Journalist*

A series about a globe-trotting photo-journalist, Mike Strait (Craig Stevens). His freelance assignments to Fashion Magazines ensure that he leads a glamourous lifestyle. Many of his assignments get him involved in murder, blackmail, espionage and intrigue.

Producer: Harry Fine. 20 x 50 min B/W film episodes.

MARKET IN HONEY LANE ATV 1967/9 *Street Market*

A soap opera that threatened the supremacy of *Coronation Street* in the ratings chart. Like the current *Eastenders*, it was set in London's East End. But unlike *Eastenders'* miserable inhabitants it focused on the vibrant Cockney workers at a fictitious Honey Lane market.

Creator: Louis Marks; Producer: John Cooper.

MRS THURSDAY ATV 1966/7 *Comedy*

Mrs Alice Thursday, (Kathleen Harrison) a charlady, was left a fortune by millionaire tycoon, George Dunrich, who left nothing to his four grabbing ex-wives. Alice also inherited all the trappings of wealth, mansions, Rolls-Royce, etc. She is protected from friends and enemies by an aide, Richard B. Hunter (Hugh Manning). The series was so popular that it knocked *Coronation Street* off the top of the ratings.

Creator: Ted Willis; Producer: Jack Williams.

NEW ADVENTURES OF CHARLIE CHAN ITC 1957/8 *Detective*

Adventures of the oriental detective, Charlie Chan (J. Carrol Naish) created by Earl Derr Biggers. Charlie was a smart, Chinese proverb-quoting detective with numerous children. He was assisted by his 'Number One Son', Barry (James Hong).

Exec. Producer: Leon Fromkess; Producers: Sidney Marshall, Rudolph Flothow. 39 x 25 min B/W films.

ON THE BRADEN BEAT ATV 1962/7 *Consumer Affairs*

Canadian Bernard Braden and his wife Barbara Kelly were very popular TV personalities and appeared in many shows. This was a consumer guidance programme, with an element of general entertainment. After five years the show was moved to the BBC and called ***Braden's Week***, there he was assisted by Esther Rantzen as a reporter/researcher. A similar show came back in 1973, ***That's Life***, with Esther Rantzen but not Bernard Braden.

Presenter: Bernard Braden; Producers: Jock Watson, Francis Coleman.

POLICE 5 ATV 1962/90 *Factual Crime*

This programme was devised and presented by Shaw Taylor. It was a short weekly programme in which the police asked for help in solving crimes. During one April 1st show whilst Shaw was presenting the programme a hand was seen to reach in the window behind him and 'pinch' the large vase he had on the window sill!

THE PRISONER ATV 1967/8 *Mystery*

The series was devised by Patrick McGoohan and offered to Lew Grade, who asked 'What's it all about?' Lew admitted that when it was explained to him he did not understand it, but knew that whatever, with Patrick McGoohan's face on screen it would be a success.

An un-named secret agent resigns his post and is abducted by sinister forces. He is taken to a curious Shangri-La civilisation; in the Village they attempt to brain-wash him. Prisoner, Number 6, (Patrick McGoohan) resists all attempts but finds that he can never escape from the Village where he is held. Escapees are caught and returned to the Village by a large balloon device, called Rover. The chief administrators of the Village are known as No 2s, and the Prisoner is given the number six, which he refuses to accept. *I am not a number, I am a free man. I am not going to be stamped, filed, indexed, briefed, debriefed or numbered. My life is my own.*

The series posed the question: *Has anyone the right to tell a man what to think, how to behave, to coerce others? Has one the right to be an individual?*

Although over 30 years old **The Prisoner** continues to remain a truly outstanding piece of television drama, and its questions are perhaps more relevant in today's 'politically correct' society! A brilliant piece of work well worth viewing time and again.

Filmed at Portmeirion in Wales, a village created as an Italian fantasy by architect Sir Clough Williams-Ellis.

Creator: Patrick McGoohan; Producer David Tomblin. 17 x 50 min colour films.

THE PLANE MAKERS ATV *Aircraft Factory*

As its name says the series was about an aircraft factory called Scott Furlong, the action taking place around the problems between the management and the trade union. The aircraft under development, the Sovereign, causes a great deal of industrial strife. The bully of a managing director John Wilder (Patrick Wymark) is a man everyone comes to hate. After the Sovereign the company's next project was the Veetol, a vertical take-off aircraft. This ended in failure and John Wilder left to become a member of the board of a city bank.

THE POWER GAME ATV *Business*

Re-titled takes up the story of John Wilder when he leaves Scott Furlong. The action of this series moves with new rivals to the city bank boardroom. John secures a knighthood and becomes involved in diplomatic circles for the Foreign Office, doing his best for Britain around the world. The series ended suddenly with the death of its star.

Creator: Wilfred Greatorex; Producer: Rex Firkin, David Reid. A 50 min series in B/W on video tape.

PROBATION OFFICER ATV 1959/62 *Probation*

A series of one hour dramas in semi-documentary style, based on real court cases, reflects the work and problems of the Probation Service, charged with the welfare of delinquents, criminals and the like. A realistic down-to-earth programme reflecting true life.

Starring: John Paul, David Davies, Iris Cope, Honor Blackman, Jessica Spencer, Bernard Brown and Jack Stewart.

Creator: Julian Bond; Producers: Anthony Kearey, Rex Firkin.

RANDALL AND HOPKIRK DECEASED ITC 1969/70 *Detective*

A private detective, Marty Hopkirk (Kenneth Cope) is killed in a hit-and-run incident. He returns as a ghost to assist his partner Jeff Randall (Mike Pratt), to bring his killers to justice. He is only visible to his partner and so he is very useful to Jeff's future cases.

Exec. Producer: Armand Schaefer; Producer: Louis Gray. 26 x 50 min colour films.

SAILOR OF FORTUNE ATV 1956/7 *Historical Adventure*

The American skipper of a freighter, Mitch Mitchell (Lorne Greene), tries to make a living sailing across the world from one cargo to the next. Intrigue seems to follow him around and there is always someone in need of his help.

Writer: Lindsay Galloway; Producer Michael Sadler. 26 x 50 min B/W films.

THE SAINT ATV 1962/9 *Crime*

An extremely popular series featuring Simon Templar (Roger Moore), the Saint from the books by Leslie Charteris and created in 1928. The unruffled, self-assured Saint, the Robin Hood of crime, is a great success and is the ladies heart-throb. Lew Grade had initially offered the series to Patrick McGoohan, but he turned it down as he did not approve of a character that had a different girlfriend every week.

Creator: Leslie Charteris; Producers: Robert S. Baker, Monty Norman. 71 x 50 min B/W films and 43 x 50 min colour films.

SENTIMENTAL AGENT ATV 1963 *Import/export*

The adventures of a smartly dressed and white-suited, charming, import-export agent, Carlos Varela (Carlos Thompson). Running an international trading company he finds himself globe-trotting and rooting out criminals. This was a spin-off from *The Man of the World* series.

Producer: Harry Fine. 13 x 50 min B/W films.

SERGEANT CORK ATV 1963/6 *Historical Police*

Set in Victorian London, Sgt. Cork (John Barrie) from Bayswater and working for Scotland Yard, being years ahead of his time, solves many crimes using scientific evidence. He dislikes bureaucracy, and finds that his modern approach to crime solving is disregarded by his colleagues and in particular by his boss. He is assisted by Bob Marriot (William Gaunt), an ex-public schoolboy and university graduate. The series captured the dark, misty, cobbled streets, top hats and cloaks, horse-drawn cabs of the time of Jack the Ripper.

Creator: Ted Willis; Producer: Jack Williams. 65 x 50 min B/W episodes.

STINGRAY ATV/ITC 1964/5 *Science Fiction*

A super-submarine of the future, operated by the World Aquanaut Security Patrol (WASP). The Earth's population has started to harvest the riches beneath the seas, where they encounter strange new enemies. WASP is the Earth's response to these new dangers of the deep. Led by Captain Troy Tempest (Don Mason) they do battle with Titan (Ray Barrett) and the evil Aquaphibians.

Creators: Gerry and Sylvia Anderson; Producer Gerry Anderson. 39 x 25 min colour films.

THE STRANGE WORLD OF GURNEY SLADE ATV 1960 *Fantasy*

This was a short-lived, six episode, series in which the title character Gurney Slade (Anthony Newley) lives in a bizarre world of his own imagination. He talks to trees and animals, fantasises about women, conjures up unusual characters as he meanders his way through weird situations.

Creator: Anthony Newley; Writers: Sid Green, Dick Hills; Producer Alan Tarrant. 6 x 25 min B/W episodes.

SULLAVAN BROTHERS ATV 1964/5 *Legal*

Hugh Manning starred as Robert Sullavan QC, head of a family-owned firm of lawyers. The three, two solicitors and a barrister work together with their various assistants to solve crimes and mete out justice for the benefit of their distressed clients.

Creator: Ted Willis; Producer Jack Williams. 26 x 50 min B/W episodes.

SUNDAY NIGHT AT THE LONDON PALLADIUM ATV 1955/1967 *Variety*

Probably the best remembered and popular television variety show in television's 50 years. More of a Sunday night ritual loved by huge audiences throughout the country.

From the world's top variety theatre in London ATV presented a showcase of international stars. Its format was always the same, the high kicking Tiller Girls opened the show with their precision dance routines, followed by two or three 'lesser' acts, then 'Beat the Clock', based upon an American quiz show, involving contestant couples performing silly tricks within a set time. That part of the show was finished with 'The Word Game', where the couple, against the clock, had to re-arrange jumbled words on a board into *'a well known phase or saying.'* The show itself then ended with a top star of the week. The final shot, with all the participants assembled on the famous revolving stage of the Palladium, brought the show to a close.

It started in 1955 and ran continuously until 1967, with a break then to 1973 when it ran for another year.

Creator: Val Parnell; Producers: Albert Locke, Francis Essex, Jon Scoffield, Colin Clews.

Comperes: Tommy Trinder, Hughie Green, Alfred Marks, Robert Morley, Arthur Haynes, Dickie Henderson, Bruce Forsyth, Don Arrol, Bob Monkhouse, Dave Allen, Norman Vaughan, Jimmy Tarbuck, Des O'Connor, Roger Moore, Jim Dale.

SUPERCAR ATV/ITC 1961/2 *Science Fiction*

Supercar was a unique vehicle; a car, a plane and a submarine in one. Its driver/test pilot was Mike Mercury (Graydon Gould). Based in a secret laboratory in the desert, the supercar team went out to help people and avert disasters all over the world.

Creator: Gerry Anderson and Reg Hill; Producer: Gerry Anderson.

VIRGIN OF THE SECRET SERVICE ATV 1968 *Historical Spy*

The dangerous assignments of a patriotic British agent, Captain Robert Virgin (Clinton Greyn) in the 1900s. As the British Empire begins to crumble he continues to defend British honour.

Creator: Ted Childs; Producer: Josephine Douglas.

WHIPLASH ATV 1960/1 *Australian Bush*

In the 1840s, an American, Chris Cobb (Peter Graves) forms Australia's first stagecoach company, Cobb & Co. Based on the true story of Cobb & Co. a stagecoach line that grew up in Australia following the 1850s Gold Rush.

The series was filmed in Alice Springs. 34 x 25 min 1960/1.

WHO-DUN-IT ATV 1969 *Murder Mystery*

This was a series of plays with a murder theme, set in the 1930s; Inspector Moon (Gary Raymond) would investigate the crime and then invite viewers to determine who had done it.

13 Episodes created by Lewis Greifer, and produced by Jack Williams.

THE WORKER ATV 1965/70 *Situation Comedy*

Charlie Drake, as the Worker, had already found, and been dismissed from 980 jobs over a 20 year period, much to the frustration of local Labour Exchange counter clerk Mr. Whittaker (Percy Herbert), whose job it was to try and find him permanent employment. In a second series 1969/70 the counter clerk was replaced by Mr Pugh (Henry McGee).

Writers: Charlie Drake and Lew Schwarz; Producers: Alan Tarrant and Shaun O'Riordan. 13 x 25min 1965. 13 x 25 min 1969/70. 10 x 15 min 1978.

THE GOLDEN SHOT ATV 1967/1975 *Game Show*

An extremely popular Sunday evening game show, originally from Elstree, which ran from 1967 to 1975. An import from Germany whose catchphrase was 'Heinz, the bolt', where the contestants fired crossbows at targets depicting cartoon scenes, in an attempt to win cash and other prizes.

The producer was ATV's Colin Clews, who is reported to have asked the presenter to join him in a 'Nazi firing squad.'

Its first presenter was Jackie Rae, but its great success was under his successor Bob Monkhouse. Later presenters were Norman Vaughan and Charlie Williams, with Bob Monkhouse returning in 1975 as the show came to an end.

On one occasion, when Norman Vaughan was taken ill, Alton Douglas who was the show's warm-up comic, stood-in and presented the show at short notice.

'Heinz the bolt' became 'Bernie the bolt.' In the games the contestants, some of them celebrities, fired the crossbows themselves, firing at apples which formed part of the highly coloured target backgrounds. Viewers could see what the bow was aiming at by a camera behind its sight. In the Jackpot game the crossbow was fired by a blindfolded marksman, who was directed by a viewer contestant at home over the telephone. The marksman responded to commands such as 'Right a bit, up a little', and when the contestant thought they could hit the target, a thin thread they

shouted 'Fire!' If they were successful in breaking the thread a treasure chest burst open and 'golden coins' poured out.

The show became very popular when it was moved from Saturday to a Sunday teatime slot which came live from Birmingham's Aston Studios.

A remarkable incident occurred during one show which has often been repeated because it had to be seen to be believed – but it really did happen! On the evening in question, the viewer contestant was to be *'Bob from Wolverhampton.'* As he started to direct Bernie the Bolt his directions were erratic in the extreme, Bob Monkhouse stopped him and asked if he was having trouble in seeing the target. Bob replied that as his television had been repossessed by Rumbelows he was not at home but in a phone box outside Currys, watching the televisions in their window. Bob Monkhouse then asked him if he could see him, the other Bob asked him to wave. It was then he realised that he was not watching the right programme! He exclaimed, *'Oh bugger, I can't see you – they've left them all switched to the bloody BBC – Fire!'* Bernie the Bolt obliged and remarkably the arrow hit the string and Bob from Wolverhampton won the Jackpot.

During its run there were three Bernies, Derek Young, Alan Bailey and perhaps the best remembered Johnny Baker. The show's presenter was always assisted by glamourous 'Golden Girls', the most famous of whom was undoubtedly Anne Aston who never got top marks for maths at school and who often had to be helped in adding up the scores on the targets. The exploding apples used on the targets sometimes caused the targets themselves to catch fire, and contestants were known to fire at the wrong target. On one occasion a pair of contestants disappeared half way through a show and were replaced by a couple hastily taken from the audience; no one seemed to notice! All this added to the charm of the show.

Besides Colin Clews there were other producers for the show, John Pullen, Edward Joffe, Mike Lloyd, Les Cocks and Dicky Leeman.

16. ABC PROGRAMMING AIMS

ABC produced many fine programmes whilst serving the North and Midlands. Howard Thomas in his article in the 'Television Annual for 1958' summed up how his company went about giving the best to its viewers:

Trends have to be watched. The sharp and sudden fluctuations of star values are reflected in sales of records, theatre appearances, mail requests. Cinema receipts show variations in audience preference, especially the rapid decline and fall of fads like 'rock 'n' roll.' The American market often a useful indication of what Britain will like, and song sales, box-office figures, etc. are carefully studied here. Even so, American crazes, like calypso singing, sometimes fall flat in Britain, and success in the United States is no guarantee of a hit over here.

In some ways it is a gamble, but a calculated gamble, to assess public taste. I do not think any of us deliberately try to play down to the lowest common denominator. The fascination of the 'game' is in the prospect of being able to guide public taste and to try to give people something better than they think they want. The trouble for all of us in this intricate business of catering for your whims is that the public never knows what it wants – until it gets it.

17. THE FIRST REVISION OF CONTRACTS

As was made clear by the ITA when it set up the regional franchise system, licences to operate a television service in a particular region were not to be regarded as permanent, they were not necessarily long-term. The performance of the licence holders was to be reviewed at intervals and if necessary changes would be made.

REPORT OF THE TELEVISION ADVISORY COMMITTEE 1960

The Government set up the Television Advisory Committee to advise the Postmaster General:

'..on the development of television and sound broadcasting at frequencies above 30 megacycles per second (Mc/s) and related matters, including competitive television services and television for public showing in cinemas and elsewhere.'

In 1960 they considered such questions concerning television over the following 25 years, such as:

- Whether to stay with the 405-line standard.
- Change to the 625-line (Bands IV and V), European standard.
- Introduction of Colour Television on Bands IV and V and the best technical means of transmission.
- Introduction of Colour Television on Bands I and III, 405-line standard.

CONCLUSIONS

The Committee reported on 17th May 1960 and came to the following conclusions:

- A change to the 625-line standard would give a definite improvement in picture quality over the 405-line standard.
- Change to the 625-line standard would enable better inter-change of programme material between the UK and Europe.
- Colour Television in the light of currently available technology should use the NTSC (USA) system.

THE PILKINGTON COMMITTEE REPORT 1962

Two months later on 13th July 1960, the Government set up The Committee on Broadcasting under the chairmanship of Sir Harry Pilkington. Its remit was:

'To consider the future of the broadcasting services in the United Kingdom, the dissemination by wire of broadcasting and other programmes, and the possibility of television for public showing; to advise on the services which should in future be provided in the United Kingdom by the BBC and the ITA; to recommend whether additional services should be provided by any other organisation; and to propose what financial and other conditions should apply to the conduct of all these services.'

The Pilkington Committee reported on 27th June 1962. After taking extensive evidence from many organisations and individuals, the Committee were clearly not impressed by the fledgling Independent Commercial Television as it then existed and recommended drastic changes to its organisation.

Amongst the more important recommendations made by the Pilkington Committee were these;

- *That the line definition standard should be changed from 405 to 625 lines, the internationally agreed standard in general use throughout Europe.*
- *That a service of colour television on 625 lines should be introduced as soon as possible.*
- *That the BBC should be authorised as soon as possible to provide a second programme of television.*
- *That independent television should be reconstituted and re-organised so that the Authority should plan programmes and sell advertising time. The programme companies would produce and sell to the Authority programme items for inclusion in the programme planned by the Authority.*
- *So long as independent television is constituted and organised as at present, it should not provide any additional services of television. But if, after independent television has been reconstituted and re-organised as the Committee recommend, and has had sufficient time to adapt itself to its new constitution, it has proved its capacity to realise the purposes of broadcasting, it should be authorised to provide a second programme.*
- *The National Broadcasting Council for Scotland should be given in respect of the BBC's television service for Scotland rights and duties comparable with those it now exercises in respect of the Home Service on sound radio.*
- *The rights and duties of the National Broadcasting Council for Wales should be similarly extended. In allotting the uncommitted frequencies in Broadcasting Band III, the first priority should be given to separating the BBC's service to Wales from that to the English Regions.*

- *One service, and one only, of local sound broadcasting should be planned; it should not be financed from advertising revenue; it should be provided by the BBC and financed from licence revenue; and be planned to serve the largest possible number of distinctive communities that technical considerations will permit.*

- *The Committee reject proposals for a service of subscription, pay-as-you-view television.*

(Source: A short version of the Report of the Pilkington Committee – HMSO 1962).

The response to the Pilkington Report was immediate and unfavourable, not only from the Broadcasters and the press, but by the public in general.

Charles Curran MP, writing in the Evening News (29th June 1962) was typical, he asked:

'Can You be Trusted to Choose?'

What is the basis on which we run this country? I blush to tell you. The words stick in my throat – now that I have read the Pilkington Report.

For we run this country on the basis that the ordinary citizen is fit to think for himself. We allow him to choose which lot of politicians shall govern him. Every now and again we have an election. A deplorable vulgar affair it is, too. Each Party tries to persuade people to vote for it.

But do we protect the ordinary citizen from this din of rival claims? No, I am afraid we do not. We leave him to sift for himself. We expect him to use his loaf.

Now this way of doing things, shocking as it is, may be all very well when we are merely deciding how the British should be governed. That after all, is a trifle!

But can we tolerate it in a matter of real importance? Can we trust the ordinary citizen to decide for himself whether to watch Coronation Street or whether to watch Z Cars?

The Pilkington Report says we cannot. Sir Harry and his fellow-investigators are shocked at the idea. They want the Government to stop this state of affairs at once; viewers must be rescued from the menacing perils of free choice. Independent TV must be nationalised. The degrading business of putting on programmes that people like must be swept away. For what are programmes that people like to watch?

The Report supplies a string of adjectives about them. They are vapid, for instance. They are puerile, unworthy, trivial, sordid, superficial, cheaply sensational. (What, by the way, would be expensively sensational? Pilkington does not tell us, alas. But I suppose it might be a millionaire shooting another millionaire in a Rolls-Royce).

Now when you look at the Pilkington Report you see that it is based on two assumptions. The first is: that the tastes and preferences of many viewers are deplorable and what is not?

Anyone is entitled, if he likes, to form the view that Westerns are deplorable. Having formed that view, he is free not to watch them. Has he any right to go beyond that? Can he say: 'Because I dislike that kind of programme, I want the power of the State to be used to impose my tastes on people who don't share them'?

In a free society, any such claim strikes me as, literally intolerable. Nor is it any good asking: 'But what about the children?' Agreed, children must be protected. Agreed, programmes unsuitable for them ought to be kept off the screen at hours when they are likely to be in front of it. But are we to run TV on the basis that nothing must ever be shown unless it is fit for children to see? We cannot apply any such rule to broadcasting any more than to printing.

The second Pilkington assumption is: that the State should run TV for the primary purpose of changing the tastes and preferences of viewers.

Why should the State do anything of the kind? Any such assumption is completely incompatible with democracy. In order to do that we should need to create a cultural paternalism in this country. The Pilkington Report reeks of paternalism. It is directed not so much against Independent TV as against the people who watch Independent TV. These people are discussed as though they were a lot of gullible dim-witted louts who must be coerced for their own good. Left to themselves they do not know what is good for them. The more of them who watch a programme, the less suitable it is.

I find throughout the report a priggish and arrogant contempt for the common man. It recurs like a decimal point. To give one minor illustration of that; the report condemns the use of background music to news on TV. Why? Because "since music speaks to the emotions, it may greatly exaggerate or diminish the feeling prompted by an otherwise dispassionate presumption of actuality." Why in the world should a free society protect the citizen against the risk of contamination by Colonel Bogey?

Mixed with the paternalism of Pilkington there is a curious hostility to the kind of society we live in. You see that particularly in the attack the Report makes on advertising. TV adverts are criticised because they stimulate acquisitiveness, and the idea of keeping up with the Joneses. Is acquisitiveness really discreditable? If it is, then every class, group and Party in Britain must be discredited. Aren't they all dedicated to the doctrine that we must raise our standard of life and as fast as we can; that we must acquire more wealth, in order to have higher wages, more to spend, more pensions, more consumer goods, more houses, and so on and so on? Why, it is the acquisitive appetite that keeps this country — and every other country — on the move.

The Pilkington Report, in fact, seems to spring from a deep disapproval of the social revolution that has taken place in this country. That revolution has put purchasing power into the pockets of the masses. They now have money to spend. Consequently, they are able to do what only the rich minority could do a generation ago; namely, to demand that their tastes, their preferences, and their desires shall be catered for.

Well, Independent TV does cater for them. It does give them the kind of programmes that they want. And why not? It is the product of the social revolution. It flourishes because it recognises that the common man now has money to spend and therefore the economic power that enables him to please himself about his tastes.

We can tax the profits of the programme contractors, by all means: and tax them heavily. We can limit their advertising time too. They are making a lot of money. Since their prosperity has been created by Parliament there is no reason why Parliament should not levy tribute on it.

But to suppose that we can cancel out our revolution by making TV into a State monopoly is an idle dream. We cannot do that – so long as we remain a free society.'

This was only one of a flood of articles in the press condemning the Pilkington report. The Government was quick to distance itself in publishing a Memorandum on the Report just one month later, in July 1962.

The Future of Independent Television

The system brought into being by the Television Act 1954, introduced a novel partnership between public and private enterprise, producing between them lively and certainly popular television. The Government recognised at the time that the system would need re-examination after some years of operation.

In many ways the system has been very successful. The evidence suggests that more people watch its programmes than those of the BBC. In some fields – for example light theatre, news and religious broadcasting – it has undeniably contributed something of value to television and by bringing competition into the world of television exercised an enlivening effect on television in general.

The Committee recommended a radical change in the future arrangements for independent television, both structurally and financially. The ITA, they say, should sell the advertising time, make some programmes themselves and buy others from the programme companies, who would continue to operate under contract to the ITA but solely as programme producers. The Committee's main argument is that in the context of the present structure it is impossible fully to reconcile the commercial purpose of the companies with the realisation of the "purposes of broadcasting."

Whether this argument is valid is a question about which there are obviously two opinions; in any case the Government feels that the practical difficulties presented by these proposals have not been fully appreciated. So fundamental a change in the structure of independent television requires the most thorough examination, and the Government wishes to be satisfied that any new structure would remedy the defects it was designed to overcome and would not throw up equally serious difficulties of its own or deprive the system of those features for which it can fairly claim credit. Full account will be taken of the views which will be expressed in public debate and the Government will later submit to Parliament a statement of its own proposals for the future of independent television.'

At Alpha Television in Birmingham, Frank Beale sent a memo to all members of staff:

'Amid all the controversy aroused by the recently published report one fact at least is certain – that less than justice was done to the achievements of ITV and to the "balance" of the programmes. To correct this impression, the ITA have assembled the true facts in booklet form and I am sending you this copy so that you can read for yourself the true comparisons between ITV and BBC broadcasting.'

The booklet was full of statistics that showed that the Pilkington Report had failed to give a clear picture of the facts.

Share of Viewing	*ITA %*	*BBC %*
1955 Oct–Dec	57	43
1956	67	33
1957	75	25
1958	72	28
1959	71	29
1960	67	33
1961	66	34
1962 Jan–Jun	63	37

London Area – Source TAM.

The ITA gave a number of examples of how programming had changed since the introduction of ITV in 1955:

1. **Religion** – *After 12 years of non-competitive television, religion hardly existed as a television subject. There were devoted to religious programmes about 30 minutes a week. There was no regular weekly programme save a brief programme of prayer on Sundays. Today there are over 5 hours of regular religious programmes in the two services, more than a tenfold increase.*

2. **School Television** – *In 1955, not even a start had been made. School television did not exist. Today about 20 different programmes are broadcast each school week, and these, being repeated, have a total running time of about 12 hours. When school television began, it was in Independent Television's second year. It was in the fourteenth year of television in this country.*

3. **Regional Television** – *After 12 years of monopoly, five hours of programmes a week were being produced in the regions. After 7 years of competition, weekly regional production has risen to more than 90 hours. In 1960–61, the last year for which figures are published, the BBC produced in its regions about 26 hours of programmes a week. Outside London, Independent Television produces in 1962 about 86 hours a week, of which 78 hours are of special local interest.*

4. **The News** – *In 1955 news in television was still embryonic, consisting of a daily "news and newsreel" at 7.30pm. Today there are four main news bulletins a day in the two services. Together with shorter bulletins, but excluding all the regional news bulletins, themselves unknown in 1955, they provide six and a half hours of news a week.*

5. **Talks, Discussions, and Documentaries** – *The news, school television, and informative programmes for children apart, programmes of discussion, talks, and documentaries, those covering religion, the arts, science and nature, social life, and current affairs at home and abroad numbered about 12–15 a week in 1955, with a duration of just over six hours. Today in both services there are each week more than 56 such programmes, with a duration of over 20 hours. If news, school programmes in term time, and informative programmes for children are included, the duration of serious television programmes has increased from about 11 hours a week to about 45 hours.*

It would be interesting to compare these benefits achieved in the first seven years of ITV with the present day, when many claim that 'serious' broadcasting has been replaced by triviality.

Pilkington Rejected – Contracts Renewed

The first revision of contracts had given the Authority the chance to review the existing pattern, and change it. But the government of the day did not accept the 'Pilkington Alternative.' The decision ensured that the original pattern of control and financing of Independent Television was to continue substantially unchanged except in one respect: the imposition of an Exchequer levy.

The ITA reviewed the licences during September 1963, and decided that no company lost its position as a local ITV contractor. All licences were extended for a further three years commencing in July 1964.

During the previous five years the companies had moved from making a loss to a position of comfort and on to one of high profitability. In the late 1950s and early 1960s the companies consolidated their position, expanded their capital investment and in several cases diversified into other fields. This raised the question whether some part of the profit should be returned to the public in recognition of the fact that it had been generated through the use of a scarce national resource, namely, broadcasting wavebands. The Television Advertisement Duty of 10 per cent (later 11 per cent) had been introduced in 1961. This was a tax on advertisers collected by the companies. It made no serious inroads into the high level of profits, which came under increasingly heavy fire – 'the licence to print money.' It was against this background that in 1964, in the wake of Pilkington, a new Television Act brought in the levy.

The ITV Companies were shocked by the abrasive criticisms of the Pilkington Report and confronted with a new and more explicit Television Act, the companies and the ITA took stock of their position. The Authority began to exercise firmer control in the balance of programming. The companies were required to produce more current affairs and other serious programmes. Axes fell on harmless but trivial quiz games.

Few would dispute that following the review ITV became more serious, more worthy, and introduced many new programmes of quality. The gains were not, however, all on the side of the viewer. ATV's **Crossroads** was banished from the London area, and it took a public outcry to get it restored! Something of the élan of the early years with their innocently popular programmes departed.

The exchequer levy began to siphon away some £30 million a year from the company's profits.

18. A NEW PRESENTATION CENTRE
IN THE MIDLANDS

Alpha had slowly progressed from a single OB Unit degutted and set-up in a wooden shed to serve as the control room for the one and only studio, into a two studio operation. This was achieved under the personal management of Bernard Greenhead and the staff at Alpha. Dressed in their old clothes and gumboots they poured concrete in every conceivable direction. But the effort expended was well worth it as Studio 2 was still in operation when ATV left the building in 1969. Two further telecine

The new building in Aston under construction.

suites were added over time. Telecine 3 was housed in a room above the area used for film assembly and Telecine 4 was housed in a purpose built hardboard room (box) protruding out into the scenes store, a very cold place in the winter.

After five years of continuous seven days a week operations, and in the light of having had its licence renewed the company believed that investing for a longer period was acceptable. It ploughed its profits back into programme making facilities. It was decided that new equipment should be obtained and installed in a new building specially provided for the purpose.

Writing in 1968 Frank Beale General Manager of Alpha recalled the time when the new building was being constructed;

The next phase was planning and building the five storey building as we know it today plus ancillary control rooms, canteen, etc. This took two-and-a-half years to complete and was absolute chaos. We neither cancelled a programme nor came off the air once.

Demolition work, builders' rubble, pile-driving, a different route around the studios every day – anything to confuse the staff just happened. The Sound Department had a ball of a time

Top Left: Artist's impression of the Alpha Studios at Aston.
(Source: Five Years at Your Fireside – ATV). Top Right: The new building – Alpha Television Studios, Aston Road North. Bottom Left: Constance Moorhouse on duty in Reception.
Bottom Right: Audience waiting to attend a show at Alpha Television Studios.

– so much so that they rigged up a klaxon alarm system which sounded off two minutes before 'airtime' when the workmen stopped hammering, pile-driving, pneumatic drilling, etc. and supped solidly from tea cans until the second blast off which signalled the end of transmission and the renewal of this devastating noise. The Same Day Cleaning Company across the Aston Road North must have made a fortune!

This may all sound amusing, but progressing in this manner, with so many operational difficulties, produced an astonishing spirit de corps among the lads and lassies of Alpha. They also had to get used to operating and working with two entirely different companies, ATV from Monday to Friday and ABC at weekends. Although straightforward enough on paper, this produced difficulties and it is to the credit of everybody concerned in the three companies that the system worked so well over thirteen years.

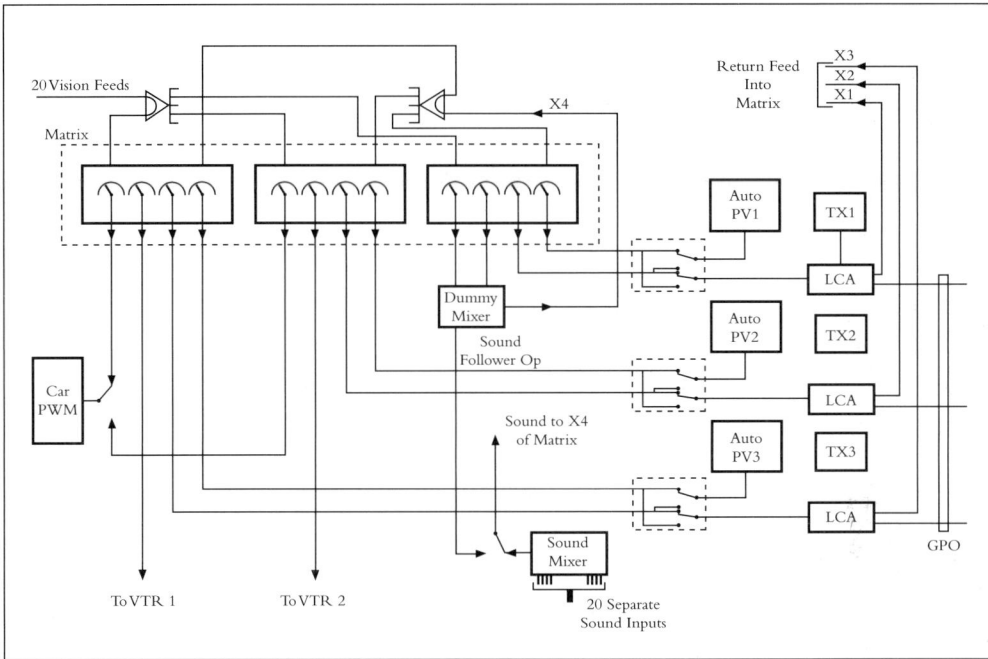

The new building was a six storey block next to the original theatre; it had an imposing look, with its black marble frontage and huge plate glass doors. Inside, the reception area was a scene of efficiency.

Tropical fish swam quietly in an aquarium, and there were fresh flowers on the desk. The receptionist greeted visitors with a smile. Two floors of the building housed offices, and the canteen, used by staff and artists alike, occupied a whole floor. Instead of the original small room which became crowded if 30 people sat down to eat, the new canteen was like a first-class restaurant where over 100 people could be seated at a time. Everywhere was spacious.

The whole of the top floor was assigned to the master control room or 'central area', as it was called. Throughout transmission eleven broadcast engineers worked there. The design of the new equipment and area, the layout of control rooms were considered carefully in the light of all the difficulties and advantages noticed in the previous years.

It was found that in the original layout the flexibility available was exploited fully in complicated presentation routines. Operational errors were few, and when they did occur, were frequently due to patching errors or wrong reselection on switching banks. The basic philosophy of operations was therefore retained, but with every effort made to simplify and rationalise the control panels.

Alpha Television Central Area's Presentation Desk.

In view of the fact that the operational staff had to spend long periods (up to 13 hours) in an alert state, comfort, pleasing appearance and ease of operations were considered of primary importance.

Apart from the new master control room and announcers' studio, the alterations did not affect the actual studio area.

On the left is the Sound Desk and Mixer, in the centre the Transmission Controller's Communication Panel and on the right the Vision Mixer. Behind the curtain is the window to the Presentation Studio.

MASTER MATRIX

The signal matrix consisted of twelve specially treated uniselectors contained in air-tight, and hence, dust-proof, boxes. The reliability of uniselectors had been very thoroughly proved in telephone systems throughout the world. Vision signals from all sources, studio outputs, telecine machines, caption scanners, remote sources, etc., being fed from distribution amplifiers to each group of four selectors. Sound was carried on the same selectors, so no additional matrix was needed.

The selectors were arranged in three boxes containing four selectors. The requirements for the twelve separate outputs were as follows:

■ Presentation vision mixer 2 outputs
■ Master Switcher 6 outputs
■ VTR machine feeds 2 outputs
■ CAR monitoring 2 outputs

VTR machines were not installed initially, CAR was the Central Apparatus Room.

PRESENTATION VISION MIXER

This was designed as a 'Next Channel' mixer with twenty-one inputs. Two outputs from the switching matrix were used to feed it.

A source was selected by operating the first pressure of one of a row of 'double-touch' keys (similar to organ-stop keys). The selected source would appear on preview and the tab key released itself. At the same time an illuminated display indicated in green below the preview monitor the designation of the selected source (e.g. Telecine 1, or Remote 3, etc.)

The second pressure on the tab key caused an immediate cut on transmission to the selected source, accompanied by a red illuminated display under the transmission monitor showing the designation of the source now on transmission.

Mixing between sources was achieved by selecting the next channel required on preview, then pressing a 'mix' button and operating a pair of faders from top to bottom. On completion the faders returned to the top by spring action.

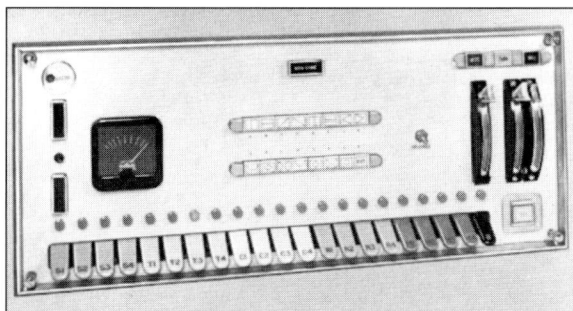

Presentation Vision Mixer.

Alternative to a 'mix', a 'fade' could be selected were the faders fade the picture content of the 'on-air' source to black at the bottom of their travel, operate a changeover switch so that the synchronising pulse or black level from the previewed source were transmitted instead. As the faders were returned to their normal positions the new picture was faded up from black.

There was a choice of fifteen shapes for 'wipes', operated from a special wipe fader. Since wipes and mixes can only be made between sources that are co-synchronous, a comparator caused a warning light to be illuminated if the sources were 'non-sync.'

Sound sources were arranged to 'follow' the vision if desired. Thus with married sound and vision sources complete presentation routines were achieved, the changeover from one sound source to the next being carried out by a rapid automatic fade down and fade up to avoid clicks and plops.

There were five groups of sources to the vision mixer:

Studios	Telecines	Captions	Remote	Miscellaneous
S.1	T.1	C.1	R.1	M.1
S.2	T.2	C.2	R.2	M.2
S.3	T.3	C.3	R.3	M.3
S.4	T.4	C.4	R.4	M.4
				Black

PRESENTATION SOUND MIXER

Companion to the vision mixer the sound mixer had twenty inputs:

Studios	Telecines	Captions	Remote	Miscellaneous
S.1	T.1	Gram. 1	R.1	M.1
S.2	T.2	Gram. 2	R.2	M.2
S.3	T.3	Tape	R.3	M.3
S.4	T.4		R.4	M.4

There was a main gain control and a peak programme meter. All sources were zero level and any source could be brought up by raising the appropriate fader. A pre-fade listen button provided the 'next' source to be connected to a small loudspeaker and amplifier in the control room, the peak programme meter was also transferred to that source.

MASTER SWITCHER

This was a routing device, having twenty-four inputs and three outputs, its control panel having three identical sections, one for each output. Only ten push-buttons were needed to select the twenty-four available sources:

In order to select a particular source all that was required was to press a letter button followed by a figure button. For example Caption 2 would require C and 2 to be pressed.

The X sources consist of the master switcher's own outputs, after passing through output amplifiers, X.1, X.2 and X.3. Then X.4 was the output from the vision and sound presentation mixers. They provided a means of cross coupling the master outputs so that the operation of one bank would be followed by one or two of the others.

Each source selected would appear on preview with its designation illuminated. Operation of the 'take' button put that source onto transmission. Sound sources were processed simultaneously and were assumed to be married. But two faders enabled the sound and vision signals to be faded separately. A third fader, fed from a patch panel enabling an unmarried sound source (e.g. announcer's voice over) to be injected.

The outputs of the Master Switcher fed the Transmitter at Lichfield and two of the Remote feeds to the Network.

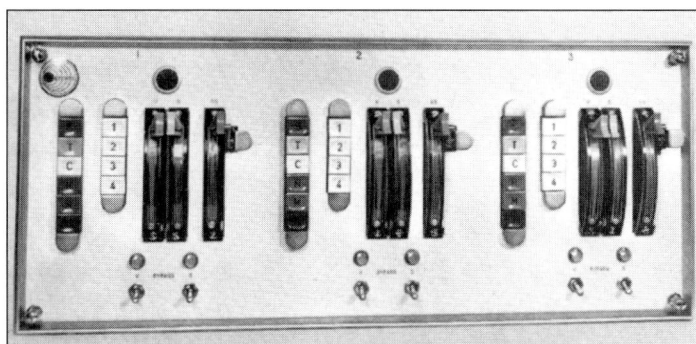

S	1
T	2
C	3
R	4
M	
X	

Master Switcher.

Alpha Television Central Area's Master Control Room. In the foreground is the Central Apparatus Room (CAR) Control Desk, through the sliding glass panel on the right is the Master Switcher Desk, and in the background is the Presentation Desk.

PRESENTATION STUDIO

The Presentation Studio was an integral part of the Central Area and was located so that it faced the Master Control Room, permitting the Transmission Controller to view it from behind its camera. It was a small studio, 15 ft. x 10 ft., equipped with a microphone, camera, a clock and a loudspeaker.

The camera was a small vidicon industrial channel (BD 871) modified for broadcast use; fitted with a zoom lens and electric servo control. A novel 'pan and tilt' head was devised in which the two principal bearings were replaced by hydraulic actuators connected by nylon flexible pipes to a joystick control. Hydraulics ensured noise was kept to a minimum; the system was very effective and had a complete absence of overshoot.

It can be said that the Presentation Studio's camera can make claim to having been used to capture the first ENG (electronic news gathering) story. When in the early sixties a house close to the Alpha Studios caught fire, the camera was hurriedly carried out of the studio to capture the unfolding drama as the Fire Brigade arrived to extinguish the flames. The output from the camera being recorded on the newly installed video tape recorders in the Central Area, to be replayed into the evening news programme.

NEW TELECINE AREA

Besides the new Master Control Room, the rest of the top floor of the new building was allocated to a new Telecine Area.

Caption Scanner – This was a 'home built' affair on a trolley, containing a vidicon camera 'looking at' the Station Clock (in fact two, one for ATV and another for ABC). In front of the clock was a caption card holder into which could be slotted 'Programme Run-down' captions, 'Announcer Name' captions, etc. It could also hold a 'chip-board' type of caption upon which emergency announcements could be made up.

In the days before 'celebrity weather-ladies' the daily summary of the weather was made-up on this chip-board and superimposed over a suitable 35mm slide. The forecast, supplied by the Met Office, was read by the Presentation Announcer as a voice-over the slide/caption. On one occasion one of the caption's letters slipped and the announcer apologised for the 'f in Fog', which of course sounded very like 'I'm sorry about the F'ing Fog', causing a few chuckles around the region.

In fact this caption scanner was extremely versatile and occasionally during the weekend ABC would have short intervals between programmes. The camera would be taken off the trolley and held out of the window to show live action pictures of the Aston Cross area. This was guaranteed to attract all the young boys in the neighbourhood to gather and wave at the camera then rush home to see if they could see themselves! On other occasions a telescope was attached to the camera to show pictures of the moon.

Presentation Studio Camera.

A view of part of the Central Apparatus Room – The Telecine Area can be seen beyond the window.

Latter two multi-caption (carousels) scanners were installed, which were able to produce extended caption sequences to be employed within programmes or on-air.

VIDEO TAPE RECORDING COMES TO THE MIDLANDS

Up until the 1970s, many television broadcasts frequently went out live and were not recorded, and for years the only television recording technology was film, and filming was too expensive just to keep programmes in vaults for the future. Video tape was introduced in the mid–1960s, but was still vastly more expensive than today's cheap home technology. It was not seen as a permanent store for television programmes. The tapes would be wiped and used again to record other programmes. Because of this most of the programmes recorded in the early years will never be seen again. It is a tragedy that at the time few people foresaw the long term cultural and historical value of its television programmes, sports and news events recorded, or their commercial potential. The future significance of such events, and the popular culture, comedy and pop-music was very much underestimated.

So consequently most programmes continued to be made on film; it was not until some years later that even feature films were transferred to video tape for transmission, and it would be many years before video tape recording and electronic editing techniques meant that programmes could be recorded scene-by-scene and

Top: View of the Telecine Control Desk for Telecines 1, 2 and 3 – Telecine 1 the Commercial machine can be seen in the centre background. Centre: Telecine 2 – multiplex suite incorporating 35mm, 16mm and slide scanner. Bottom: Telecine 3 – multiplex suite incorporating 35mm, 16mm and slide scanner.

edited into a complete programme. Any faults or problems could then simply be re-recorded, i.e. as 'take two' or whatever. These techniques have created a whole new programme genre around the 'out-takes', and have kept Denis Norden and others in a job for many years.

Video tape recording drastically changed the way things were done in television. There was no need to transmit programmes live with all the problems that were inherent in the process, they could be recorded well in advance of the transmission time, but to an industry brought up on live transmissions it was regarded as a means of simply delaying the playout of live programmes; they were recorded onto video as though they were live. The editing of video tape in its early days was a complicated process and involved the 'high-technology' of safety-razor blades, iron fillings and sticky-tape. Editing meant physically cutting the tape and re-joining; this was difficult and time-consuming, those people who could do it effectively were few and came at a price. So editing only rarely occurred, it was sometimes easier to re-record a whole programme.

It was not until 1968, when ATV won the seven-day franchise for the Midlands and its London week-end franchise was transferred to LWT (London Weekend Television) that VTR (video tape recording) came to the Midlands. Until this time any video tape requirements were carried out in London at ATV's Ogle Street facilities.

19. REVIEW OF CONTRACTS 1968

Early in 1967 the ITA invited applications for new contracts. These were to a revised pattern which was to add one further central company to the existing 'Big Four.' The ensuing convulsion shook every company, affected most of the senior programme executives in ITV and involved many in the BBC. Plans were laid. Rival consortia formed and reformed, prospectuses were written and rewritten. Swept into cabals, closeted with accountants, senior programme-makers were distracted from programme planning, and executives from the running of companies which were now facing an unpredictable future.

As long ago as December, 1966, when the Independent Television Authority announced that the North and Midlands would no longer be split into weekday – weekend contracts both ATV and ABC had lived with the prospect of change. When the Authority's decisions were announced ITV was transformed!

THE SYSTEM IS SHAKEN-UP

1968 was the year of the biggest shake-up in ITV's history; unlike the 1964 'roll-over' of contracts, this review created dramatic changes to ITV and its structure. The new contracts were to run from the end of July 1968.

The changes were:

- An end to the chronological split in the Midlands between ATV and ABC.
- An end to the chronological split in the north between Granada and ABC.
- The North was split by the geographical divide of the Pennines.
- The London weekdays contractor was handed Friday evenings.

This involved considerable changes to a number of contract companies:

- ABC Television no longer had contracts for the Midlands and North at weekends.
- ABC and Rediffusion formed a joint company called Thames Television to run London on weekdays.
- London Weekend Television was created to operate in London at weekends.
- ATV was awarded the Midlands contract for seven days a week.

- Granada's area was drastically reduced to cover Lancashire only seven days a week.
- Yorkshire Television was contracted to operate east of the Pennines in Yorkshire.
- Lord Thompson lost control of Scottish Television.
- Television West and Wales (TWW) was replaced by a new contractor called Harlech.

Until this time each region had produced its own local programme listing and guide. These were now abolished and a new company, Independent Television Publications was created. This was to produce a national TV Times magazine with regional editions.

The effect of the changes was to have considerable implications for television in the Midlands region. The Independent Television Authority awarded ATV Network Ltd (ATV Midlands) the contract for the Midlands area. This was on the condition that they established their headquarters in the region. In the early years of television strong regulation was required to ensure that the industry operated outside London; and it was this that brought investment up to the Midlands. A single company operating in the region was considered by most people to be a benefit, even though it meant losing a producer of such high quality as ABC.

The shake-up in the system created a feeling of uneasiness both within the Companies and the staff. It had come as a shock to realise that no contract was to be taken for granted, and that any company could at a stroke lose its franchise without any way of appealing against the decision. After thirteen years or so in the business companies were beginning to settle into complacency, but also to plan for the future, investing for the long-term. But this shake-up stopped them in their tracks and they reverted to short-term planning again, not knowing whether their investment would be wasted and them out of business at the next round of contract reviews.

The staff were also effected, the companies they had worked for over many years during which they were planning their careers, their lives, their mortgages and their families were suddenly being thrown out of business or transferred to the other end of the country. There was considerable uncertainty immediately following the ITA's announcements and during the period of change-over, staff were worried that their new bosses might not want them, were they going to have to uproot their family and move to another part of the country?

20. ABC TELEVISION SAY GOODBYE
TO THE MIDLANDS

When ABC started broadcasting to the Midlands in the 1950s, things were very different to today. Obviously the programmes were different, but the actual concept of television was also different. At that time watching television was considered to be a separate activity, people scheduled time for it, the set was likely to be switched on only to watch specific shows, in the same way the radio was used. It was unlikely that either the radio or the television was left switched on for long periods or less likely for the whole day, operating in the background to be listened to as background music or glanced at in passing.

Viewing hours were also limited, there was no 24 hour television, broadcasting commenced in the mid-morning, closing down in the afternoon, coming on again with children's programmes and further adult programmes in the evening, to close down by midnight after the *Epilogue* and the playing of the National Anthem. Broadcasting was not continuous, there would be scheduled breaks, interludes, and of course the occasional unscheduled break when we were treated to the caption which read *'Please do not adjust your set. Normal Service will be resumed as soon as possible.'*

It has been said that the 1950s were the innocent childhood of television, but that the 1960s were definitely the period of rebellious adolescence. As the country underwent dramatic social and cultural change, so television led the way into and reflecting the *'Swinging Sixties.'*

Throughout its period in the Midlands ABC reflected these changes by way of its responsible, high quality and progressive programming. So when the lights went out for the last time at Didsbury Studios in Manchester and for ABC at Alpha Studios in Birmingham there were a lot of people who went all sentimental.

ABC had seen the birth of *Armchair Theatre*, of *Boy Meets Girl*, of *Big Night Out*, *Just Jimmy*, *Opportunity Knocks* and so many well loved shows that made the viewers laugh and entertained them.

In 1959 they brought popular culture into the living room; rock arrived in *Boy Meets Girl*, when so many rock legends and many now forgotten performers of the sixties certainly brought a new perspective to television for younger viewers.

In July 1968 as ABC's time in the North and Midlands came to an end, its Managing Director Howard Thomas said:

'Plus ca change, plus c'est la meme chose.' (The more things change, the more they are the same.)

Everything is changed – but the objectives of us all remain as they were, to give the public the finest programmes and the best programme service. Like every other company in Independent Television, ABC has had its vicissitudes, but very few among us have ever lost sight of the fact that we all work for the public and, with rare exceptions over 12 years, contentious issues have been set aside so that services to viewers should continue.

What now?

A new chapter; not again the early struggling years of ABC with new, untrained staff, learning as they went along. Now, skilled and seasoned veterans, with hundreds of programmes under their belts, go forth with new Companies. They have learned the ways, mastered their jobs and become the professionals of television......... inevitably to form the nucleus of a new company, for every new army, however brilliantly led, depends upon its elite of battle-hardened warriors.

He was leaving three teams of 'battle-hardened', television professionals. In the North the ABC contingent would form the nucleus of the new company of Yorkshire Television. In the South, the expert technicians of Teddington would join forces with the equally expert operators from Wembley, and the veterans of Television House would be rejuvenated with some top talent from ABC.

In the Midlands, of course, he was leaving intact a complete television station, which had worked for them at week-ends and ATV Midlands during the week. This was being left to the new company, now called ATV Network Ltd.

A LOOK BACK ON TWELVE YEARS OF ABC

1956

Didsbury, Manchester, goes on the air, it's first-ever show, **Hometown Saturday Night**, started with a swing.

This was soon followed by a series of shows in the same vein called **Holiday Town Parade**.

Saturdays started with **Housewives Call the Tune**, an early morning disc programme presented by Joan Edwards.

Each Saturday morning she dusted away to the strains of *Poor People of Paris, Cherry Pink* and *Que Sera Sera* all pre 1956 vintage pop, pre-rock, from Tin Pan Alley.

1957

This year marked the introduction of what was becoming one of the most popular Advertising Magazine programmes (Admags), **What's In Store**, hosted by Doris Rogers.

Admags are programmes that are used to promote commercial products. They were commonplace in Britain after the advent of ITV, but were eventually prohibited by Parliament in 1963.

Amongst the well-known Admags were **Jim's Inn**, where Jimmy and Maggie Hanley kept a pub into which the locals from the village would come and discuss their latest bargains. Others were **Homes and Gardens** with Noel Gordon, **Where Shall We Go?** With Peter Butterworth and Janet Brown, John Slater's **Slater's Bazaar** and the cartoon **Arnold Doodle Show**.

On ABC the Advertising Magazine was accompanied by a unique way of exchanging unwanted items in Elizabeth Allen's **Swop Shop**.

1958

ABC went out into the countryside to bring viewers the world's first live Outside Broadcast farming series, **The Other Man's Farm**.

The pop pioneer, Jack Good brought a dynamic new form of entertainment to the ABC screens, the famous **Oh Boy!** programme; which introduced a Calcutta choirboy Harry Webb, who was to go on to become the world-famous Cliff Richard.

Oh Boy! was Britain's first total Rock 'n' Roll programme; described as a lively show full of energy, where each song blended smoothly into the next. The top recording artists of the time sang not only their current recording but sang together with other artists. It was a fast one hour show, presenting a mixture of the latest from the *Hit Parade* and older music. All the shows came from the Hackney Empire.

It was an immediate hit not only with the teenagers but also with the adult audience. Regulars on the show were Marty Wilde, The Vernon's Girls, the Dallas Boys, Cherry Wainer, Red Price, Tony Hall, Ronnie Carroll, and Neville Taylor and the Cutters. Providing the music was Harry Robinson's Band, which Jack Good changed into the famous Lord Rockingham's XI, which had hits of its own.

Cliff Richard.

Joe Brown and Alvin Stardust with The Vernon's Girls.

1959

ABC introduced a Religious Training Scheme, whereby clerics of all denominations gained TV experience and know-how.

The picture shows the televising of the inaugural meeting with left to right: Howard Thomas, the Bishop of Manchester, Dr. Eric Fletcher, MP, and Rev. L.G. Tyler, Anglican Adviser to ABC Television.

Religious Training Scheme.

Time Out For Peggy, was a Situation Comedy series, starring Warwickshire born, Billie Whitelaw and Diana King.

Billie Whitelaw also appeared in many of the single-dramas in the ABC Armchair series.

1960

Sunday Break was the first attempt on television to bring religion to the country's youth. Actually starting earlier in 1958, it was in its heyday and had become a household programme throughout the land.

Also popular were the very many memorable one hour plays on Sunday nights under the umbrella title of ***Armchair Theatre***. It was an influential series, and became compulsive viewing on Sunday evenings.

The series featured many top performers, including Tyrone Power, Flora Robson, Gracie Fields, Joan Greenwood, Ian Hendry, Billie Whitelaw, Donald Pleasence, Tom Courtenay and Diana Rigg.

Some of the early plays were transmitted live, and the perils in doing so were highlighted in 1958, when actor Gareth Jones collapsed and died during the performance of ***Underground***.

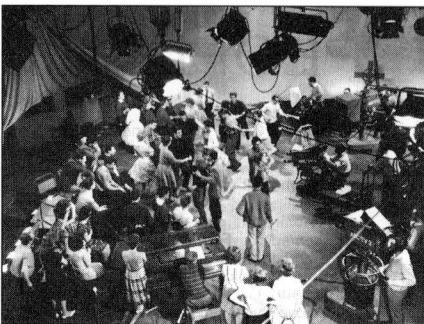

Producers of the show were: Dennis Vance, Sydney Newman, Leonard White and Lloyd Shirley.

No Tram To Lime Street, starred Jack Hedley and Billie Whitelaw.

Not forgetting, of course, Light Entertainment; the arrival of rock brought such greats as ***Boy Meets Girl*** and ***Wham!!***

David Nixon was an ABC regular, who must have lost count of the programmes he has appeared in. Amongst them were ***Comedy Bandbox, Candid Camera, The David Nixon Show*** and many guest appearances.

Candid Camera was imported from America and featured hidden-camera stunts at the expense of members of the general public. Bob

A remarkable line up from Boy Meets Girl: Left to right: Billy Fury, Jess Conrad, Gene Vincent, Joe Brown, Eddie Cochrane, Adam Faith and Marty Wilde.

Monkhouse was its host and Jonathan Routh roamed the country to find gullible people. People were faced with impossible situations and hidden-cameras filmed their reactions.

Memorable situations include the man appearing to grab and eat goldfish from a tank, which were actually pieces of carrot floating in the water; the pole-vaulter trying to get his enormous pole into a taxi; a man taking food from another persons plate in a café and of course the famous car without an engine which rolled down a hill and arrived at a garage where the mechanic was asked to find out why it would not start.

The filmed material was put into the show and shown on a large screen before a live audience at Alpha Studios, Aston; producing real, live, spontaneous audience reaction, as opposed to 'canned laughter.'

Police Surgeon followed the adventures of Dr Geoffrey Brent (Ian Hendry) working for the Metropolitan Police at Bayswater and getting caught up in criminal investigations. Created by Sydney Newman, and using scripts written by a real-life police surgeon. There were 13 x 25 min B/W episodes. See ***Avengers*** overleaf.

1961

Steamboat Shuffle, a musical programme for the young at heart, came from the banks of the River Thames. It was hosted by Peter Elliott and Don Rennie.

Another programme with a watery theme was *City Beneath the Sea*, starring Stewart Guidotti and Gerald Flood.

It was an adventure series for younger viewers and was a follow-up to the highly successful *Pathfinders* series, which covered the escapades of Professor Wedgwood's family (Peter Williams) in outer space. *Pathfinders* was produced by Sydney Newman, who created *Doctor Who*.

Also in 1961 Dora Bryan, one of Britain's favourite comediennes of the 1950s –70s, starred in *Happily Ever After*, as Dora Morgan, with her doctor husband, Pete Murray.

1962

This was the year that ABC Television brought off one of its greatest scoops by presenting Frank Sinatra in his British TV debut, *This is Sinatra*.

Another member of the Rat Pack was also featured in *Sammy Davis Comes to London*.

The Avengers became a top-rate viewing habit with the British public.

It starred Patrick MacNee as the now famous John Steed and Honor Blackman, as Catherine Gale, as the original female foil.

This very successful series grew out of another earlier ABC series called *Police Surgeon*, made in 1960. This starred Ian Hendry as Dr. Geoffrey Brent, a man avenging his wife's murder, but a supporting character which caught the eye was that of Patrick MacNee as a dandified secret service agent (bowler hat and cane borrowed from a performance by Ralph Richardson in the film Q *Planes*).

Created by Sydney Newman and Leonard White, *The Avengers* was produced from January 1961 to September 1969. The first series centred upon two main characters, John Steed played by Patrick MacNee, and Dr. David Keel played by Ian Hendry. Ian Hendry's character was also avenging the murder of his girlfriend by a drugs gang, his practice nurse but he was not the same character as in **Police Surgeon**.

Ian Hendry did not wish to continue with a new series, and Patrick MacNee became the lead character in the one-hour series entitled **The Avengers**. Honor Blackman became his aide, and her judo skills and leather outfits became talking-points; she left the show after one series whilst it was still in black and white and broadcast from VTR.

Thereafter **The Avengers** went to colour film and lasted a further two seasons with Diana Rigg, as Emma Peel,

and one with Linda Thorson as Tara King; Patrick MacNee was in every episode. It had developed into a secret agent spoof, with fantasy violence, zany villains and macabre plots solved by amusing and ambiguous leading characters whose hair never got ruffled. Responsible for its image was Philip Levene.

In 1976 Albert Fenell and Brian Clemens, who had been very much involved with the production and writing of the old series, put together **The New Avengers**, with Patrick MacNee assisted by Joanna Lumley as Purdey and Gareth Hunt as Mike Gambit, which ran for 26 episodes.

1963

Portugal's most famous singer, Amalia Rodrigues, who made Fado – the Portuguese equivalent of Flamenco – famous around the world, appeared on **Tempo**, a fortnightly arts magazine show.

It was a 50 minute arts indulgence presented by the Earl of Harewood,

besides the classic arts of painting, sculpture, ballet and music, it reviewed films, literature and drama.

Its aim was to allow the mass television audience to appreciate the artistic world without being brow-beaten by academic opinion.

A popular series called the **Human Jungle**, about the case book of a Harley Street psychiatrist, D Roger Corder (Herbert Lom) commenced this year. It exhibited a wide range of human interest stories as he attempted to unravel the complicated problems of his disturbed patients. There were 26 episodes on B/W film.

In Birmingham, pop stars from this country and America – including The Beatles – topped the **Thank Your Lucky Stars** Tam ratings under the guidance of Keith Fordyce and later, Brian Matthews, their fellow DJs and Brum's own *'Oi'll Give it Foive'* girl, Janice Nicholls.

Other presenters were Jimmy Savile, Pete Murray, Alan Dell, Sam Costa, Barry Alldis, Ken Walton, Jimmy Young and Don Moss.

A part of the show was called Spin a Disc, in which a panel of celebrities accompanied by local teenagers gave their views on new record releases and gave them marks. Janice Nicholls was a 16 year-old office clerk with a wonderful rich Black Country accent, and when she first appeared on the panel she became an instant favourite, after which she became a regular.

The current stars of the pop-music scene mimed to their latest tracks, recorded prior to transmission. The show gave The Beatles their first national television appearance, on January 19th 1963, when they mimed to their second single, *From Me To You*.

The Beatles topped the bill in June 1963 in a programme called **Summer Spin Liverpool Special**. Supporting artists were Lee Curtis, The Big Three, Kenneth Cope and the Breakaways, Billy J. Kramer, The Vernon's Girls and Gerry and the Pacemakers. The show is recorded as having some six million viewers.

This prompted ABC to come back with another ***Merseybeat Special*** in December 1963. This again featured The Beatles along with Gerry and the Pacemakers, Billy J Kramer, The Dakotas, Cilla Black, Tommy Quickly, The Fourmosts and the Breakaways. This show proved that the Merseybeat was a national phenomenon.

1964

The Gazette from Didsbury starred the then lesser known Scaffold group of Roger McGough, Mike McGear, John Gorman and Sheila Fearn.

Programmes about the Army were ever popular and the controversial ***Redcap*** gained much public interest and respect with John Thaw as its star, as a tough, no-nonsense military policeman, Sgt. John Mann.

It had stories of the Military Police investigations into crime in the armed forces, brisk yarns of characters in action, as cool and crisp as one would expect, with action in Malaya, Borneo, Aden and Cyprus.

Created by Jack Bell and produced by John Bryce, it was broadcast in black and white from VTR and there were approximately 30 x 50 minute episodes.

1965

Midlands super sleuth, Inquiry Agent Frank Marker (Alfred Burke) starred in ***Public Eye***, one of ABC's most successful drama series.

He was a poorly paid, down-at-heel private investigator, a likeable hero in realistic detective dramas, who even went to prison at the end of the series.

Twelve episodes were in black and white and twenty-one in colour. Each episode ran for 50 minutes. It was created by Roger Marshall and Anthony Marriott.

With regards to comedy, Mike and Bernie Winters, strengthened their household name along with many of their comedy colleagues.

Here seen with Kenneth More during the summer show, which they hosted, **Blackpool Night Out**, the forerunner of **The Blackpool Show**.

Mike and Bernie had arrived on ABC screens in 1963 as hosts of **Big Night Out**. This show was the first to feature regularly the ABC Television Showband – a group of Manchester based musicians put together and led by Bob Sharples.

1966

Producer Margery Baker won the year's best adult education programme award, presented by the National Institute of Adult Education in conjunction with the Guild of Television Producers and Directors, for her programme **Grammar of Cookery** featuring Philip Harben.

Philip was a familiar face on British television, as one of the first TV cooks, always wearing his striped butcher's apron.

Intrigue was a series in which Edward Judd played Gavin Grant investigating and ferreting out industrial spies from the world of big business. It was short lived with only 12 x 50 min episodes.

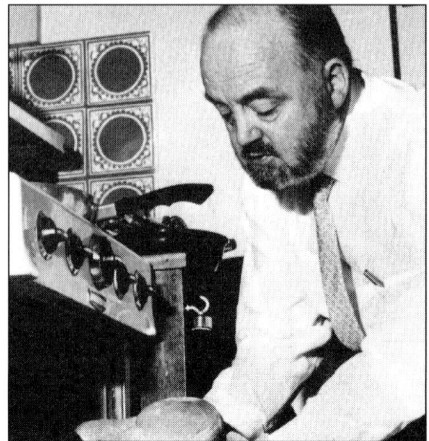

ABC was also concerned with education and its **First Steps in Physics** was another programme to gain the interest of viewers. It was an audience participation GCE "O" Level programme by G.H. Hacker, B.Sc. and presented by Prof. James Ring.

1967/8

Ken Dodd from Knotty Ash, king of the Jam-Butty Mines and creator of the Diddy Men, had his own highly-successful series on ABC, which was introduced by 'Little Diddy' David Hamilton.

Stalwart of many variety shows and singer of sentimental songs with his fly-away hair and tickling stick brought much pleasure to viewers of ABC.

Other comedians to appear on ABC where Tommy Cooper, Frankie Howard and Bruce Forsyth.

First shown in 1956, the top-ranking long-running, talent show, **Opportunity Knocks**, hosted, for over five series to 1977, by Hughie Green, and responsible for much of the country's new talent, drew to a close.

It had a simple format; Hughie introduced six acts each week each of which was sponsored by a studio guest who presented background information about the performers. At the end of the show the audience were asked to applaud each act in turn; the applause being measured on a 'clapometer.' The act recording the highest reading was declared as 'the studio winner.' But the true winner was the act voted highest by viewers who posted their votes on postcards. The following week the winner was announced and joined the next group of acts. This meant that a popular act could return week after week. At the end of the series there would be an 'all-winners' show to determine the overall winner.

Finds of talent from the show included Les Dawson, Russ Abbot, Freddie Star, The Bachelors, Frank Carson, Mary Hopkin, Little and Large, Paul Daniels, Freddie Davies, Peters and Lee, Lena Zavaroni, Ken Goodwin, Pam Ayres, Bonni Langford, Paul Melba, Tom O'Connor and Paper Lace.

Memorable musical muscle-man Tony Holland was first introduced to viewers on **Opportunity Knocks** when he flexed his muscles to the popular *Wheels Cha-cha-cha*.

A singer called Gerry Dorsey failed even the audition, but he changed his name and did a little better for himself; his new name was Engelbert Humperdinck. Sue Pollard was allegedly beaten by a 'singing dog.'

World of Sport provided many Saturday afternoons of fine entertainment from many venues brought Wrestling, Horse Racing, Rugby League and Motor Racing to the screen by ITV's largest OB fleet. It was fronted in the studio by Eamonn Andrews, who also had his own **Eamonn Andrews Show**.

For four years **Just Jimmy** was one of the big rating-pullers on ABC. The appearance of the show in the Tam Top 20 was a feature in Jimmy Clitheroe's schoolboy cap. He appeared with Danny Ross and Mollie Sugden.

Other comedy series from ABC were **My Sister and I** and **Life With Cooper.** Light entertainment included **Blackpool Night Out** and the **Dave King Show**. **Glamour All the Way** presented Miss TV Times with Patrick Macnee and Adam Faith.

The last Alpha Central Area shift to operate with ABC Television in Birmingham.
Left to right: John Pettinger (Telecine), Tony Smith (Telecine), Tommy Temple
(House Electrician), Arthur Owen (MCR), Phil Grocutt (Shift Supervisory Engineer),
John Rock (VTR), Shelia Kennedy (Presentation Announcer), Alan Watson (CAR),
Ray Coleman (CAR), Roger Roe (Transmission Controller), Larry Ridout (VTR),
Chas Lindsay (Telecine); Kneeling and seated: Gerald Aitken (MCR), Mike Speake
(Telecine, later Continuity Announcer).

21. THE END OF ALPHA –
BUT A CONTINUATION AS ATV

Frank Beale General Manager of Alpha recalled in the final edition of the *ABC TV News* of July 1968:

......it is to the credit of everyone concerned in the three companies (Alpha, ATV and ABC) that the system worked so well over thirteen years.

Every type of production – drama, light entertainment, religion, education, documentary – you name it – we've done it! Needless to say, some productions in the drama field and light entertainment shows such as Val Parnell's Startime were so cramped in the very limited studio areas that they were soon moved elsewhere – but at least we tried. The original World of Sport type of programme came from Alpha every Saturday afternoon, having spent most of Friday night turning Studio 1 into a glorified 'in vision' control room and linking studio, then converting back to a normal studio for Sunday productions.

We surely must hold the record for long-running shows – Thank Your Lucky Stars every Sunday for over five years, Lunch Box every weekday for eight years. Crossroads, a five-episode-a-week serial, recently reduced to four a week, has been running nearly three and a half years and has notched up 900 episodes.

And what about people? Well, Alpha has turned out some pretty smart runners from its stable. What about Bernard Greenhead, Eric Parry and Howard Steele for a start? I think it is true to say that every television company in the country has at least one ex-member of Alpha and most have done very well for themselves. There is a lot more of this potential, and I hope some of them will get the opportunities to make the higher grades in the years to come.

As you read this, the new licence period will be commencing and Alpha will suddenly be absorbed into ATV Network Ltd's new and exciting operation in the Midlands. In a way, it is sad that Alpha's identity will vanish but progress is progress and in years to come it will only be remembered by ex-Alpha men and women who will recall 'what television used to be like in my young days.'

I know that everyone here in Birmingham would want me to wish you all tremendous success under the new Thames Television banner and, for myself, I wish the Alpha staff every success under their new ATV banner.

Ah, me – things will never be the same......

Having worked for Alpha and with this man, what can one say? He knew what television was all about; he was a human being, most respected by those who worked with him. He is one of the 'greats' of the industry!

With the end of the split arrangement with ATV during weekdays and ABC at weekends; at first, the staff were concerned that they would no longer have a job. ATV already had staff at Foley Street in London and at the Elstree Studio Centre. Communication from the ATV management was not able to satisfy their concerns. Relations between staff and management had already taken a knock at the time of the move from the original technical areas into the new building. Staff had wished to install all their equipment but the Alpha management did not give sufficient support, the staff felt that they were rushed and not given the tools to do the job properly.

Things were no better for the ATV London staff at Foley Street and Ogle Street, they too realised that they would no longer be required in London and there were already staff operating seven days a week in Birmingham; their security had suddenly been taken away. But ATV realised that there were no VTR facilities in Birmingham and staff would be required for that facility when it was installed. London staff were then given the option of moving to Birmingham or Elstree. Those that chose Birmingham were quickly absorbed into the existing Alpha staff who were themselves transferred to ATV.

But uncertainty remained and as the changeover to ATV seven-day-week operation approached the staff became increasingly apprehensive and talks, between Management and the unions (ACTT, NATKE and ETU) were started to find a way to smooth the transition. The Unions were keen that the change-over went smoothly and set out their position jointly:

'Briefly, in July 1968, ATV would acquire the premises and staff which had previously operated as Alpha Television Services (Birmingham) Ltd. All members of the Alpha staff hoped that this would solve most of the problems and disadvantages that working for a holding company bring. In many ways the signs of a happy, though hard working future were auspicious and…. ACTT staff were determined to work under heavier pressure with less staff and in poor conditions to show that their new employer's faith in them was justified. Indeed, on the 7th May, 1968, prior to the takeover, talks were started to obtain a local one year productivity agreement which would enable the company to maintain a smooth output, while preparing for a complicated move to a new studio complex in the centre of Birmingham. As talks on this agreement had started, the union, wishing to show its trust and respect in ATV, abandoned many of the protections offered to it under the terms of the National Agreement, and ensured for the company an increase in production hours of 27% and another increase in transmission hours of 10%.'

Things looked promising in the Midlands, the staff at Alpha realised that working for a single company, particularly one the size and standing in the industry as ATV was to be an improvement, and were prepared to work with them, and those who had come from London were on the whole pleasantly surprised with their new surroundings and settled in well. They realised that life did exist outside of London, and found it to their liking. But elsewhere, throughout the network things were also changing and all was not well.

22. INDUSTRIAL DISPUTE 1968

The shake-up in independent television created an attitude change within the industry which was to result in a serious industrial dispute. It was always the case that franchise holders were not permanent and liable to review; they all knew that it was possible that at a review their licence could be withdrawn and their whole business would, at a stroke, cease to exist. It started when Lord Hill of the ITA terminated the franchise of Television West and Wales; this was followed by the virtual dismissal of Rediffusion from London, ABC from the North and Midlands and the halving of Granada's region. These actions wiped out over-night a feeling of permanence which had been slowly growing among the original ITV contractors. The struggles and financial losses of the early days and the later period of inflated profits were both forgotten. The Companies licences to print money had been simply renewed in 1964, and it appeared that a time had arrived when they could begin to consider long-term plans.

Now, suddenly they were faced with a completely different situation, making it necessary to think only for the short term again. They accepted that it was fair to plan for maximum profits during the six-year period remaining on their contracts, with the reasonable possibility that they would not be extended. They could then be thrown out of business without any course of appeal.

The staff, throughout the network were also affected, they sensed the mood change and also began to see things differently; their employers who had seemed to be there for the long term were suddenly being rejected by the ITA, or moved to a franchise at the other end of the country. They realised that they too were vulnerable and that there was no longer a guarantee of continued employment with a company that held the franchise for their region. At the next review of contracts, the company they worked for could be rejected and thrown out of business.

Considering that, in 1955, many of the early staff of the Independent Companies, as young unmarried men and women had taken a big career gamble. They had skipped into uncertain world of commercial television from the secure worlds of the BBC, films and other large concerns, which in those days would have been an irreversible move. Now in 1968 they were approaching middle age, married and with growing families and mortgaged. At the next uncertain licence renewal round they would be over 40 years old, and the round after that…. Their employment situation was suddenly filled with anxiety. No wonder they were keen to improve their conditions and maximise their earnings, over what could probably be a very short career.

Things came to a head as the old contractors were about to move on and the new ones about to prove themselves to the viewers. Also at this moment in time the agreement between the Television Unions and the Independent Television Companys' Association (ITCA) was about to come to the end of its term on 29th July 1968.

The Association of Cinematograph Television and Allied Technicians (ACTT) took the lead and started negotiations with the ITCA. They claimed a 7% pay increase for its members, a reduction of five hours on the working week to 35 hours, and other improvements in working conditions. On the whole television technicians were well paid and their conditions were by no means the worst in the country.

Faced with a lack of satisfactory response from the Companies the ACTT carried out a number of 'guerrilla strikes' across the network to attract their attention. On 24th July 1968 at least six ITV regions were affected by limited spontaneous withdrawals of labour. The ITN News around 18:00 was not transmitted as the staff was called to a summoned union meeting, between 17:40 and 18:00. Anglia Television staff withdrew from 15:45 for one hour and Grampian was unable to broadcast a documentary programme.

The ITCA claimed that some 3000 staff were involved and that the union's claim would cost the Companies at least £1m a year. Within no time the situation developed into deadlock. Alan Sapper, deputy general of ACTT said, *'The ball is in the employer's court.'* Ronald Carrington the labour relations adviser to the ITCA replied, *'We regard the ball as being in the union's court. We made them an offer, which they said was not acceptable, and they made counter-proposals which we found unacceptable, and we asked them to reconsider our offer. They are in breach of our current agreement.'*

In the days that followed up to the end of the Agreement term further action was taken by union members, the output of commercials was affected in a number of areas. The newest of the new ITV Companies, London Weekend Television was blacked-out as soon as it went on the air for the first time. Viewers heard and saw: *'Welcome to London Weekend Television'*, from an announcer as the station's symbol came up. *'Now it's over to* We Have Ways of Making You Laugh *with Frank Muir….'* The screens then dimmed and up popped a caption card saying *'Watch this space – back in a trice.'* This caption was a joke by studio technicians on the company's best known shareholder David Frost who coined the quote, and their way of saying they were walking out. They returned half an hour later.

In a suddenly uncertain future the ITV Companies did not want to be under constant threat from the Unions and decided that in this time of change they should be brought under control and set out to reduce their power. It was widely believed that they decided to engineer a dispute which would work in their favour. Now that video tape recording was well established they believed there were sufficient stocks of recorded material and film for them to operate the Network from a single site and keep the union members locked-out until they were desperate to return.

Throughout the following days things got progressively worse. At Alpha Television in Birmingham the management appeared in the Central Area with a clip board containing a list of staff on duty. They called upon each person, explained that they were taking over the operation of the station and proposed to take programme material from other management run stations on the network; then asked the individual if they were prepared to work under those conditions. If the person refused they were sacked.

But the management's lack of understanding and lack of sense of humour was exposed when they called for a particular person; lets call him 'Joe Bloggs', a voice from amongst the staff asked 'Which Joe Bloggs?' The management with furrowed brows consulted the list on the clip board and could only find one. Looks of confusion followed and they retired to consult their personnel records. Having 'been-had' they soon returned, this time with the police; the staff were not sure whether the police had been called to intimidate them, protect the management or to make sure they were not 'had again'! In due course the whole shift was dismissed, as each person refused to work under the management's conditions, they were handed a notice of dismissal. As handed the notice each person stepped back and refused to handle the notice, and one by one the pieces of paper fluttered to the floor.

The shift refused to leave the building saying that they were prepared to work under normal conditions, and defying the police to eject them. The police refused to do so and stood aside embarrassed by the situation. The whole shift then retired to the canteen where they were joined by staff from the ATV offices at Edmund Street in the city. They remained 'ready for work' for the next five hours until their shift ended.

The same tough tactics of the managers was repeated across the network and one by one the managers took over the television stations and broadcast a stock of pre-recorded programmes and films. They ferried programme material from stores and studio centres by private cars, but in the London area alerted by the union, the police made sure that only vehicles with 'C' Licences could carry goods. The union made sure that the strike breakers did not also break the law.

ATV Network Limited

ATV House
17 Great Cumberland Place
London W1

telephone 01-262 8040
cables and telegrams
Ayteevee London W1
telex 23782

a subsidiary of
Associated TeleVision Corporation Limited

Directors
Lord Renwick KBE Chairman
Lew Grade Deputy Chairman
and Joint Managing Director
Robin D Gill
Joint Managing Director
Jack Gill Finance Director
Sir Eric Clayson
Norman Collins
Leonard Matthews
Bill Ward

31st July 1968

Dear   Mr. Pettinger,

The Company together with all other Independent Television Companies has been engaged in negotiation with the A.C.T.T. for a new Agreement. It has not been possible to reach agreement before the expiration of the old Agreement on the 29th July 1968.

The Company has already indicated that it will continue to employ you on the basis of the terms and conditions of the expired Agreement and this constitutes your individual contract of employment with the Company.

The Independent Television Companies are not prepared to countenance any longer the unofficial stoppage of work, the refusals to carry out instructions and other departures from normal working which have occurred over the past few days. It has been decided therefore, that, in the event that you withdraw your labour, or refuse to carry out instructions, or depart from normal working in circumstances which constitute a breach of your individual contract of employment, the Company would view such action as a repudiation by you of your individual contract of employment.

The Company would accept such repudiation and you would be deemed to have immediately terminated your own employment.

Yours truly,

John Walton

John Walton,
Group Staff Relations Controller.

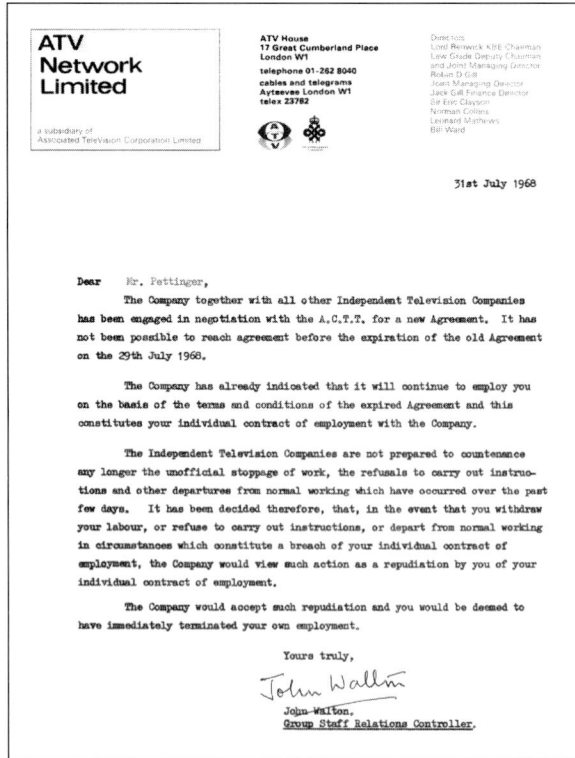

Each day the staff reported as usual and presented themselves for work. They were refused entry by the management and so the 'lock-out' commenced.

The situation just got worse, 350 staff were dismissed by ATV at their Elstree centre, including all grades, producers, cameramen, production assistants, floor managers, sound and vision engineers, and the like. But those who had planned the strategy had not thought it through sufficiently, the union members stayed out longer than expected and the lock-out could not last much longer as staff employed at film laboratories refused to work overtime to process films. Managers from Alpha Television, General Manager Leonard Matthews, his deputy Colin Wills, Gerry Kaye and Cliff Fox were amongst those controlling the 'strike bound' ITV's emergency national programme network from the company's former London control room in Foley Street. They worked their way through the dwindling stock of recorded material and films. By the 13th August it was estimated that the management could keep on-air for at least a further week; but pre-recorded series such as Coronation Street and Crossroads were running out and no further episodes were being

Left: Staff ready for work outside offices in Edmund Street – take a coffee break.
Right: Locked-out staff outside Alpha Studios ready for work addressed by Mike Lloyd.
Visible are, Left to Right: Percy Thomas (film editor), John Rock (video tape),
Larry Ridout (video tape), Kevin Latimer (film editor), Barbara Bradbury (P.A.), Peter
Rubery (sound), John Lightbourne (telecine), Mike Lloyd (director), Johnny Clarke (cameras).

produced. There was a real likelihood that some series may have to be scrapped for good. Artists were turning up for work each day, being paid and sent home again. This was quite apart from the massive loss of advertising revenue and the financial blow to the new companies which came into operation at the end of July.

Pressure from within the industry was mounting on the Companies to return to normal working. Too many concerns were losing large amounts of money. The enormous cost of the dispute mounted daily as:

- Expensive spectaculars were scrapped.
- Entertainers daily reported for work, were paid to do nothing.
- Artists and their agents lost money because no new contracts could be negotiated.
- Fears grew in all sections of the industry that long-established series would be killed off.
- Advertising agencies faced an overproduction of commercials which might never be screened.
- Expensive advertising 'summer campaigns' were scrapped.

It was a brave effort by a few managers, most of whom were pioneers in commercial television, but the result was a forgone conclusion, it was not possible for them to replace 3000 staff across the network. They had dwindling stocks of pre-recorded programmes and film, and were not skilled enough or in large enough numbers to produce the large quantity of programme material to feed the demands of the network. Resources were haemorrhaging away at an alarming rate.

Eventually both sides agreed that a return to normal working was in both their best interests. The ITCA agreed to withdraw their letter to individuals which led to their dismissal, and all ACTT members were reinstated without loss of right or benefit. In return ACTT withdrew its industrial action. An early date was set for the recommencement of negotiations for a new agreement to last more than one year. So a trial of strength had taken place, the Companies had lost a considerable amount of money, their managers must have been tired out, the advertisers had their promotions disrupted, and the staff had lost nothing, found solidarity and strength, along with some time off to dig the garden or paint the house.

The situation after all the disruption was back to where it started with negotiations for a new agreement about to start.

It was estimated that the August strike of television technicians had cost ATV Network more than £250,000, Associated Television Corporation Chairman Lord Renwick reported at the Annual Meeting.

ITV EMERGENCY PROGRAMME

This emergency programme will be screened by independent television in all regions because of the recent dispute. The schedule may be subject to locally-announced alterations.

1.5   **Great Temples of the World** : Sir Kenneth Clark.

2.0   **All Our Yesterdays** : Brian Inglis looks at the world of 25 years ago—August 1943.

2.30   **Football** : Highlights of the game between Arsenal and Leeds for the League Cup.

3.15   **Film** : ' **Quartet.**' First of the three omnibus films made from Somerset Maugham short stories. Basil Radford and Mai Zetterling figure in ' The Facts of Life,' Dirk Bogarde in ' The Alien Corn,' George Cole in ' The Kite ' and Cecil Parker in ' The Colonel's Lady.' The film is now 20 years old and its style has dated as badly as that of the original stories.

5.30   **Forest Rangers.**

6.0   **News.**

6.15   **Knock Three Times** : part 3 : ' The House in the Wood,' starring Hattie Jacques.

6.40   **The Rain on the Leaves** : Tonight's subject—Grief.

7.0   **Choirs on Sunday** : Peter Glossop introduces choirs from Sheffield.

7.25   **Film** : ' **Chicago Syndicate.**' Made 1955. Stars Dennis O'Keefe, Abbe Lane. One man's attempt to smash a $10 billion crime network of a Chicago syndicate.

9.0   **Goodbye Again** : Peter Cook and Dudley Moore in their own show. Also stars Georgie Fame, Salina Jones.

10.0   **News.**

10.10   **Play** : ' **Anything but the Woods,**' by Peter Eckersley and Kenneth Cope. A comedy starring Milo O'Shea, Jack Watling, Ralph Michael, Adrienne Corri.

11.10   **The Auction Game** : Jimmy Edwards brings the hammer down on general knowledge questions bid for by Shirley Anne Field, David Hutcheson, George Melly, Stephen Potter.

Emergency Programmes 18th August 1968.

23. ATV NETWORK LTD – SEVEN-DAYS-A-WEEK IN THE MIDLANDS

When in 1967 ATV 'won' its franchise to broadcast to the Midlands with a seven-day-a-week contract, it was on the condition that they had headquarters, not in London, but in the Midlands.

It had been argued that even in the formative years of independent television strong regulation was required to drag the industry kicking and screaming out of London. It was this strong regulation that brought the investment to Birmingham and the Midlands.

The politicians had never appreciated that in its formative years the television industry as a whole had had to struggle. Frank Beale in 1968 recalled that:

Since those days of 'do it yourself' techniques, so much has changed and one must remember, too, that the Independent Television Companies really had to struggle in this early period to make ends meet. This statement may seem to offer ribald laughter and ruderies from some of the younger members of the industry – I can just hear them saying 'but look at them now.' Please remember, though, that had it not been for the ability of Company Directors and all the original 'old hands' to 'tighten the belt', Independent Television could well have gone into liquidation and people would not be enjoying a thriving industry with the high rates of pay which exist today.

Economics played an important role in the development of Independent Television. Consider the costs of re-locating the headquarters of a company from London to Birmingham when modern communications (via the Birmingham to London microwave link) reduced the distance between the two cities to zero. Even in those early days, ATV House was and could be in immediate communication with what was taking place in Birmingham. And by being located in London it was also in communication with the current heart of the industry, theatre and the artists. ATV had established considerable programme making facilities around London, where it could produce programmes of quality for the Network at reasonable cost, bringing to the public world renowned artists from America and elsewhere at minimal cost.

It had been argued by Government Committees, local politicians and critics of independent television (who it seemed hardly ever watched) that the programme output was of poor quality. They had not realised that to run a television network, even on the then current minimal hours, was extremely costly, taking into consideration the slender resources and staff available to Companies at the time. As Bill Ward recalled, writing in 1976, that the going had been very hard during the first three years. He had worked close to Lew Grade and Val Parnell in Kingsway, where ATV had the fifth and sixth floors above Associated Rediffusion. He said that there had been many heart-searching discussions at board level. Money was running out, and ATV had to find additional support by bringing in the Mirror Group. Ironically, he added, if they had waited another month they wouldn't have needed the additional support because the breakthrough came, which led to Lord Thompson's famous remark about an ITV station licence being a licence to print money.

There was bound to be a predominance of pre-recorded (on film) programmes, particularly from North America. Limited resources and facilities meant that day-to-day material purchased from other countries would appear relatively cheap to Companies strapped for cash and without the necessary facilities to make all their own programmes.

Looking back it is difficult to follow the reasoning of politicians and government committees in their decisions as to which company should broadcast in which area. Often from this perspective they seem to be completely out of touch with 'real people'; did they ever watch any of the output from any station. They certainly listened to 'experts' in universities, but never queried where they obtained their information or its true validity.

But those individuals who operated ATV really had their 'finger on the pulse', they knew from years of experience in theatre and cinema what the people wanted, how they wished to be entertained, educated and informed. They had proved themselves by filling theatres and cinemas; they had had failures and had learned from them. They were a universe away from the professors in the university who from their 'ivory towers', felt that they, 'knew what people wanted and needed.' But it was the 'experts', those who thought they knew what was best for the public that those in control listened to.

Things are little, if at all, better today; Melvyn Bragg has recently said while researching for his recent programme ***The Story of ITV, The People's Channel***:

If you want to find the 646 most ignorant people about television then go down to Parliament and meet them. They hear about it, they complain about it, but they don't watch it. I was very furious about the ignorance of the influence of ITV on television. I think the contribution of ITV has been unjustly underestimated. I decided then that I wanted to show what ITV stands for. ITV is a great story, a great British invention. No commercial channel in the world does what we do, offering hit shows as well as public service programmes.'

At the forefront of ITV's development was Lew Grade who founded ATV, one of ITV's original broadcasters, in 1955. ATV brought the world's top stars into people's homes, with song-and-dance spectaculars as well as programmes such as **The Morecambe and Wise Show, The Saint** and **Thunderbirds**. Lew Grade once said, *'All my shows are great, some are bad, but they are all great.'*

With his serious show business connections ATV was able to put on-air the weekly Sunday night spectacular **Sunday Night at the London Palladium**, hosted by a young Bruce Forsyth. Each week the show was topped by a world famous star proceeded by highly entertaining but simple games and other supporting acts.

ATV's Lew Grade had a northern rival in Sidney Bernstein at Granada Television. It has been said that what Lew was to showbiz, light-hearted, happy, 'sit back and smile' entertainment; Sidney was to confrontational, dower, questioning, 'put the world to right' and grumpy broadcasting.

Each would continually try to out do the other. But Lew, it seems always had the measure of Sidney. For example, in the early days long before mobile phones, Lew had installed an in-car radio telephone in his Rolls Royce to keep in touch with the office whilst travelling, but mainly as a status symbol. Sidney who was not to be outdone, followed suit and rang Lew from his car on his newly installed radio telephone, to show off. Lew's secretary, answered the radio call and told Lew that Sidney would like to speak to him, Lew, not to be outdone responded by saying, 'Tell him I'm on the other line!' In the North they tell the story the other way round, well they would! But my money is on Lew.

Granada Television's output had a completely different tone to that of ATV; on the Network it was regarded as the brash Northern upstart that replaced the superb earlier contractor ABC Television. Michael Parkinson has described Granada as *'Arrogant, blunt, salty. It wore clogs.'* Granada was hit hard in 1968 when its self created state, 'Granadaland' covering most of the North, was cut in half and restricted to the area west of the Pennines. Sidney was so upset that it was rumoured that he threatened to take the matter to the United Nations. But the ITA were aware that Granada programming attracted many more complaints from viewers than all the other programme contractors put together.

Granada's output was always more serious than the rest of the network; they produced many noteworthy current affairs programmes, it seemed as though they wanted to force the viewers to confront serious issues and drew them into highbrow debates, thrust the classics at them, and tried to educate them and change their views. When all the viewers wanted to do was settle into their chairs after a hard day at work and with a can of beer be entertained, to laugh and to simply relax, they did not want to 'get heavy.' But Granada did have one spectacular success in more light-hearted television, it produced the very popular and long running **Coronation Street**, which has been the most popular television series ever; unfortunately it does as little to reflect the Manchester area or its culture as the BBC's, also popular, **Eastenders** does to reflect the culture and life in London. Neither is what might be classed as a Regional programme; both surely, hopefully, do not reflect what life is really like in the North or in the South.

FURTHER TROUBLE

Following the unfortunate dispute of 1968 and the changeover to ATV there was still a feeling of unease at the Studios in Aston. In April 1969, despite the productivity agreement with the union agreed the previous year, the company appeared to have taken advantage of the relaxation of the National Agreement conditions by the union. The staff were required to work excessive overtime hours, morale was very low and to top it all there were rumours that ATV was about to be joined by RCA, the giant recording company Radio Corporation of America in developing Birmingham's biggest hotel, which would dominate a new television centre in Birmingham.

Robin Gill, then joint managing director of ATV said, *"We are looking forward to having RCA as partners."* News of the negotiations with RCA sparked more speculation about ATV Network's future as the Midlands ITV programme contractor.

The protracted rumbling dispute with the technicians at Alpha Television Studios was made worse by the news, they feared that ATV was about to lose its franchise. The technicians had 'blacked out' commercials on two evenings in mid–April, and the management had claimed that the action had lost the company £100,000 in advertising revenue. Mr Gill dismissed the rumours of an *'ATV withdrawal'* as entirely groundless. *'There is no question of giving up our franchise'*, he said.

The company issued letters to all staff, delivered by hand, via taxis, throughout the nights of 27th and 28th April, warning staff that if they continued in their action the company would have to inform the ITA that the company could not operate at Aston and that all staff would be laid-off.

The Union was incensed by the way in which the letters had been delivered, and maintained that its members were working in accordance with the National Agreement. It again stressed that if the company were to employ more staff in order to reduce overtime, many of its problems would be solved.

Robin Gill.

Eventually the company agreed to recruit extra staff as soon as practicable, and not to use systematic overtime as a substitute for employing sufficient staff. It also agreed to apply the same conditions of employment and remuneration in Birmingham as was in operation at its Elstree Studios. The company and the union agreed to work together to resolve the immediate difficulties.

Robin Gill, in an interview with Blair Thomson of the Birmingham Mail, spelt out how he saw the future of ATV. He stressed that the company intended to be in every sense the Midlands contractor; there would be a strong Midlands representation on the board, and that the whole operation of the company would be controlled from the Midlands.

He confirmed that the new Midlands Centre in Birmingham would have facilities which would be capable of handling any type of programme, including major drama productions and light entertainment. It would also be fully equipped for colour programme production and transmission and that it would have its own outside broadcast unit. All this would be in addition to those facilities that already existed in Aston.

With regards to Midlands influence in the actual programming Mr Gill promised that there would be an emphasis on Midlands current affairs and many exclusive Midlands programmes in the schedule.

24. A NEW CENTRE FOR THE NEW CONTRACT, WITH ADDED COLOUR

At this time Midlands' television was still operating in monochrome, 405-lines. But with the new contract and the requirement to move headquarters to Birmingham, came plans for the new ATV Centre, right in the heart of Birmingham, extended facilities for the coverage of the region and full capability for the change to colour television which was soon to come. Two long-serving ATV executives, Bill Ward and Len Matthews, were largely responsible for implementing those ambitious plans – Bill Ward as Executive Director and Director of Programmes and Len Matthews as Director and General Manager.

A BIT MORE HISTORY

The site chosen for the new Television Centre was between the corner of Broad Street where it joins Suffolk Street and Paradise Street, and Bridge Street further along Broad Street.

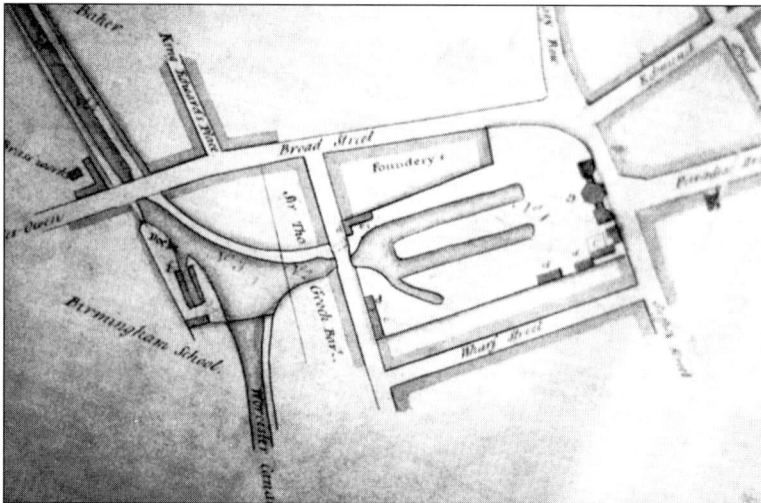

Plan of the Old Wharf beyond Bridge Street.

The offices of the Birmingham Canal Company at the Paradise Street end of the Old Wharf.

Back in 1772 when the canal was constructed the Birmingham Canal Company built a terminus area, as an extension of what is now Gas Street Basin, with a large twin armed wharf shaped like a tuning fork. At one time the basin was called Paradise Street Wharf, but later and more commonly it was known as the Old Wharf. At the far end of the two long basins stood the Birmingham Canal Company's offices, opened in 1773.

The site continued to be used by the Canal Company until the mid 1850s, when it became associated with the area's theatrical and entertainment history.

The Curzon Hall was opened there in 1865 to house the Birmingham Dog Show; it was a huge barn of a building capable of accommodating as many as three thousand people. It soon became noted as a place that set the standard for all that was large and spectacular in entertainment, including screen spectacles, panoramas and magic lantern shows. For many years at Christmas time it was home to Harry H. Hamilton's 'excursions', which were the wonder of the age. They were a series of huge colour pictures on canvas sheets revolved on pillars each side of the stage which passed across an illuminated 20 x 20 foot screen; they depicted scenes from the 'excursion' and places of interest were pointed out by the top-hatted commentator's cane and were accompanied by music, lighting and sound effects. On one occasion an amazed audience watched a rider mounted upon a white horse jump from the theatre gallery into a pool of water set into the floor of the auditorium. Another tearful audience were enthralled as Sergeant Major Parkinson, who had been present when the Six Hundred brave men charged into the Valley of Death, recited *'The Charge of the Light Brigade'*.

In 1899, Waller Jeffs, a pioneer in the world of film, introduced 'Edison's animated pictures' to Birmingham. Jeffs was a journalist who became a lecturer and then a showman; by the end of the 19th century he had become adept at the Victorian world of Pleasure Travel kind of shows presented at the Curzon Hall. He acquired his first cinematograph in 1898 and as touring manager for Thomas Edison Animated Photo Company he started showing moving pictures alongside his lantern shows.

He roamed the streets of Birmingham, in all weathers and in all areas, filming the City's men, women and children; and then invited audiences to come into Curzon Hall to view themselves, their work colleagues and neighbours upon the flickering screen. He also shot from the top of a new electric tramcar heading down the Bristol Road towards the city centre. Other local films were shot in Chamberlain Square, the Old Square and at the Aston Villa v Sheffield United football cup-tie. Not content with these elaborate 'home movies', he had the Hall repainted to resemble a cathedral, installed an orchestra and choir behind the screen when he showed **The Miracle**.

During the First World War the Hall closed as a cinema and became a Recruiting Office; many young Birmingham men signed on there, to fight in the muddy trenches of France and Belgium, so many of whom were never to see their homeland again. At the end of hostilities Curzon Hall became a labour exchange.

It reopened as a cinema in the year 1924 as the West End; first 'talkies' were introduced to be followed by every cinematograph advancement that came along.

PARADISE CENTRE – ATV CENTRE

In view of the limited facilities at Aston, ATV decided that a new, larger TV Centre and headquarters was required for a seven-day contract. The ITA had expressed the view that it wanted the programme contractor to move to a new centre where it could provide the best possible service.

ATV's new studio centre was one of the world's most up-to-date purpose-built for colour; equipment alone cost some £3 million. It was part of a planned £15 million

LET'S FACE IT!   by Lewis Williams

"Good evening —— and welcome to the first programme from Paradise Centre!"

ATV Network Limited
LONDON 17 Great Cumberland Place, London W1H 8AA
Telephone: 01-262 8040
BIRMINGHAM 150 Edmund Street, Birmingham 3
Telephone: 021-236 5191
MANCHESTER Mount Street, Manchester 2
Telephone: 061-834 3130

ATV's new Birmingham Studios, which will form part of the magnificent entertainment complex now being constructed in the heart of the city, will contain the most up-to-date equipment to meet all requirements for colour production. Technical equipment alone for the studios will cost approximately £2,500,000.
In addition to our Mobile Colour Vehicle (equipped for both colour and black and white recording), studios C and D at ATV's Elstree Studio Centre are also in operation for electronic colour TV Productions. These two studios will be able to record for both the 525 American NTSC system and the British 625 PAL standard. Shows can thus be taped simultaneously for screening here and in the U.S.A.

ATV COLOUR

For nearly three years ATV have been producing colour *filmed* series which are being (and will be) screened in over 83 Countries throughout the World. These include "Danger Man" starring Patrick McGoohan, "The Saint" starring Roger Moore, "Man in A Suitcase" starring Richard Bradford, "The Champions" starring Stuart Damon, Alexandra Bastedo, William Gaunt, "Department S" starring Peter Wyngarde, Joel Fabiani and Rosemary Nicols - and many more.
Since early in 1966 ATV have also been making *electronic* colour TV productions such as:—"Ivanov" a ninety-minute play starring Sir John Gielgud and Claire Bloom, six one-hour Palladium Shows, several programmes in the "Love Story" series, "Twelfth Night" starring Sir Alec Guinness, Tommy Steele, Sir Ralph Richardson and Joan Plowright, several "Morecambe and Wise" shows, a series of fourteen hour-long Spectaculars "This is Tom Jones" and ten shows starring Liberace. In fact, seventy-five "taped" productions have been completed since 1966.

487

British Film and Television Year Book 1969 – Advertisement for the ATV Centre.

entertainments complex on the site of the former West End Cinema and its extensive car park on the corner of Broad Street and Suffolk Street. The centre had taken two years to plan, build and fit-out. Planning had begun, in anticipation, before the TV contracts were awarded by the ITA in 1968. From a hole in the ground in October 1968 work progressed at a fast rate so that a year later in October 1969 most of the staff had moved in and live programmes were being transmitted. Its dead-line had been the switch-over to colour on 625-line transmission in 1969.

The site had been offered to ATV by Birmingham City Council, and Bentray Investments, ATV Group's property company was responsible for the overall project. Architects for the project design were Richard Seifert and Partners. The complex was given the name of *Paradise Centre*, after the adjacent Paradise Circus. This was later changed to *ATV Centre* following a competition announced by Sir Lew Grade, the winner being a public relations officer, who won the £250 prize.

ATV Centre Birmingham with Alpha Tower on the left and Holiday Inn centre.
(Source: This is ATV).

It was the operations headquarters of the ATV Network, through which all broadcast material passed. Productions made at Elstree were transported on tape to Birmingham and transmitted from the centre.

The new Studio Centre was brought into operation on a phased basis, firstly the Central Technical Apparatus Room, including telecine machines and video tape recording equipment, with the Master Control Room and announcer studio, were all in operation by mid September 1969.

The first presentations from the centre were continuity announcements in mid 1969, as the three studios were gradually brought into full use. The first programmes transmitted from the centre were a **News Bulletin** and **ATV Today**, news and current affairs programme.

The centre consisted of three main studios, together totalling 11,000 sq. ft. of floor space. In addition there was a presentation studio. The extra large production space meant that there was greater opportunity for Midlands productions. Two light entertainment shows were planned from the start; they would star Dave King and Mike Yarwood.

Besides the extensive studios and their state-of-the-art control rooms, all those things necessary to operate a successful professional television studio centre were included in the design of the new building.

A massive capital outlay went into equipping the studios for full colour operation. Each of the twelve new colour cameras cost £17,000 and each of the six new video tape machines £60,000. In total ATV spent well over £2 million on its colour equipment, considered to have been the finest available in the world.

Lighting for colour television is very important and ATV invested in the latest computer-controlled lighting system, able to memorise any particular lighting scene set-up, and reproduce it at the touch of a button. The main studio had available on this system 100 different lighting combinations. As programmes were rehearsed skilled Lighting Directors would light each scene to the required settings; these would then be recorded in the computer and reproduced instantly on transmission or during the video recording session.

Studio 1 was 93 feet by 50 feet, with a further 16 feet 'pull-back' area under the control room; equipped with four EMI cameras and seating capacity for an audience of 192 people; Studio 2 also had four EMI cameras and Studio 3 three EMI cameras. All of the studio cameras were maintained and their technical output was carried out by the Vision Control Department. Professional and experienced cameramen operated them on the studio floor under the show's Director.

Studio 3 was dedicated to News Programmes, which were produced by a team of journalists, reporters, presenters, film crews, production assistants, editors and secretaries.

Top: Transmission Controller Peter Laws in the Master Control Room at ATV Centre. Centre: Studio 1 ATV Centre – some of the many sets that make up Crossroads. Bottom: Studio 3 ATV Centre – home of nightly news magazine programme – Team at Six.

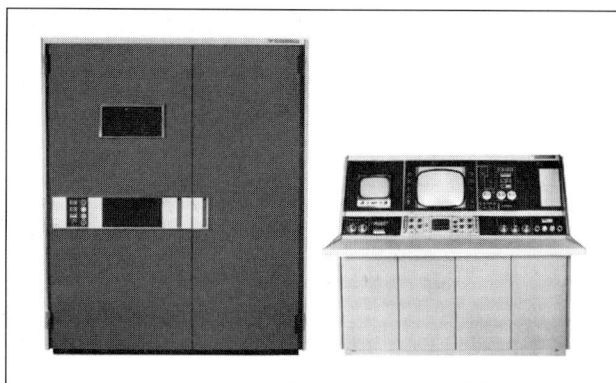

Rank Cintel Flying Spot Telecine.

The Presentation Studio was equipped with a single EMI camera, and was located in front of the Master Control desk so that the Transmission Controller could see the Announcer.

Outside Broadcast Units operated out of the Studio Centre; two units each with four Philips colour cameras. From locations the outputs of the units were either linked back to the centre by Post Office Lines, or via microwave links.

Telecine Equipment, was highly expensive, and enabled filmed material to be shown on screen or transferred to video tape. The telecine machines installed in the new studio complex were the latest colour flying-spot machines from Rank Cintel. There were both 16mm and 35mm along with 35mm slide scanners. Also there were two caption scanners capable of converting simple black and white caption cards into colour and able to show multi-caption sequences.

Most film material was at the time transmitted live from the Telecine Department. The material included all feature films, series, documentaries, cartoons, news items, inserts into programmes and of course the all important commercials.

Transmitting film was an art, as many aspects of the picture could be altered during transmission. An incorrect colour cast could be corrected; picture low and high lights could be varied as could the overall gamma. Widescreen and cinemascope films presented television broadcasters with a problem; many viewers complained that, they did not like the resulting black bars at top and bottom of picture. It was decided that such films would be transmitted as full-screen; but this meant that not all the available picture could be transmitted. Films consequently had to be panned live to show the important action; there was obviously a delay from the moment the operator saw a change in action and panning to it. This resulted in ridiculous situations where the action moved about so fast that the operator could not keep up and missed it all or just showed two noses either side of the screen. The ATV Telecine Department developed a system, to minimise this, where the film transmitted was also recorded in widescreen onto a video cassette recorder. The Recording was started a few seconds before the actual film and the operator panned the film by watching the recording; this meant that he was always panning into the action on the actual film!

Telecine Transmission Control Desk – right John Lightbourne Telecine Supervisor and left Roy Davis (later to be Central Television's Manager of Operations Department). (Source: ITA).

In later years Rank Cintel developed sophisticated computer programming systems which enabled cinemascope and 'letter-box' formatted films to be re-programmed and transmitted in 4:3 television aspect ratio. The programmer selecting the 'important' action to be shown and with the capacity to pan or cut to the next action, avoiding the necessity to show such films with black bars above and below the picture. In effect the programmer became a 'director' working with the material available on the original film.

Feature films, series, documentaries and cartoons, had to be prepared and edited to fit the transmission time slot and time between commercial breaks; commercials had to be 'made-up' into the order of transmission within the commercial break; and news items following shooting and development had to be edited and assembled into the order required within the new programme.

All this required a considerable number of specialist Film Editing Suites. Editing rooms with sound dubbing and transfer facilities, were provided to deal with 35mm and 16mm film with both separate (sepmag) and combined (commag) magnetic sound, two preview rooms and a fully equipped viewing theatre.

The News and Sports Departments had their own dedicated film editing suites where the tempo was always hectic and driven by tight deadlines for items to be on-air.

The Film Library contained copies of some 3,500 commercials and over 20,000 other cans of film material, and the staff could locate any given piece within minutes.

The huge amount of prepared film material, many hours each day, was delivered to the Telecine Department ready for transmission. It was extremely important that each reel of film was accurately labelled to ensure that they were transmitted in the correct order. Very few mistakes in 'make-up' were ever made, but over the years some did occur. In one episode of **Wagon Trail** individuals were killed off when the wagon in which they were riding went over a cliff in Part I, only to re-appear again in Part II. The last episode of the **Hollywood Wives** series was marred to the annoyance of many viewers when the last reel was transmitted before the last but one!

The technical areas of the Central Area and control rooms had specialised flooring consisting of interlocking die cast aluminium modules supported on adjustable pedestals. Each module was removable by a single person using a suction cup tool, giving immediate and easy access to all under floor services such as electrical and technical vision and sound cabling and piping.

Transmissions from the centre were broadcast from the Lichfield transmitter operating in black and white on 405 lines and the Sutton Coldfield transmitter in

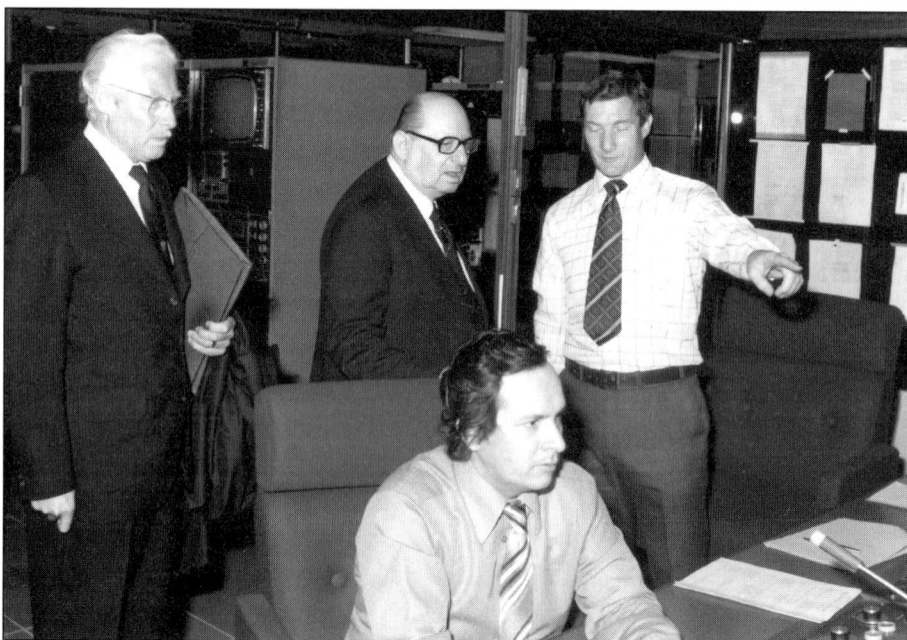

John Pettinger explains Telecine Operations to Lew Grade, Jerry Mayfield operates the control desk whilst Len Matthews looks on.

Len Matthews explains Telecine Operations to The Duke of Edinburgh.

colour on 625 lines UHF. A new transmitter at Waltham was also brought into commission providing a UHF colour service to Nottinghamshire and Leicestershire. This was soon followed by another bringing the UHF colour service to the southern area of the Midlands region including Oxford.

The Wardrobe Department, run by specialists in historic and modern clothing fashions had a wide selection of costumes, from period dresses to the latest 'mod' gear.

The Make-up Department was operated by trained staff skilled in the specialised art of making-up necessary for the critical eye of the colour cameras. Artists were provided with fully equipped and comfortable dressing rooms, and had the use of rehearsal rooms.

An extensive Design Department prepared detailed layout plans for each studio set required for each production and designed the scenery to be used in that set. The plans and designs were then passed to the fully equipped Carpenter's Shop where the scenery was constructed and then painted by Scenic Artists.

Scenes Department personnel with the help of the designer's plans expertly built each set for the scenes of a production. This was a highly skilled job requiring precision and expert construction techniques; it is a myth that Crossroads sets always wobbled – Health and Safety would not allow it to happen and the staff were too skilled.

The Property (Props) Department was an Aladdin's Cave run by magicians who were able to conjure up anything from a period clock for a Victorian sitting room or a Sherman Tank for a World War II scene. If they did not have one in their Store, Tony Eaton and Peter Tipping knew a man who could get one in time for next week's show.

An important facility for programme makers was the Special Effects Department, where many weird and wonderful devices and strange effects were conjured up. Whether some nasty 'gung' was required for throwing about on Tiswas or a Motel needed burning down, this was the department that made it happen, safely!

No job was too big or too small for the fully equipped Mechanical Workshop, lathes, cutters, drills and hammers along with hoists, pulleys and workbenches could produce almost everything with a little help from the highly skilled mechanical engineers employed there.

Viewing rooms were provided where artists, their agents, producers, directors etc. could view in comfort and under ideal conditions rehearsals, playbacks, inserts as required. All film transmitted from the Centre was also previewed here by Assistant Transmission Controllers, for timing and to check content for suitability. There was also a larger Film Viewing theatre available for use by a large audience.

Satellite and Eurovision Links were located within the building and links for ITN and OB vehicles to connect into the studios as required were located within their garage.

All of this was backed up by the important work carried out by a first class team of Cleaners and House Maintenance Staff, and everyone, staff, artists and visitors were all fed in a modern Canteen, serviced by a large kitchen, Chefs and staff.

When completed the new Studio complex was so modern and state of the art that it was visited by television engineers and executives from around the World, politicians, dignitaries and Royalty, who all came to 'see how it was done.' Its official opening was even a Royal Occasion.

25. ROYAL OPENING OF THE ATV CENTRE

Princess Alexandra officially opened the £6 million ATV Centre on 19th March 1970. During her visit to the Studio complex she admitted that she had never watched Britain's longest-running daily serial, *Crossroads*, but she promised that she would tune in to watch the episode she watched being recorded.

Lord Renwick, chairman of the Associated Television Corporation said that the opening was *'truly a Midlands occasion.'* Civic leaders of Birmingham, Stoke-on-Trent, Nottingham, Solihull and Sutton Coldfield were among the many guests.

The Princess, who was wearing a navy blue coat with a white and black hat, had arrived by air from London. She was received at the centre, which stands on the former West End cinema site, by Lord and Lady Renwick, Sir Lew Grade, chief executive of ATV, and Lady Grade.

Princess Alexandra chats with Lord Renwick.

She was introduced to the guests by Lord Renwick, and conducted the opening ceremony by cutting an electronically-wired tape suspended between two model transmitter aerials; this unveiled a plaque in the entrance hall of the centre.

The Princess congratulated Birmingham City Council on making the site for the centre available. The Council had recognised the important role which television plays in the national and regional life of the country, she said.

The opening ceremony was followed by a lunch for 250 guests held in one of the centre's studios. Lord Renwick proposed the toast to the guests and the response was given by the Vice-Lieutenant of Warwickshire, the Earl of Aylesford.

At the opening of the Centre the Lord Mayor of Birmingham, Alderman Neville Bosworth, gave this message:

*The Princess was presented with a bouquet by eight-year-old Karen Pettinger,
the daughter of John Pettinger an ATV telecine engineer.*

The official opening of the new ATV Centre by Princess Alexandra is just another important milestone in the development of Birmingham which has been a continuing process for the past 25 years, gradually growing in momentum until today we look around us and see a scale of development unprecedented in modern times anywhere else in the country.

Amongst the guests was John Stonehouse MP, Postmaster General, who was interviewed by ATV's Political Editor, Reg Harcourt:

Mr Stonehouse what do you think of this new Colour TV Centre in Birmingham?

I think it is magnificent and I am delighted that the Midlands are being provided with this facility – I think it will be a great addition to facilities here.

Now one is often hearing how great the British television service is – how true is this?

I think that the view that our TV service is about the best in the world is correct. Certainly all those who know what is going on in the United States would agree with this view. In the

ATV STUDIO CENTRE

Opening by Her Royal Highness Princess Alexandra

Luncheon

On the occasion of the opening of
ATV Network Studios, Birmingham, by
Her Royal Highness Princess Alexandra,
at ATV Centre, Birmingham, on Thursday, 19th March, 1970.

12 noon for 12.15 p.m.

Your table is
G

Luncheon on the occasion of the opening of
ATV Network Studios, Birmingham, by
H.R.H. Princess Alexandra

ATV Centre, Birmingham · 19th March, 1970

Grace

by The Right Reverend
The Lord Bishop of Birmingham

Toasts

The Queen
H.R.H. Princess Alexandra
The Guests
proposed by
The Lord Renwick of Coombe, K.B.E.

Response by
The Rt. Hon. The Earl of Aylesford,
Vice Lieutenant of Warwickshire

Menu

Vraie Tortue Verte des Indes
Paillettes au Parmesan
Amontillado

Suprême de Volaille Jeannette
Petits Pois au Beurre
Pommes Nouvelles Persillées
Salade Française
Pouilly Fuissé 1966
St. Julien 1964

Timbale de Cerises Noires
Glace Vanille
Petits Fours
Café
Cockburn 1955
Hine

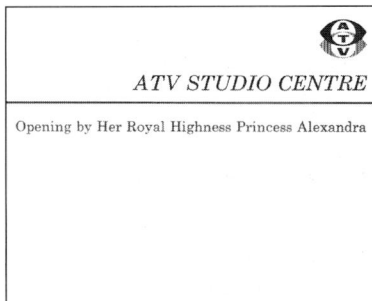

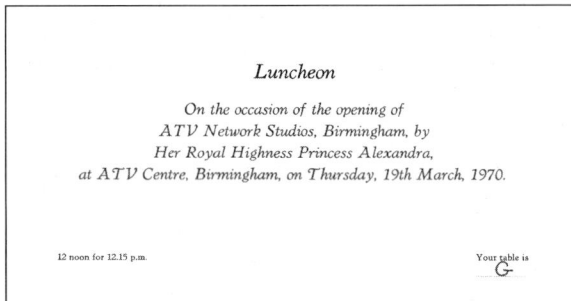

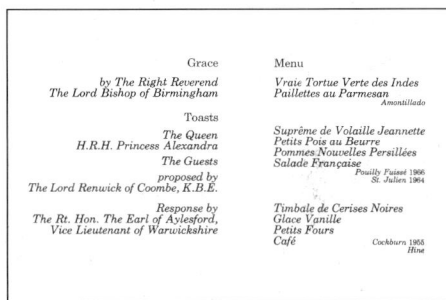

United States where the standards are deplorably low, here in this country we have, through the BBC and the ITA managed to develop the right sort of competitive situation and the right sort of controls, which ensures that standards are kept fairly high. Of course there is room for improvement, I am not suggesting that it is all 100% perfect, but I think we have achieved an enormous success.

You are talking about programme standards, but how do you see television developing in the future in this country?

I think the situation will be changed enormously by the changes in technology, in particular I think the consumer the individual viewer at home will have enormously increased opportunities of choice. Whereas at the moment the broadcaster either through the BBC or the ITV determines what he can see, I think in the future the consumer will have much more choice through the development of cassette, and through the development of on-wire systems. With the cassette of course he will be able to buy or hire a programme of his choice and show it at the time he desires. Through the on-wire system he will be free to dial in to a computer controlled library and see any programme he wants, at any time he wants on his own TV set at home and this is going to change the character of broadcasting and I think it will be a change for the better. Because it will enable minority groups and will enable individual viewers, householders to have an infinitive choice. I think this will be all to the good.

You don't see more channels then?

I think the technical limitations on broadcasting will restrict us to four or five broadcasts on air, but through wire-systems and I believe this is going to be economically feasible through the developments that the Post Office are considering it will be possible to have nearly every home in Britain, in years to come; I am not suggesting that this is tomorrow, but in years to come they will be linked up with TV studios and facilities which will enable them to dial in to the programme that they want to see.

Reg Harcourt and John Stonehouse.

What about the responsibilities of the broadcasters there, they often come into the limelight as sometimes a good deal of controversy, are they doing their job fairly well at the moment?

I think that broadcasting in this country is reasonably good, of course there are mistakes from time to time, and I believe that there is too much violence on our TV programmes. I think we sometimes get this out of line, I do not think it reflects the situation in our society. But generally speaking I think that we do a reasonably good job. What I think we want to ensure is that the system of control in the future helps us to be among the best if not the best TV system in the world.

After lunch the Princess toured the centre accompanied by Mr. Leonard Matthews, ATV's general manager in the Midlands. In Studio Two she was introduced to the staff of **Crossroads** by the serial's star Miss Noel Gordon, and watched them record an episode.

26. AN UNEASY PERIOD OF READJUSTMENT

Following the contract changes of 1968, and the damage done to industrial relations by the strike/lock-out, ITV suffered an uneasy period of readjustment which lasted three years and of which the BBC took full advantage. There was difficulty in absorbing the fifth major producing unit (Yorkshire), which had taken over 'Granadaland' to the east of the Pennines, into the network scheme; and another of the new-comers (London Weekend), granted an awkward franchise, suffered acute problems in coming to terms with it – problems which affected the whole network for some two years.

With the introduction and growth of colour in 1968 the BBC enjoyed rising revenue from increased fees for colour licences. ITV, on the other hand, decided to make no premium charge for advertisements in colour, and when the economy became less buoyant its revenue began to sag alarmingly. In 1970 an interim reduction in the levy from £30 million to £24 million brought some relief. ITV's finances were subjected to the scrutiny of the National Board for Prices and Incomes.

The NBPI Report pointed out that a regional structure such as ITV's inevitably involved some higher costs than those applying to a centralised operation like the BBC's. As a result of the NBPI hearings, the ITA suggested that in a business where the cost of the main product (programmes) is virtually unrelated to revenue from the sale of a by-product (time), an Exchequer levy would be more appropriately applied to profits than to revenue. By this method, in a period of low revenue, a company's entire programme costs would be met before any levy was paid. This proposal for a profit-based levy was agreed in principle by the Minister of Posts and by the industry and introduced by Act of Parliament in the summer of 1974.

In the Autumn of 1972 the Government removed an arbitrary restriction on broadcasting hours. Fear of 'unfair' competition with the BBC had prompted a ban on any ITV programme hours in excess of the output of BBC1. This had resulted in no afternoon or late night transmissions, and the immediate result of the changes was to add at least 40 hours a week to ITV's programmes. ATV took full advantage of the fresh opportunities for new programmes, afternoon dramas, chat shows and children's programmes, both regional and network.

27. REVIEW OF CONTRACTS 1974

The Sound Broadcasting Act 1972, creating the new commercial Independent Local Radio stations and gave the regulating powers to the ITA. Accordingly the ITA changed its name to the Independent Broadcasting Authority (IBA). The Belmont television transmitter in Lincolnshire was reassigned from the Anglia region to the Yorkshire region. This almost doubled the area served by the smallest of the now 'Big Five' companies. As in 1964 the review of licences resulted in a roll-over of them all. The teletext service ORACLE was launched in 1974.

THE ANNAN COMMITTEE

On the 10th April 1974, the then Home Secretary, Mr Roy Jenkins set up the next Committee to look into the future of television, in preparation for the next round of licence applications:

'To consider the future of the broadcasting services in the United Kingdom, including the dissemination by wire of broadcast and other programmes and of television for public showing; to consider the implications for present or any recommended additional services of new techniques; and to propose what constitutional, organisational and financial arrangements and what conditions should apply to the conduct of all these services.'

This was the Annan Committee, chaired by The Lord Annan OBE, The Committee set out to consider the future of broadcasting for the 12 years between 1979 and 1991.

The Independent Television Companies Association submitted evidence to the Annan Committee on the Future of Broadcasting in March 1975. As part of this evidence each company wrote its own profile, a self-portrait from that company's point of view, it is interesting to note how ATV saw itself:

ATV

ATV was granted its first franchise as long ago as 1954. This was for weekends in London and weekdays in the Midlands. Broadcasting began in London in September 1955, in the Midlands in February 1956. Since 1968 the company has held a franchise for seven days a week in the Midlands. ATV has thus had nearly twenty years' experience of television broadcasting, nineteen of them with the nine million viewers in the Midlands region.

In 1973–74 programme production totalled 1,085 hours. Of these 786 were networked and 299 designed exclusively for the Midlands audience. The breakdown of network production by categories was: drama 222 hours, outside broadcasts 210 hours, light entertainment 154.5 hours, education 114 hours, children's programmes 44 hours, documentaries 29.5 hours and religion 12 hours.

Birmingham

Following the award of the 1968 franchise, a new studio centre was built in Birmingham, completed in March 1970 at a cost of £6.5 million. The spread of programmes produced is comprehensive, the single unifying factor being a reflection of Midlands tastes, problems and conditions. **Crossroads** *appears more regularly than any other programme in the Top Twenty charts: its 2,000th episode was screened in October 1973. Almost as popular with Midlands viewers is the daily feature,* **ATV**

ATV's Elstree Studio Complex.
(Source: ATV Yearbook 1975–76).

Today, **Farming Today**, **Gardening Today and Angling Today** *cater for those with special interests. The weekly programme* **Citizens' Rights** *was introduced in 1972 as a forum for a free discussion of individual local grievances. ATV educational programmes are viewed in 4,500 registered schools. Total output from Birmingham amounts to some 800 programmes or 400 hours a year, supplemented by 150 programmes or nearly 200 hours of outside broadcasts.*

Elstree

The Elstree studio complex is the home of costly international productions and of programmes like the thirteen-part **Edward VII** *which require special technical facilities. Together with the productions of the film division of ATV and co-productions with European state broadcasting organisations, these are made available to ATV Network in the Midlands and through it to the whole ITV network. Programmes from Elstree include television versions of the National*

171

Theatre's **Long Day's Journey into Night** and **The Merchant of Venice** and the Royal Shakespeare Company's **Anthony and Cleopatra**.

Programmes for the international market amount to less than 3 per cent of the company's output, but they are those on which much of the export success of British television rests. ATV's place in the world market of television was recognised by the Queen's Award to Industry of Export Achievement in 1967, 1969 and 1971.

An indication of the standing of ATV amongst the ITV Companies and its commitment to the industry and its viewers may be judged from the Schedule of capital equipment as set out in Appendix F of the ITCA submission to the Annan Committee:

Appendix F – Schedule of capital equipment						
	Studios	OB Units	Colour Cameras	Colour Telecines	Colour VTRs	Cassette Video Recorders
Anglia	2	1	13	6	3	1
ATV Network	**7**	**4**	**36**	**11**	**14**	**2**
Border	2	–	3	4	2	–
Grampian	2	1	4	4	3	–
Granada	4	1	24	6	9	2
HTV	4	1	19	8	6	2
LWT	5	3	27	7	7	2
Scottish	3	1	14	5	4	–
Southern	4	1	14	9	4	2
Thames	5	5	33	10	13	2
Tyne Tees	2	1	11	6	4	–
Ulster	2	–	7	4	2	–
Westward	2	1	5	5	3	1
Yorkshire	4	3	22	7	8	2
ITN	2	1	8	4	6	–
Total	**50**	**24**	**240**	**96**	**88**	**16**

ATV was clearly a major and probably the most important programme producer on the ITV Network.

28. AWARD OF CONTRACTS FOR THE PERIOD 1982 TO 1991

Since the last review of contracts, many changes had taken place within the ITV network. Colour broadcasting had begun in 1969 on both the BBC and ITV. In 1972 the IBA took on the role of regulating the new commercial radio stations throughout the country. The Teletext service had commenced in 1974, and the ITV franchises had simply been renewed in 1974.

CRITICISM OF ATV'S REGIONAL COMMITMENT

During the 1970s dissatisfaction was expressed concerning the commitment to the Midlands region by ATV. Many complaints came from the East Midlands that they were not being adequately represented by the company. The Midlands area was one of the least homogeneous of the ITV regions and there were many similar complaints from Derby, Stoke, Hereford, Oxford and so on. But the pressure from the East Midlands was orchestrated and became very concentrated.

ATV, along with other television companies were in a dilemma, how to satisfy those who argue, persuasively and aggressively, for more regional and community television – and at the same time cater for the mass taste for costly features, series, ambitious documentaries, soap operas and the like. They could not find enough hours in the day.

The company felt that the rising tide of criticism within the region was ill-founded. But ATV was far too complacent, it believed it had done a good job during its franchise, but it had not completely won over the Midlands politicians. Its well established and respected base in Birmingham, was producing many regional programmes and news, as well as programmes for the Network. But the company had retained its large, well established and successful production facilities at Elstree in Hertfordshire. It was not responding to the growing voice of discontent from the East Midlands pressure groups who believed that they were being neglected. If ATV had opened up a News facility in the Nottingham area and followed it with the early promise of a production facility in the area things today might be so different. But the opportunity was missed, ATV only started to talk about 'The Double Eye for The Double Region' after the IBA had declared that that was the way it was going to be.

ATV then put a set of plans to the IBA, saying that they wished to provide a television service for 'local' areas in the Midlands. To enable this to take place the IBA would have to re-align its transmitters so that the company could broadcast programmes to specific areas. They believed that the plan would provide the best of both worlds, accommodate the proponents of regional and community television and the great majority of viewers who were most interested in 'blockbusters' and nationally networked light entertainment. From the IBA's perspective it was too little too late!

But as the licence renewal process proceeded ATV began to realise that the strength of political and media criticism against it was very strong, and began to try and put the record straight as they saw it. In its Yearbook of 1977/8 it said the following:

For 22 years ATV Network has served the Midlands area with television programming. In February 1956 the company first began transmitting to the area on weekdays only. Since 30th July 1968, when the IBA granted it the franchise for the entire week, ATV Network has been responsible for the 13,000 square miles of its region with an audience of 9 million people.

The company utilises not merely the ATV Centre studio complex at its Birmingham base but also the internationally famous Elstree studios which between them amount to a studio capacity of just over 42,500 square feet.

To ensure that the diverse nature of the Midlands area is comprehensively covered ATV Network decided in January 1978 to expand its activities and facilities in the East Midlands and in the Oxford area. Bob Gillman, Executive Producer of News and Current Affairs, was appointed to a new executive post with special responsibilities for the development of ATV's programme coverage throughout the region.....

ATV Today, *the longest running local news programme, continues to provide a compilation of regional items every weekday evening including discussions and previews of the weekend's sport on Mondays and Fridays.*

One wonders if this statement was not simply confirming what its critics had been saying!

ATV, although at the time, embattled by the critics and commentators, with hostile pressure groups doing all they could to ensure its Midland franchise was brought to an end, had high hopes of being awarded the second ITV channel. It had submitted its plans, evidence and record to the IBA and was quietly confident.

ATV vainly believed that they had done such a good job that the fourth channel (now Channel Four) was theirs for the taking. They believed that they should be judged on their record, which by all standards was exemplary, but which did not fit well with that expected by the IBA who were being flooded with criticism from the East Midlands.

But the Annan Committee reported to Parliament in March 1977, and recommended that the Fourth Channel should be run by a separate body called The Open Broadcasting Authority. This would control the programmes on the channel, which would be paid for by a combination of sponsorship, advertising, subscription and government grant. The IBA would effectively be demoted to be the regulator of local broadcasting. The then Labour Government was against setting up another regulator and the plan to start a fourth channel remained unfilled. The Annan Committee's recommendations were set aside.

In February 1979 the IBA announced that, as part of the process leading up to the award of the new contracts to commence from January 1982, it would be inviting the public to make known their opinions on the present ITV service and how it might develop in the future.

By January 1980 over 20,000 people had attended public meetings, over 7,500 had been interviewed in the course of the research survey of the public's views, and a smaller number have been involved in additional surveys carried out in particular places where further guidance from local opinion was felt to be of particular importance. Many individuals and organisations had in addition written to express their views.

The Authority's aim was to improve still further the regional service provided by Independent Television while at the same time preserving the strengths of the national ITV service. It therefore decided to maintain the number of contract areas. But, to allow even greater attention to be paid to matters of regional concern, it decided that it would convert two of the contract areas into dual regions, in which separate output and separate identity for different parts of the area would be provided by a single contractor. There were to be separate studio centres for

IBA INDEPENDENT BROADCASTING AUTHORITY

THE FUTURE OF INDEPENDENT TELEVISION

You are invited to attend a public meeting to discuss the future of ITV in your region

7pm WEDNESDAY 17th JANUARY 1979
CIVIC HALL, TROWBRIDGE

NO TICKETS NEEDED

YOUR VIEWS AND QUESTIONS WELCOME

each part of the region, and in addition it was its intention that the contractor's Board structure should represent the dual nature of the franchise area. Each studio centre would have to produce a certain amount of programming specially designed for the audience in its area, and each part of the region would be able to have separate advertising. The Midlands Area would be one of the new dual regions, with studio centres in the East and West Midlands.

Before the new contracts could be awarded the IBA were to examine the records of the existing holders, ATV included. Anthony Everitt of the Birmingham Post interviewed Charles Denton ATV's Controller of Programmes about his company's achievements and plans for the future. The question for ATV was, had the Lord Grade Empire fulfilled its obligations to the Midlands viewers? Charles Denton argued that they were in fact doing a great job within the limitations imposed upon them. With regards to the regional content of ATV's output, he went on to say:

We have a statutory requirement to transmit a minimum of six and a half hours of regional programmes. In fact, we average at rather more than eight. We're in business to reflect the region to itself.

Don't forget that, along with the other big companies, we are also under an obligation to produce a significant percentage of ITV's nationally networked service.

We show our regular documentary series, **England Their England***, to a majority audience at a peak viewing time. We carefully scheduled the programme early in the evening between a popular drama series (***Crossroads***) and a popular comedy series.*

If we moved **Left, Right and Centre** *(a political Talking Heads programme) to say nine o'clock, our belief is that the viewing figures would not significantly rise. That means we would be annoying a lot of people who would be expecting a programme they would like to view at that time. We would be wilfully rejecting half our potential audience.*

With regards to the regional news coverage by the company, another arguably weak spot, Mr Denton said, that without specific regional coverage many stories transmitted tended to be 'soft.' The Midlands was an amorphous region. Viewers in one part, for example Derby were not very likely to be interested in an event taking place in Oxford, unless it was one of national importance. He said that the magazine programme **ATV Today**, which followed the early evening news was popular throughout the region because it entertained by focusing on 'soft' issues of human interest; he believed that human interest was the keynote of any ATV news magazine.

In the light of the IBA's consultation exercise, ATV launched a public relations exercise to put its proposals and record before the public; producing a booklet entitled 'This is ATV.' The introduction was entitled 'ATV the Double Eye for the dual region':

The following lists include most of ATV's output 1968-1978. The year noted serves only as an indication of the first programme. Many projects span several years.

Drama

1968
Danger Man
The Prisoner
Mrs. Thursday

1969
Male of the Species
The Fraud Squad
Strange Report
Department S
The Saint
Randall & Hopkirk (deceased)
Market in Honey Lane

1970
The Champions
U.F.O.
The Misfit

1971
Twelfth Night
Crime of Passion
Happy Ever After
Jason King
Hamlet

1972
The Protectors
The Adventurers

1973
The Zoo Gang
Space 1999
General Hospital

1974
Long Day's Journey Into Night
The Strauss Family
Hunters Walk
Origins of the Mafia

1975
The Merchant of Venice
Antony and Cleopatra
Clayhanger
Edward the Seventh

1976
The Cedar Tree
Beasts

1977
Cottage to Let
The Bass Player and the Blonde

1978
Return of the Saint
Scorpion Tales
The Foundation
Law Centre
Blue Skies from Now On
Partisans
Why Here?
Are You Stone Cold Santa Claus?

The Marrying Kind
The Comedy of Errors
Will Shakespeare
Disraeli
The One and Only Buster Barnes

Documentaries

1968
It's Dark Down There
Big Fish Little Fish
The Lion and the Dragon
Welcome to Britain
Power from Beyond: —
The Guavara
The Kennedys
Franz Fanon
Arkle and The Duchess
Warwick University
Man of the Month: —
George Wallace
Jack Odell
Dr. Norman Boriaug

1969
Man of the Month (cont): —
Mrs. Frances Bourne
Anything Can Happen
Old Boys
Man of the Month (cont): —
Allon (Israel)
Gen. Lemnitzer
Dr. Lindt
Harry Wheatcroft
Brig. Afrifa
American Tourist
The Bonapartes
Moynihan
The Lord Mayor
Hospital
Last of the Big Punters
Wild and Free
Dave Allen in the Melting Pot
Man of the Decade

1970
The Violent Earth
Send Up the Sun
The Snooper Society
The Tribe that Hides from Man
Turn Around Man
Bernadette Devlin
See Through Fashion
Doing Her Own Thing
Spiro Agnew Answers Bernard Levin
Celluloid Village of Dreams
Enoch Powell
It's a Sort of Disease

A Privileged Village
Bernard Levin in a Think Tank

1971
In Search of Paradise
The Important Thing is Love
What We Need is More Red Tape
The Passing of Simpkin & James
The Magnificent Gift
The Great Train Race
A Completely Different Way of Life
The Most Important Briton in America
Black Mayor
D'Oliveira
Peggy Seeger
Sir Oswald Mosley
Great Hair Do
Mirror of Maigret
Beaton by Bailey
Germaine Greer vs. U.S.A.
Other Side of The Medal
Kingdom in the Jungle
Animal War

1972
The Next Wave?
Senator Edward Kennedy
Inside the World of Your Dreams
Stand Up and be Counted
Whatever Happened to Tin Pan Alley?
Algeria – Ten Years After
Too Late Tomorrow
Radical Lawyer
Scottsboro Case
Battle of Kursk
Siege of Dien Bien Phu
Go Go Go With Arthur
The Dead End Lads
Drugs Via Satellite
We Take This Child
Options Part 1
The Life and Times of J.W. Rainbird
Options Part 2
Neighbours
Cambridge Union Debate
Cleo and John

1973
4th M/F Shared Flat
Seychelles – Isle of Love
The Search for Revenge
Enclosed
Warhol
Crime Squad
Double Sentence
St. Moritz
(In the Beginning There Was Snow)
Mike and Sue

A Kind of Freedom: —
Lady Allen
Richard Neville
The Bates Family
Champion Jack Dupree
Jane
Could Your Street be Next?
The Unlucky Australians
Bitter Harvest
'Thank You, Ron'
Elton John & Bernie Taupin Say . . .
Happy Being Happy

1974
The Slimming Disease
Graham (Hill)
Evidence of Your Eyes
Retirement – End or Beginning?
Where Harry Stood
Just One Kid
Almost a Sickness
(Confessions of a compulsive
gamesplayer – Omar Sharif)
Pilger (six programmes)
New Faces
Dave Allen in Search
of The Great English Eccentric
The Opium Warlords
Telling It Like It Is: —
Cudlipp's Crusade
Peshmerga: —
Those Who Face Death
Caged: —
Man and Other Animals
The Selling of Las Vegas
Heroes of our Time
Dave Allen: —
Eccentrics at Play

1975
Battle Over Water
A Family Doctor
Pilger (six programmes)
Motor Industry Special
Napoleon: The Man on the Rock
St Helena: A Tale of a Colony
To Be Seven in Belfast Part 1
To Be Seven in Belfast Part 2
Class Roots
Mangling of the Middle Classes
Britain on the Brink
Three Characters
in Search of a Treasure
One Man's View (three programmes)
Chicago Streets
Where on Earth . . .
It's a Lovely Day Tomorrow

Do We Have Lions in the Garden?
Into the Unknown Part 1
Into the Unknown Part 2
Earl 'Fatha' Hines

1976
Death Of An Informer
Death Of An Informer (Discussion)
Hopi – People of Peace
Busker
Pilger in Australia
The Masked Dance
Lure of the Dolphin
Angola – Spring of 1976
This is Waugh (three programmes)
Pilger (three programmes)
Into the Unknown Part 3
Mussolini – The Road to Glory
Mussolini – The Turning to
Catastrophe
Rise & Rise of Laura Ashley
The Black Panther

1977
Dave Allen and Friends
(thirteen programmes)
Just One More War
The Last Round?
City in a Dream
Islay – A personal impression
of a Hebridean Island
City of Angels
Angels' Defence
The Rather Reassuring Programme
Ned Sherrin Asks (six programmes)
Fire Fighters
Personal Report (six programmes)
Peter, Tina & Steve
The Price of Power
Dummy
The South African Experience
(in four parts)

1978
Dave Allen (thirteen programmes)
Personal Report:
Dr. Peter Henriot – Human Rights
Auberon Waugh – Workers
Playtime
The Children of Aberfan
Personal Report: Peter O'Dell –
7 Sisters and the Blue-eyed Arabs
Havoc (eleven programmes)
Dave Allen in the Enchanted Garden
Opium Trilogy: —
The White Powder Opera
The Warlords
The Politicians

The Secret Life of Edward James
Great Expectations (six programmes)
Fly On The Wall
Memories of Violence
We've Always Done It This Way
Haven't We?
Debate on above
Do You Remember Vietnam?
After the Hijack
Breaking Point
The Gentle Killers

Comedy Light Entertainment and Music

1968
The Tom Jones Show
The London Palladium Show
All Square
Secombe and Friends
The Des O'Connor Show
George and The Dragon
The Morecambe and Wise Show
The Gang Show
Spotlight
The Frank Ifield Show
Who is Sylvia?
My Man Joe
Here Comes Kathy (Kirby)
The Heart of Show Business
Cliff
Sam and Janet
The Golden Shot
A Date with Janie Marden
The Dickie Valentine Show

1969
This is Tom Jones
The Liberace Show
It's the Bachelors
Goodbye Again
(Peter Cooke and Dudley Moore)
The Big Show
The Jimmy Tarbuck Show
The Real Mike Yarwood
'Stars' with Maurice Woodruff
With Bird Will Travel (John Bird)
John Brown's Body
(Peggy Mount and Naunton Wayne)
It Must be Dusty

1970
Saturday Stars
This is . . . Tom Jones
The Mireille Mathieu Show
The John Davidson Show

At the centre of Independent Television, ATV stands as a major Network company, making an integral contribution to ITV as a whole as well as serving directly millions of viewers in the heart of Britain. To meet these commitments ATV employs a staff of more than 1,800 people. There are modern studios in Birmingham and in accordance with the Independent Broadcasting Authority's plans for a dual region in the East and West Midlands, a substantial studio centre will also be developed in the East Midlands.

At least three million of ATV's regional viewers had not been born when the now familiar 'double eye' symbol was seen on the screen for the first time in 1955. ATV is the only company to have maintained a continuous service since the inception of ITV in 1955. Today technical developments and changing tastes and ideas provide a challenge for the future which ATV is in a strong position to meet.

The purpose of this booklet is to outline who we are and what we do.

Any television company should be willing to be judged by its record. This is ATV.....

The lists of programmes shown in the booklet are reproduced here as they record the many and diverse productions broadcast by ATV in the ten years between 1968 and

Music Hall
Hold On — It's The Dave Clark Five
The Liberace Show
Join Jim Dale
Goodbye Again
The Royal Variety Performance
[___ 1971 ___]
Lonnie
The Dave King Show
The Engelbert Humperdinck Show
An Evening with
  Burt Bacharach & The Stars
The Worker
Girls About Town
Norman
The Best Things in Life
The Gold Diggers
From a Bird's Eye View
The Peggy Mount Series
[___ 1972 ___]
The Val Doonican Show
The Marty Feldman Comedy
  Machine
The Melodies Linger On
Petula
Coppers End
It's Tarbuck
Slapstick and Old Lace
You're Only Young Twice
Alexander the Greatest
Lollipop Loves Mr. Mole
[___ 1973 ___]
Saturday Variety
Ken Dodd
Kopykats
Burt Bacharach
Shut That Door
My Good Woman
[___ 1974 ___]
The Julie Andrews Hour
It's All in Life
Spirit of London
The Bruce Forsyth Show
The Mike and Bernie Show
James Paul McCartney
Miss TV Europe
Larry's Christmas Party
Sleeping Beauty on Ice
Christmas Company
Tony and Lena
Singalongamax
The Barbra Streisand Show
The Glen Campbell Show
The Reg Varney Show

Lunchtime with Wogan
Nobody is Norman Wisdom
[___ 1975 ___]
Up the Workers
New Faces
The Squirrels
Julie on Sesame Street
Julie and Dick in Covent Garden
The Jimmy Tarbuck Show
Singalongamax
Nobody is Norman Wisdom
H.M.S. Pinafore
Max
The Max Bygraves Hour
Julie and Jackie... Together
Ann Margret Special
Cilla Black
Carry On
Peters and Lee Christmas Show
Danny La Rue Christmas Show
[___ 1976 ___]
Carry on Laughing
New Faces
Salute — A Tribute to Sir Lew Grade
Shut That Door
Down the Gate
Comedy Premiere
The Squirrels
Love and Marriage
The Summer Show
Celebrity Squares
The Big Band Show
[___ 1977 ___]
Jack Parnell & the Big Band Show
Meet Peters and Lee
Steve and Eydie
The Muppet Show
Summer Night Out
Nobody Does It Like Marti
Ann — Margaret Smith
[___ 1978 ___]
The Comedy Connection
I'm Bob He's Dickie
The Entertainers
Bing Crosby
Heart and Soul
The Beatles for Ever
You're Never Too Old
Make 'Em Laugh
The Band Show
Sapphire and Steel
Turtle's Progress

Children's Entertainment

[___ 1968 ___]
Thunderbirds
The Tingha and Tucker Club
(until 1971)
Topo Gigio Comes to Town
[___ 1969 ___]
Joe 90
[___ 1970 ___]
The Secret Service
[___ 1971 ___]
The Adventures Of Rupert Bear
(until 1977)
If I were you
The Secrets of the Deep
Timeslip
[___ 1973 ___]
Escape Into Night
Tightrope
Fly Into Danger
Tiswas
[___ 1974 ___]
The Kids from 47A
The Jensen Code
Cuddles & Co.
[___ 1976 ___]
Here Comes Mumfie
The Siege of Golden Hill
[___ 1977 ___]
Four Idle Hands
[___ 1978 ___]
Bunch of Fives
Raven
Come Back Lucy
Cloppa Castle

Adult Education

[___ 1969 ___]
Your Living Body
Taste and Style
Better Driving
[___ 1970 ___]
Music Room
Camping and Caravanning
The Communicators
[___ 1971 ___]
Take a Cine Camera
It's Your Money
Bridge for Beginners

Pioneers of Modern Painting
Something to Sing About
Rules of the Game
Holidays Abroad
The Melodies Linger On
[___ 1972 ___]
Foreign Flavour
The Piano Can Be Fun
Take Better Photographs
Romantic Versus Classic Art
Getting Your Money's Worth
[___ 1973 ___]
Improve Your Bridge
Advanced Driving With
  Graham Hill
Have You Seen This?
Enjoy Your Retirement
[___ 1974 ___]
Checkmate
Here's Good Health
Understanding Ourselves
[___ 1975 ___]
A Present From The Past
Pub Crawl
[___ 1976 ___]
All About Babies
In Focus With Harry Secombe
It's Alive and Kicking
[___ 1977 ___]
Out of Work?
Doctor!
[___ 1978 ___]
For Better For Worse

School Series

[___ 1969 ___]
Just Imagine
Primary French Year 1
Primary French Year 2
And The Living Of It
Ici La France
[___ 1970 ___]
Towards Mathematics
Rules, Rules, Rules
Karl and Christa
[___ 1971 ___]
Stop, Look, Listen
Conflict
The Time Of Your Life
[___ 1972 ___]
Figure It Out
High, Wide and Deep
You're Telling Me

Believe It Or Not
[___ 1973 ___]
Look Around
Exploration Man
Starting Out
Over To You
[___ 1974 ___]
Believe It Or Not
Good Health
[___ 1976 ___]
Alive and Kicking
[___ 1977 ___]
Work
[___ 1978 ___]
Leapfrog
Watch Your Language!

Pre-School

[___ 1975 ___]
Pipkins (still running)

Religion

[___ 1970 ___]
Beyond Belief
[___ 1970 ___]
Turn of the Year
[___ 1971 ___]
Thou Shalt Not
A Completely Different Way
  of Life
Got the Message?
Songs that Matter
A Play for Sunday
Who Knows
[___ 1972 ___]
According to Mark
Stories Worth Telling
Sue Jay Reports
[___ 1973 ___]
Dilip
Peter Plant Reports
Ian Phelps Reports
Christians at Large
Epilogues
[___ 1974 ___]
Let's Celebrate
Songs for Sunday
Women of the Bible
How I See It
[___ 1975 ___]
The Gospel in Song
What is Faith?
Saints Alive

[___ 1976 ___]
Children of the Bible
[___ 1977 ___]
Moses, The Law-Giver
(six parts)
Jesus of Nazareth
God, Our Help?
Something Different
[___ 1978 ___]
Parables
Jaywalking

1978. In the light of the current television production situation in the Midlands Region, readers might like to peruse the lists and decide whether the IBA was right back in 1981.

ATV continued to emphasise that they were one of the 'Big Five' companies, who had a responsibility to provide top rating programmes for the ITV Network as well as its own viewers in the Heart of England. ATV was proud of its achievements and its contribution to the success of Independent Television, it claimed that it produced eight hours a week of 'purely local programmes' from the regional centre in Birmingham. The rest of ATV's contribution, some nine hours a week was split between Birmingham and Elstree.

ATV finally knew which way the wind was blowing and recognised the strength of the political opposition it faced, but true to its commitment to its Midlands viewers and recognising the position of both Nottingham and Birmingham on the national communications and transportation systems, it made a commitment to build a studio centre at Nottingham and to close down its operation at Elstree. Its intention was to try to shift the centre of gravity of television production from London into the Midlands.

What We Do
Programmes 1979/80

Drama
Crossroads
Turtle's Progress
Heartland
Honky Tonk Heroes
Sounding Brass
For Maddie with Love
The Flickers
Sapphire and Steel
Quiz Kids
The Purple Twilight
The Family Dance
Donkey's Years
All the Fun of the Fair
New Girl in Town
Visitors for Anderson
Janie and Mike
Friends in Space
The Lady

TV Films
The Hard Way
Very Like a Whale
Bloody Kids
The Shillingbury Blowers

Documentaries
England Their England (regional series)
Year of the Child
John Pilger —
    Year Zero (Cambodia)
Mexico
America Me Me Me Me Me
The Mighty Micro (series of six)
Frontiers
Here Today, Here Tomorrow
Heritage in Danger (series of six)
Jack on the Box (Jack Trevor Story) (series of six)
Around the World with Ridgway
The Will to Live
Borderline (Namibian Independence)
The Moonies
Behind the Lines
Country of Birth
The Talking Whale
Auditions
The Gamekeeper
Death of a Princess
Girl Talk (series of six)
Stress
Fostering (series of six)
Why England? (James Cameron)
Before the Monsoon (Trilogy)
Project Aries

News, Current Affairs and Features
ATV Today
Left, Right and Centre
Format V
ATV Newsdesk
Election Specials
Gardening Today
Farming Today
Angling Today
Nurse of the Year
Miss ATV
Hobson's Choice

Public Service Programmes
Police Five
Link
Getting On
Public Service Announcements
    (and see also other programmes under the headings of Adult Education and Schools)

Comedy Light Entertainment and Music
The Dancing Princesses
The Yeomen of the Guard
Traces of Love
Leslie Crowther's Scrapbook
Bob Hope at the London Palladium
Variety Club Tribute to Morecambe and Wise
Eurogala
Nurse of the Year
Showtime — Peter Cook & Dudley Moore
Showtime — Don MacLean
Cleo Laine Specials
Oh Boy!
The Muppet Show
Celebrity Squares
The Masterspy
Bonkers!
The Losers
A Sharp Intake of Breath
Spooner's Patch
Tropic
Family Fortunes
Giselle (with Rudolph Nureyev)
Nureyev
And the Bands Played On
Young at Heart
Crowther & Matthews
Leo Sayer Special
Talent Shows —
    Arrivals 1
    Arrivals 2

Children's Entertainment
Tiswas
Words on War
Why Can't I Go Home
The Further Adventures of Oliver Twist
Kid's World

Pre-School
Pipkins
The Munch Bunch

Adult Education
Beyond the Moon?
All About Toddlers
Doctor! (2nd series)
Your Child and Maths
Pets and Vets
Supersavers

Schools
Starting Out
Alive and Kicking
Over to You
Stop, Look and Listen
Good Health
Look Around
Work
Watch Your Language!
Believe It or Not
Leapfrog

Religion
Jaywalking
Something Different
Church Services

Sport and Outside Broadcasts
ATV Sport (in ATV Today)
Butlin's Grand Masters Darts
Professional Snooker Challenge
Professional Wrestling
Star Soccer
Mid Week Soccer Specials
International Basketball
International Showjumping
International Speedway
Horse Racing
Motor Racing
Motor Cycle Racing
Benson & Hedges International Open Golf
Dunlop Masters Golf
International Golf (from the Belfry)
Sunday Sport
F.A. Cup Final
Soccer Player of the Year
Royal Agricultural Show
Royal Windsor Horse Show

The production base at Elstree had been retained, partly on sound commercial grounds and partly because of the reluctance of artists to move away from the London area. Elstree was well established and had an awesome stature in the international world of television, recognised as a centre of excellence and reliability. Not only did it produce world class productions for the ITV Network, it produced them for the world market. Many top-rated American artists were willing and happy to come to Elstree to make programmes, where the workforce was highly skilled in all kinds of production and worked as a highly professional, expert and happy crew.

In the light of the present day situation and the current franchise holder's very light, almost non-existent, commitment to the region, together with the closure of ATV's Nottingham Television Centre at Lenton Lane, the earlier closure of the Birmingham Television Centre and finally the ceasing of transmission from the Birmingham Central Court Studios, the criticisms of that time appear to be weak in the extreme, and where are they now?

An artists impression of the proposed Nottingham Studio Centre.

Following the report of the Annan Committee in 1977, the Labour Government invited comments on its conclusions and recommendations, and then presented its own proposals in a White Paper in 1978. But more was about to happen; following Mrs Thatcher's triumph in the polls in 1979, she announced that the fourth broadcasting channel would be awarded to independent television.

In January 1980 the IBA advertised the new ITV contract areas. For the Midlands region, it received three applications: ATV Midlands Ltd. Mercia Television, and Midlands Televisions (MTV).

But at the end of the day it was for the IBA to make their decision as to whom they would award the Midlands contract, they would have to decide how well ATV had performed overall, since 1970.

Their conclusion was that they had done a great deal, but not paid sufficient attention to regional television programmes that sufficiently reflected the nature of the whole of its region.

But before the IBA made its decision the ITV Network was rocked by a major industrial dispute, the longest in its history, which was to put the service off the air for eleven weeks between 10th August and 19th October and which resulted in a loss of revenue estimated at £90-100 million.

29. ATV REGIONAL PROGRAMMING

Back in October 1954 the Independent Television Authority made a decision that the new ITV network was to be divided on a Regional basis. It adopted what it called the 'plural' system, because it wanted to realise the benefits of a decentralised form of organisation, to encourage the development of a service which would portray a variety, a diversity, of character and attitude, rather than concentrate on those of London, the Home Counties or any other region.

Each of the companies serving the thirteen regions of the UK was to provide a local television service for their particular region. Each regional service was to have its own on-screen identity to distinguish it from the other regions. They were to provide from within their region such programmes as local news and documentaries, using local facilities and people.

After five years on-air weekdays in the Midlands Philip Dorte OBE, Midlands Controller of ATV pointed out that prior to ITV there was no regional programming at all. But things changed as ATV introduced local programming for the Midlands, introducing regional announcers, presenters and newscasters in order to give the whole regional operation a clear individual identity.

In those early years as well as providing its required proportion of quality programmes for the whole network, ATV produced in its regional centre, Birmingham, a wealth of programmes for regional consumption. A selection of these programmes has been mentioned earlier.

By 1962 the ITA were pleased to note that their original aim was being realised, regional television had increased since the introduction of ITV from around five hours of programmes a week, after seven years of competition, weekly regional production had risen to more than 90 hours. During 1960/1 the BBC had produced in the regions about 26 hours of programmes a week. Outside London ITV produced in 1962, 86 hours a week, of which 78 hours were of special local interest.

Following the award of contracts in 1968, ATV built a new studio centre in Birmingham, which produced a comprehensive spread of programmes which reflected Midland tastes, problems and conditions. By the mid-1970s *Crossroads* was appearing regularly in the Top Twenty charts. Besides the daily feature *ATV Today*, there were **Farming Today**, **Gardening Today** and **Angling Today** all programmes catering for those with special interests. There was the weekly **Citizen's Rights** programme, a forum for a free discussion of individual local grievances.

By 1973/4 ATV produced 299 hours of programmes exclusively for its Midlands audience. In 1979/80, the list of local programmes for the region had further increased to include **ATV Today**, **Left**, **Right and Centre**, **Format V**, **ATV Newsdesk**, **Election Specials**, **Gardening Today**, **Farming Today**, **Angling Today**, **Nurse of the Year**, **Miss ATV**, **Hobson's Choice**, **Police Five**, **Link**, **Getting On**, **Jaywalking**, **Something Different** and **Church Services**.

Besides this the Sports Department produced **ATV Sports**, **Darts**, **International Basketball**, **Show Jumping**, **Speedway** and **Golf**, **Professional Snooker** and **Wrestling**, **Star Soccer**, **Midweek Soccer**, **Horse**, **Motor** and **Motor Cycling Racing**, **Soccer Player of the Year**. Many of these were Outside Broadcasts, which also covered the Royal Agricultural Show.

ATV NEWS AND SPORTS

Of course it was the News and Sports Departments of ATV that produced the core of the company's regional programming. By 1978 there were formidable teams of editors, reporters, presenters, researchers and experts in both departments.

ATV Today the daily local news programme had built a reputation as one of the most successful news and current affairs programmes in Britain. It was on the air for about 150 hours each year, reflecting the burdens and the pleasures of life in the heart of England, and was supplemented by other news and regional current affairs programmes concentrating on specific subjects.

The programme's Managing Editor was a typical 'old-school journalist' and pioneer of regional independent television, Ted Trimmer. He was a great, jovial man always sporting a bow tie. He was full of anecdotes about his days in Fleet Street and his Hollywood connections brought about by being the brother of Oscar nominated actress Deborah Kerr, who starred in **The King and I**.

In the summer of 2004, Ted, at the age of 78, was tragically killed after being punched in the face during a road rage attack.

The Editor of the **ATV Today** programme was Mike Warman, brother of Bob the presenter. Its political editor was the very popular Reg Harcourt. Derek Hobson was the main presenter of **ATV Today** along with reporter/presenter Bob Warman, who has gone on to become anchorman of **Central News**, and the longest serving presenter of regional news in the Midlands. Other well-known reporters and

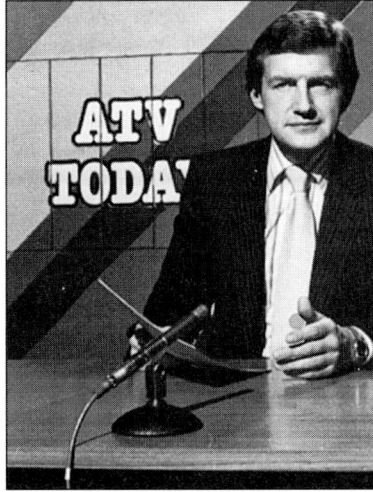

Anchorman Bob Warman.

presenters were Chris Tarrant, who specialised in 'off-beat' stories, Peter Plant, Wendy Jones, Wendy Nelson and John Swallow who always found an amusing tale to tell.

In regional terms ATV covered a huge, diverse area, within which news stories could occur anywhere. Even in 1978 news assignments were limited by distance and hence travelling time. Reporters needed to rush their film items back into Birmingham in good time for the film to be processed, which could take an hour, before it arrived in the studio centre's editing rooms to be cut. Films were transferred by dispatch riders, one of which was Mike Inman, who is now one of the ITV Sports senior producers.

HISTORICAL CONTEXT

The historical context in which ATV Today operated between taking over the Midlands contract seven-days a week and its changeover to Central can be summarised:

By 1968 Enoch Powell, MP for Wolverhampton, had made his 'rivers of blood' speech on immigration and was dismissed from the Conservative Shadow Cabinet, George Brown resigned as Labour Foreign Secretary, and the Race Relations Bill was published. The British Concord (002) aircraft was wheeled out of its hangar; the two-class postal system was introduced and a time bomb reduced Birmingham's water supply from the reservoirs in Wales.

1969 was the year in which men first walked upon the moon, the country began conversion from coal-gas to natural, North Sea, gas; the old halfpenny and the half-crown coins disappeared from the UK currency and the European Common Market agreed to let Britain negotiate its entry.

The voting age was reduced from 21 down to 18, and in June 1970 the Conservatives were returned to government at the general election, Ted Heath replaced Harold Wilson as Prime Minister.

The first 'official' miners' strike since 1926 led to the Government declaring a State of Emergency. The IRA spread its bombing campaign for the first time to the British mainland and there were signs of serious problems at the British Leyland car factories in the Midlands. The 'Battle of Saltley' produced extraordinary scenes as 'pickets' from all over Britain forced the closure of a coke depot at the Saltley Gas Works.

In 1974 at the first of two general elections within eight months, Harold Wilson returned as Prime Minister with a Labour Government. The IRA outrages got worse, with bombings in Coventry and Solihull, and twenty-one people died when two Birmingham pubs were bombed.

This atrocity caused problems for **ATV Today** as the public had a right to be informed, but a hysterical reaction had to be avoided. Viewers saw harrowing scenes and interviews with badly injured survivors and rescue workers. A violent backlash against the innocent Irish community in the Midlands had to be avoided. Viewers saw the Anglican Bishop of Birmingham and the Roman Catholic Archbishop standing beside each other outside one of the wrecked pubs in the City Centre to offer prayers.

1976 was a year of severe drought, with hose-pipe bans and stand-pipes in the streets; the John Stonehouse affair, the resignation of the Liberal leader, Jeremy Thorpe, and the handover of power from Harold Wilson to James Callaghan.

After the kidnapping from her home and disappearance of a 17 year-old Shropshire girl, Lesley Whittle, ATV co-operated with the police in the prolonged search for her and the man responsible for her eventual murder. This proved to be Donald Neilson, who was known as 'The Black Panther.'

ATV SPORTS

ATV's Head of Sport and Outside Broadcasts was Billy Wright, the famous England footballer, who played for Wolves for 21 years and during this time he appeared for England in 105 matches, 90 of them as captain – a world record. He made a highly regarded second career in television sport after retiring from the game. The company always gave sport a high priority, recognising its popularity to the viewers. With its OB units at sports events all year round and across the region it produced many hours of entertainment for the Midlands. During the summer months ATV covered athletics, speedway, powerboat racing, motor cycle racing and motor racing, canoeing, rowing, cycling and flying. In winter months the emphasis was on soccer and horse racing.

Star Soccer was for many years an integral part of Sunday afternoon family viewing, with recorded highlights of three of the weekend's top football matches. Recorded from across the region, on Saturday afternoon, the matches were edited overnight for broadcast the following afternoon.

There was regular sports coverage in the local magazine programme *ATV Today* which on Friday evenings devoted its last half hour to Midlands sport.

Sports presenters were Trevor East, Bob Hall, Garry Newbon and Nick Owen, and the main commentator for football was Hugh Johns. Jimmy Greaves worked with the team as an expert analyst of soccer. Terry Thomas was the angling expert, who has been described as a middle-aged country gentleman, who wore tweeds and sported a moustache on his often red face. He was a terrific character very popular with the viewers, a relaxed broadcaster with an elegant turn of phrase.

LEFT, RIGHT AND CENTRE

This political programme followed a succession which started in 1966 with *Midlands Member*, next came *Today's MP*, and in 1975 came *Platform for Today*: *Question Time*. *Left, Right and Centre* challenged those who maintained that most viewers were bored by politics.

A 40 minute programme, hosted by Dick Taverne, MP for Lincoln, discussed current political, industrial and social issues that were important to Midland viewers. The team included Andrew Roth, the well-known Westminster lobby correspondent and Reg Harcourt, ATV's political editor.

GARDENING, FARMING AND ANGLING TODAY

These were three long-standing favourites with regional viewers. *Gardening Today* established the remarkably successful partnership of Bob Price, a professional gardener, and Cyril Fletcher, a versatile entertainer who was also a keen amateur gardener. ATV specially created a garden in Birmingham's Kings Heath Park, which became well-known to viewers in the region.

Farming Today appealed to another group in the region which includes some of Britain's most fertile agricultural land. The programme featured veteran broadcaster Leslie Thomas, who was Regional Information Officer of the Farmers' Union when he presented *Midlands Farming* for ATV back in the 1950s. It built up a loyal and enthusiastic following among farmers who were able to view in their own precious 'spare' time on Sunday mornings. Alan Jones, journalist and farmer, brought his own fresh approach to traditional problems when he took over from Leslie Thomas.

As previously mentioned, *Angling Today* featured Terry Thomas, the man whose friends suggest is the original of the 'Colonel' in the box at the Muppet Show. Terry a world-ranking angling expert wrote on the subject for Encyclopaedia Britannica. Hundreds of thousands of ATV's viewers are fishing enthusiasts who will echo Terry's greeting of 'tight lines.' The show was filmed in many fishing locations throughout the region. Terry and the exquisite film cameraman, John Varnish, made a wonderful

team, producing magnificent shots from the Midlands riverbanks. On one occasion Terry was being filmed standing on the river bank by John Varnish when two swans came in to land on the river behind him, John saw them and panned with them from behind Terry along the river until they settled on the water. Terry, in his unflappable manner continued with his remarks, ending up as voice-over a truly pleasant piece of opportunist filming.

LINK AND GETTING ON

These were public service programmes, started in 1975, campaigning to make life easier and fairer for people with disabilities, that is people of all ages suffering from any kind of handicap, physical or medical. The programme examined numerous aids available for people with disabilities.

One of the presenters was Rosaline Wilkins, herself a wheelchair user.

Alternating with **Link** was another public service programme called **Getting On**, which was aimed at people beyond retirement age. It encouraged older people to get the best out of life and to pass on their skills, memories and experiences. Above all, it aimed to show that despite all its difficulties, old age can be a good age.

The programme was co-presented by Madge Wicke, then aged 73.

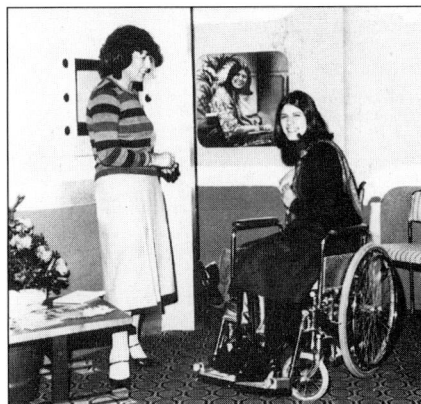

30. THE BIG DISPUTE OF 1979

This was a year when the Labour Government was in real trouble, the British economy was in tatters and the International Monetary Fund had been called in to help sort things out.

In January 1979 the Country was paralysed when a strike by national lorry drivers was followed by many more, including water workers, ambulance drivers, dustmen and even grave diggers. As uncollected rubbish piled up and rats ran freely in the streets, people were deeply shocked by what seemed a never-ending trail of decay and decline in living standards.

The prices of goods on the High Street had shot up and discontented and frustrated workers, throughout the country, desperately trying to care for their families, frequently went on strike to keep their wages in line with rising inflation. Current inflation projections were 17% to 20% by the end of the year. The Labour Government through consistent borrowing and spending, had dragged the country into deep debt, and seemed to have no answer to the crisis.

WE'LL DO THE STEERING, JIM—YOU CHANGE GEAR

James Callaghan had replaced Harold Wilson as Labour leader in 1976, and the situation had progressively got worse. He called a General Election for May 1979.

The new Conservative leader, Margaret Thatcher, promised a firm line with the unions and 'a change in direction.' The British people ousted the Labour Government, and replaced it by a Conservative Government which was faced with the task of sorting the mess out.

Margaret Thatcher's message was simple; she reminded the people that a country's finances were just like those of any family. A sensible family would cut back on spending rather than increase its debts. Yet previous governments had gone on spending when it was obvious the country could not afford it.

Her Government had a mammoth task ahead of it to put right the damage to the economy and the way of life created by the Labour Government. There were no instant fixes and things got worse before they started to

One more week of watching Play School and Open University and they'll be back.

improve. The July Retail Price Index figure increased by 4.6%, which was the largest monthly increase ever recorded. The previous highest was the month before – June – when it rose by a mere 1.7%. The Unions made it clear that with inflation at such a high level a pay rise of 35% would leave its members no better off by July 1980 than they were in July 1975.

It is difficult to realise, at a time when inflation has been fairly static at around 2% for many years, what effect on the lives of the people this rampant inflation meant.

Perhaps, still smarting from its lack of success in the previous dispute in 1968, the ITV Companies saw the situation as a good time to test the strength of the Unions and in particular the ACTT. The ITV licences were due to be re-allocated the following year. Following the previous re-allocation none of the ITV companies could be sure of keeping their existing licences. To lose a franchise meant not only a loss of business without any means of appeal, but job losses, redundancy payments, etc. It seemed that the companies manipulated a situation to force a confrontation at a time convenient to themselves and to break the union. It was also clear that Mrs Thatcher's new Government was going to be hard on the unions and hence sympathetic to employers who tried to break the power of the unions.

"Go on, do him again — you know how mother loves Albert Tatlock!"

By 4pm on Friday 10th August 1979 the vast majority of ACTT members were already suspended, or on strike in support of others who had been suspended earlier. The remainder would have been locked-out by the ITCA on the following Wednesday.

On this occasion the Companies were not going to be drawn into providing the viewers with a management run emergency service, they thought, perhaps, that blank screens would turn the viewers against the union staff.

But after blank screens for twelve days the workforce at all 15 ITV companies faced a total lock-out from 22nd August. The companies had offered 15% increase in pay. Although the screens went blank, it is interesting to note that viewing figures showed that over one million people chose to watch a blank screen rather than tune into the BBC.

It has been suggested that the companies chose August for the confrontation because it was the slackest time for advertising, and therefore would reduce their losses.

The ITV companies had behaved as if they expected the employees to come crawling back in a few weeks with their tails between their legs. But as the dispute dragged on through September most of the union members had finished painting the house, redesigning the garden and taken summer holidays; and with the children back to school a large majority took part-time jobs to tide them over. Members had varying experiences with jobs. One had a part-time job in a sauna bath, one castrating sheep. Two got jobs as lorry drivers only to find themselves on strike again within two days! Two more advertised as home decorators in the local paper and had £1,000 worth of business lined up within a week. They then had to turn work away. One member deputised for the local preacher at the Sunday service for £13.50 cash in hand and no questions asked. Another became a gardener and found himself mowing his Managing Director's lawn; his friend took a job as a waiter at the local Holiday Inn and to his horror found himself serving a table full of senior executives from his studios. One went for a job interview to discover he was being interviewed by another member from his shop, who had been quicker off the mark.

Even as the dispute dragged into October the workers had not come crawling back with their tails between their legs. In fact when 5,000 members in 25 shops up and down the country voted, they did so overwhelmingly, over 85%, in favour of not accepting the companies 'fifth', final offer. By 10th October a stockbroker's report showed that the companies had already lost £10 million in profits during the first eight weeks of the dispute that they started, and losses where rising to nearly £4 million per week. It should be remembered that as the ITV Levy was based on profits most of these losses actually came out of money the companies would have paid to the Chancellor in taxes.

Some managers thought the time had come to put the show back on the road themselves and mount their own network as had been tried back in 1968. But those wiser heads who had been there and done that

We can't let the BBC have it all their own way at Christmas.

ATV

5.45	NEWS.
6.5	THE MUPPET SHOW. New series with Kermit, Miss Piggy and other favourite characters. Guest: Dudley Moore.
6.35	CROSSROADS. A narrated refresher course on events at the Crossroads Motel seen in the last screened episodes, followed by tonight's episode.
7.0	GEORGE AND MILDRED. New series of comedies, with Yootha Joyce and Brian Murphy as the argumentative couple George and Mildred Roper.
7.30	CORONATION STREET. Viewers are brought up to date with a brief narration of the last episodes, and then it's business as usual down at the Rovers' Return.
8.0	3 - 2 - 1. New series of this popular quiz game, hosted by Ted Rogers.
9.0	QUATERMASS, with John Mills in the role of the scientist. This is a new Nigel Kneale science-fiction story.
10.0	NEWS.
10.30 ★	FILM: "Chinatown" (1974), starring Jack Nicholson and Faye Dunaway. A detective story set in Los Angeles in the 1930's. 12.30 CLOSEDOWN.

*ATV Programmes for
24th October 1979.*

advised strongly against Management ITV. In fact during the last days of the dispute the ITV companies pulled out the hardliners, reported to be Paul Fox and Bryan Cowgill, from the negotiations with the Unions.

The dispute was sensibly brought to an end. The headline read: ***ITV Members Accept 45%***. At the end of the unprecedented dispute which completely closed down ITV's national network, members in ITV voted overwhelmingly to return to work on the basis of a formula covering pay, holidays and new technology. It was a two year package which guaranteed pay increases of 17.5% from July 1979, 7.5% from January 1980 and a further 15% from July 1980. This was considered to be a slight improvement on the 7% the companies were offering before hostilities started. Besides this the return to work cost the companies huge amounts in overtime payments in order to catch up with work and delayed production.

ATV returned on 24th October 1979, with the ***Muppet Show***, followed by an update on ***Crossroads***, ***George and Mildred***, ***Coronation Street***, ***3–2–1*** with Ted Rogers, a new ***Quatermass*** story starring John Mills, some news and the film ***Chinatown***.

The companies had failed miserably to 'crack' the union, had lost an enormous amount of money in lost revenue and had upset the advertisers and artists into the bargain; and untold damage to its viewers. Instead of weakening the unions the ITV companies only in the long run succeeded in weakening themselves.

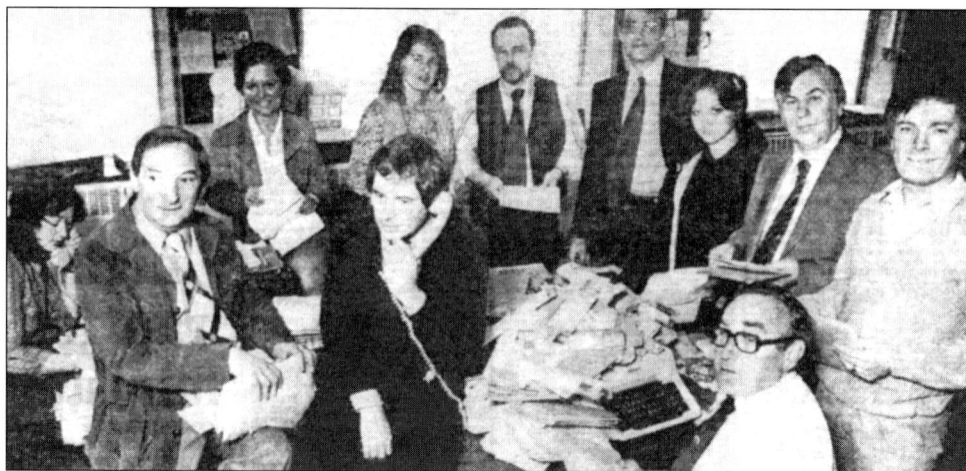

The ATV Today News Team prepares to catch up with the mail! Left to Right: ?, Peter Green, Wendy Jones, Wendy Nelson?, Mark Gottschalk, Mike Warman, ?, Reg Harcourt, Trevor East. In front: Nick Owen, and Billy Wright.

31. THE IBA'S DECISION ON NEW CONTRACTS

When the Conservatives returned to power in 1979 they challenged the IBA to come up with a plan for the fourth channel. The IBA recommended that the fourth channel would buy its programmes, would have a responsibility to embrace minority interests, and would be required to be innovative, educational, and not to duplicate the type of programmes broadcast by ITV. Importantly the channel was to take a large proportion of its programmes from independent producers. It would be financed by subscription from the ITV companies, who would in return sell its advertising airtime.

The Conservative Government accepted the proposal and Channel Four, awarded to ITV came into being.

With regards to the other contracts, after the completion of their consultation exercise the IBA reviewed the ITV licences, and changes were made:

- ATV was considered by the IBA to have not focused on their region enough, and in order to retain their licence were instructed to change.
- Southern Television lost its contract to Television South.
- Westward Television lost its contract to Television South West.
- A Breakfast Television service licence was granted to TV-am to start in May 1983.

The IBA had considered that with regards to the Midlands, although there was some merit in both the proposals from the other two applicants, Mercia and MTV, they did not have sufficient financial and programme depth. Consequently ATV was awarded the contract for the new dual Midlands Area, but not on their terms. There was more to come; the IBA imposed a stipulation that ATV's parent company Associated Communications Corporation Ltd. would only be permitted to hold 51% of the new licence, and that the name of the company should be changed, indicating a substantially new form of company. The IBA wanted the remaining 49% of the company to be taken up by Midlands based companies. Strangely there was not a great deal of interest from local companies and the shares were bought up by Sears, Ladbrookes, BPC (Robert Maxwell) and DC Thompson.

Following a number of rejections for managing director, the head of Sun Printing and ITP (Independent Television Publications) Bob Phillis was appointed.

All this had been a 'kick in the teeth' for ATV, perhaps they only had themselves to blame, but they had to get on with things as they were. They were determined to continue making the very best of programmes for the Midlands and for the entire network.

CENTRAL DAWNS

So ATV, on IBA instructions changed its name, it became Central Independent Television and commenced operations on 1st January 1982. The parent company ACC retained ITC, but following a number of later take-overs and management buy-outs its library was disposed of to Carlton for the sum of £90.5 million.

Central purchased a freehold 17-acre site at Lenton Lane from Nottingham City Council, and promised to build the most modern complex in Britain to be in operation in the Autumn of 1983. It would then close the studio centre at Elstree and transfer many of its experienced staff from the south to the Midlands.

WELCOME TO CENTRAL

Bob Phillis as the new Managing Director of Central Independent Television had the following to say with regards to the future:

Our future policy is bold and simple – to shift the centre of gravity of Independent Television to the heart of England and establish ourselves as the first choice of the best programme makers working in British television. Above all we will never forget that the viewer is central to us.

One of the main terms under which Central was awarded the contract by the Independent Broadcasting Authority for the East and West Midlands was to operate studio centres, one for the East and one for the West. Besides this it was also obliged to move the company's headquarters to the Midlands.

The Chairman of Central Independent Television, Sir Gordon Hobday, remarked that the new company would draw upon the skills and experience of the previous franchise holder, ATV, but would be broadened by the new resources required by the IBA.

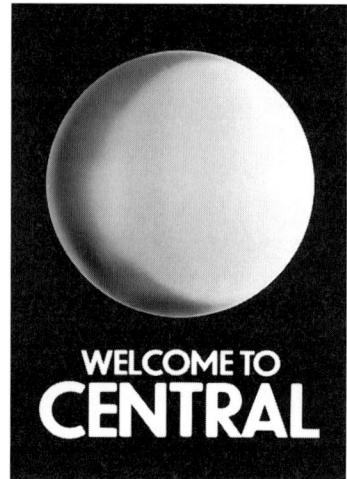

NEW HEADQUARTERS AND EXPANSION AT BIRMINGHAM

The site chosen to house the new headquarters of Central Independent Television was on Broad Street, a site steeped in history, adjacent to the existing Birmingham Television Centre. The building was originally constructed for the Freemasons of Warwickshire. Its foundation stone had been laid in 1926 by Colonel Wyley, the Provincial Grand Master of Warwickshire, and the building was officially opened a year later by the Right Honourable Lord Ampthill. It was then used as a Masonic Hall until the Second World War, when with just seven days notice; it was requisitioned by the Government for the Ministry of Food on 26th October 1939.

The Ministry of Food occupied the building throughout the war as the Birmingham Food Office and National Registration department. They eventually left in 1954. The site remained undeveloped until the 1960s when the building was taken over by The Engineering and Building Centre. It became an important centre for the study and promotion of all activities associated with the engineering and construction trades.

In the 1970s ATV took a lease on the building, but it was not until 1981 that a link bridge was constructed to join the building to the studios and refurbishment, in line with the IBA's requirements for Central's new Headquarters, commenced.

Refurbishment of the office accommodation was not all, the changed company also made many other changes to the Midlands operation. A new Master Control Room and Continuity Studio, and a new Central Apparatus Room were built, which in effect replaced the heart of the operation with the latest technology. The latest innovations in telecine computer programming equipment and updated video tape recorders were installed. The transmission of the all important commercials was transferred from film to a video tape system called ACR (Automatic Cassette

Recording). This was a system where each commercial was recorded onto its own individual 2" video tape cassette. These cassettes could then be loaded into an ACR machine for each commercial break, in the required order and transmitted as an automatic sequence on cue from the Master Control Room.

Terry Johnson, Controller of News and Current Affairs, confirmed that **Central News** programmes would be the flagships of the company's local programme output. Two nightly magazine programmes would be transmitted from studio centres in Birmingham and Nottingham. Each would have its own separate staff of journalists and will present to their own local areas the news stories, issues, personalities and events of the day. Central was setting up the largest regional news operation in the country.

Another very important change to the Midlands operation came with the introduction of ENG (Electronic News Gathering). Film cameramen replaced their film cameras with light-weight electronic cameras. This saved considerable time as the film processing time was eliminated. ENG news stories could be quickly returned to the TV Centre by dispatch rider, electronically edited and ready for transmission in a fraction of the time it would have taken using film. This also meant that news crews could travel further afield within the Midlands Region

Top: Brian Villis operates an ACR Suite.
Centre: Lord Grade discusses new ACR 25 equipment with Senior Engineer Keith Horton and Len Matthews, Lord Windlesham and Francis Essex talk in the background.
Bottom: Keith Horton operates the Paltex system and Grass Valley mixer in PPS 2 Edit Suite. (Courtesy: Keith Horton).

to collect their stories. Further, as later regional News Rooms were built in Nottingham and Oxford, ENG news material could be quickly transferred electronically between them. In Birmingham a new dedicated ENG playout suite was built within the Telecine Department to service the news programmes.

News would be serviced by more than 70 journalists working at both Birmingham and Nottingham studio centres. But in addition to those main centres there would be news offices in Leicester and Oxford with their own reporters. With regards to Sport, Terry Johnson confirmed that it would have an important place in the weekly programming. Bob Hall would join the sports team and, with Garry Newbon he would add strength to the Friday edition of **Central News**.

Central's current affairs output would probe behind the news in the region. **Left, Right and Centre**, the main political programme, would feature the regional MPs and **Venture** would highlight people and stories concerning industry and commerce. But Central's constant concern would be to watch, guard and portray the interests and needs of the 10 million people who lived within its transmission area.

THE PLANS FOR STUDIOS IN THE EAST

Central decided that it would build studios in the East capable not only of providing a significant number of programmes for its own area but also major programmes for the national ITV Network.

Jeremy Taylor was appointed General Manager, Central (East), he had this to say:

On January 1st 1982 Central opens temporary studios at Giltbrook near Eastwood, Nottingham. These studios, which have been hired for two years while the East Midlands

Artist's impression of Central's Lenton Lane Studios.

Television Centre is being built at Lenton Lane, will produce regional programmes for Central. About 150 people will work at Giltbrook producing four hours a week of programmes specially for the East Midlands viewer.

Central will also have its own local announcers on air from Giltbrook.

The decision to operate the East Midlands on video tape was made so that the studios could be equipped with the latest Electronic News Gathering (ENG) units and the most up-to-date video editing. This means that local news can go on air with the minimum of delay.

Central has purchased the freehold site at Lenton Lane from Nottingham City Council. It is well placed on the Nottingham Ring Road providing good access to the City Centre and to other major East Midlands towns like Leicester and Derby.

Initially we plan to build on only about half of the 17 acre site but with our commitments to the ITV Fourth Channel and the opportunities offered by cable and satellite, it is almost inevitable that we will have to expand our studio area.

The East Midlands Television Centre will be the most modern complex in Britain, producing about half the programming output for the dual Central areas. It is planned to open in the Autumn of 1983 and then Central will no longer use its studios in London and the whole of its operations will be based in the Midlands.

We plan to build three studios at Lenton Lane; two of 7,000 square feet and one of 3,000 square feet. The two 7,000 square foot studios are large enough and capable of making any kind of television programme. The 3,000 square foot studio is for the production of the regional news magazine and other programmes which need less floor space.

In addition to these studios facilities and the ENG units which will operate throughout the whole area, there will be three EFP (Electronic Field Production) units which will be used to make Drama and Entertainment series on location around the country.

I am confident that our studios and staff at Giltbrook and Lenton Lane will provide some of the best television to be seen locally, nationally and internationally.

32. EAST MIDLANDS TELEVISION CENTRE

Central Independent Television opened the East Midlands Television Centre in 1982. On the 1st January 1982 temporary studios were opened at Giltbrook near Eastwood, which were on hire for two years while the East Midlands Television Centre was being built at Lenton Lane. Work began on the 17 acre site at Lenton Lane in April 1982 after the laying of the foundation stone by Lord Thomson of Monifieth, Chairman of the IBA, in February of that year.

Giltbrook produced about four hours a week of regional programmes and some 150 people worked there. Presentation announcers, Linda Cunningham and Helen Lloyd, and newsreaders were appointed and a decision was made at the start to operate the East Midlands entirely on video tape. Giltbrook was equipped with Electronic News Gathering (ENG) along with the most up-to-date video editing facilities from day one. This meant that news stories were on-air sooner, not being delayed by film processing and editing.

Each weekday evening Giltbrook transmitted *Central News East*, devoted exclusively to the area's news, personalities and events. News gathering units were established in Nottingham, Leicester and Derby. Nick Owen and Anne Diamond spearheaded a news team of some fifty reporters, journalists and technicians. The News programme on Mondays was extended to one hour, incorporating a thirty minute current affairs magazine. The Friday evening show was also extended by thirty minutes of East Midlands sport.

OFFICIAL ROYAL OPENING

The East Midlands Television Centre at Lenton Lane was officially opened in the presence of H.R.H. The Duke of Edinburgh, on 2nd March 1984. The Duke spent two hours touring the site accompanied by Sir Gordon Hobday, Central's chairman, in his capacity as Lord Lieutenant of Nottinghamshire. The press report said:

Europe's Most Advanced Studio Complex
The growth of the East Midlands Television Centre reflects the growth of Central since it was awarded the ITV franchise for the Midlands.

The Independent Broadcasting Authority, which decides which companies, should be allowed to broadcast on ITV, set Central an exciting and challenging task. For the IBA said the company should operate from two studio centres — one in the East and one in the West with head offices in the region.

This week's official opening is the most significant landmark in Central's undertaking to serve the people of the East Midlands.

Expansion plans are under way in Birmingham following the opening of the company's new £1 million head office last year.

Central's production will be evenly split between the two studio centres as the company provides not only a first class service to its own region but also top quality programmes to the whole of the ITV network.

Central is one of the five ITV networking companies which between them contribute the majority of programmes screened by all the ITV companies throughout the country.

The extent of Central's commitment to the East Midlands can be gauged in the £21 million centre that the region can now call its own.

Its construction in less than two years has been a remarkable feat by all of those involved.

The first programme, an edition of **Family Fortunes***, hosted by Max Bygraves was recorded on 4th November, 1983. As the other studios were completed more programmes were recorded, and among the first guests to appear there were Chancellor of the Exchequer, Nigel Lawson in Central's business magazine* **Venture***, and Labour leader Neil Kinnock in* **Central News***.*

Central then had two major, modern production centres in the Midlands area. It closed its operation at Elstree and the staff was in the main transferred to Nottingham. At long last the Midlands stood alone as a major television producer without facilities in London.

The new centre at Lenton Lane had, larger than originally planned, two studios of 10,000 sq. feet, for producing all kinds of programme, and one of 4,500 sq. feet for the production of the regional programmes. The operation of all three studios was completely electronic, using video tape only, and the two large studios were capable of using six cameras, while the smaller studio could use four.

There were separate control suites for the three studios, and the directors working there had up-to-date vision, sound and lighting equipment. In addition, the acoustic

Left: Aerial view of the new Studio Centre at Lenton Lane.
Right: Prince Philip visiting Make-Up, talks with Carolyn Smith.

treatment in the studios had been carefully calculated to provide the viewer with the best possible sound to match the standard of the pictures. There was also a music recording studio, with an area of 2,500 square feet.

The heart of the studio complex was the central technical area. The equipment there included 15 video tape recording machines, character generators for captions and frame stores for still pictures. The sound department with 24 track recording and multiple cartridge effects machine, a sound recording and music dubbing studio and post production area in which there were computer based editing suites and two sound dubbing theatres.

To provide news stories there were four electronic news gathering (ENG) editing suites, each with a sound booth, and an ENG playout suite which could exchange material with the Birmingham, all other ITV companies and ITN.

It was as has been said *a full kit of parts* to produce modern television programmes.

33. A SUB-REGION IN THE SOUTH

In 1989, a third sub-region covering the Southern part of the Midlands Region came into being. As soon as approval was given to create the sub-region, a location for the main studio was found and building work commenced. The project cost £5 million and included a state-of-the-art production centre in Abingdon in Oxfordshire which was connected to studio centres in Gloucester and Swindon.

Transmission commenced with the first edition of Central News South on Monday 9th January 1989. Its opening night was a disaster when the technology installed to play the video items failed.

Despite its bad start the Central News South programme won the prestigious Award from the Royal Television Society for technical innovation, being at the time the most automated news operation in the country.

Central News South continued to pioneer new technology, keeping it at the forefront of digital newsgathering in regional news. In the spring of 2001, the Abingdon Central South studios were re-equipped with the latest digital technology, the most modern Quantel video servers and edit suites were installed along with up-to-date cameras and video tape machines.

But in just a few years it was announced that Central News South was to cease on 6th June 2006, after seventeen years. It was merged with other regions. Meridian North took Oxfordshire, Buckinghamshire and Swindon; ITV West took Gloucestershire, and Herefordshire returned to Central News West from Birmingham. The last regional news bulletin was transmitted on Sunday 3rd December, 2006.

Presenters Hannah Shellswell and Wesley Smith.

34. THE BROADCASTING ACT 1990

Within no time, it seemed, it was time to review the contracts of the Television company's franchises once more. Parliament, with its usual wisdom, regarding television matters, decided that the system had to change once again. Following the publication of a White Paper in November 1988, they introduced the Broadcasting Act of 1990.

It has been said that this Act brought enormous change to the ITV system, and paved the way for the deregulation of the British broadcasting industry. In time it spelled the end of television being run by creative, show business oriented people and opened the door to the 'bean counters.' The Act made the following changes:

- The IBA was abolished and replaced by the Independent Television Commission (ITC), a new 'light touch' regulator.
- The ITV Network was renamed Channel 3.
- The manner of licence allocation was changed and replaced by 'highest-bidder' auctions to determine the winner of each regional franchise.
- ITN no longer had to be owned exclusively by the ITV companies.
- Channel 4 became a Government owned corporation patterned on the BBC.

There was a considerable outcry concerning the auction element of the allocation of franchises; resulting in the ITC agreeing to ensure that applicants had to first pass a 'quality threshold' to ensure that high bidders who had poor programme plans could not secure a licence by money alone.

35. 'THE CHALLENGE OF CHANGE' –
CENTRAL UNVEILS MAJOR PLAN FOR THE FUTURE

On 26th November 1990, Central Independent Television announced its plan for the 1990s, designed to win the Channel 3 television licence for the Midlands Region for the following ten years. The Central Group was to be restructured before the renewal process began and would reduce its workforce (already reduced from well over 2,000 to 1,500 over the previous two and a half years) by a further 467, to just under 1,000, most of whom would work in the Midlands at Birmingham, Nottingham and Abingdon. As soon as they had been awarded the licence Central would begin work on building a new television centre in Birmingham. The restructured company would be made up of three divisions:

- **Central Broadcasting** – the Group's Headquarters, based in Birmingham, and responsible for the operation of the Channel 3 Licence. To commission, schedule and transmit all the company's ITV programmes. Also responsible for the production of Central's regional programmes, news service operating from Birmingham, Nottingham and Abingdon; producing more than 700 hours of regional news a year and a further 200 hours of other regional programmes.
- **Central Productions** – based in Nottingham, producing Central's programmes for the ITV Network as well as other UK and international broadcasters.
- **Central Television Enterprises** – based in London selling programme rights to broadcasters, cable operators and video distributors throughout the world.
- **021 Television Ltd** – a subsidiary company, providing the industry's most modern outside broadcast production facilities, based in Birmingham.

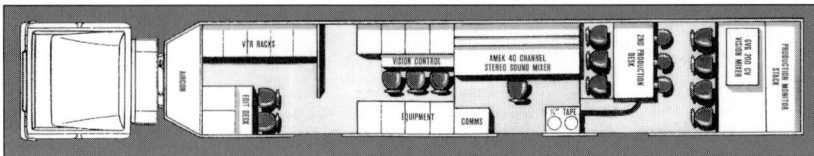

O21 Television state-of-the-art Outside Broadcast facilities van.

Central was beginning to experience problems in marketing its spare studio capacity, it claimed that there was insufficient profitable work available; to survive it needed to become lean, fit and talented in the radically changing world of television. There were, rapidly developing, adverse factors in the market amongst which were:

- The Government's requirement that 25% of all broadcast output be made by independent producers.
- Changes in the ITV Network resulting in the removal of a guaranteed programme supply for the major companies, resulting in a decreasing and unreliable workload.
- An increase in the Government's Levy, to increase by £15m in 1990 alone.
- Over capacity of studio space.
- BSkyB.

Not surprisingly, the company had not been able to shift the centre of television production to the Midlands by its move to Nottingham. It no longer had a production base in London, which was bound to be the first choice for the independent producers to make their increased programme share for the ITV Network. But the company was no longer headed by Showmen, and did not have people at the top who understood the entertainment business and how to adapt to the changing world of show business around them. Their instinct was to contract, to cut costs; but in doing so they lost their most precious asset in television, as Howard Thomas (ABC) years ago had called them, 'their battle-hardened elite staff.' That precious asset either left the business altogether or became freelance to work for the independent producers.

In hindsight, costs and the IBA permitting, it might have been more sensible not to have cut off the London production arm completely by closing Elstree and move everything to Nottingham. A News Room and an East Midland Regional programme operation at Nottingham would have satisfied the local MPs and critics in the East as well as the media; but ATV had burnt its bridges!

All this aside, Central's immediate objective was to secure the licence to operate Channel 3 in the Midlands for the next ten years.

36. LICENCE APPLICATION 1991

On the 15th May 1991, Leslie Hill, Chairman and Chief Executive of Central Independent Television, handed in its application for the Channel 3 licence for the East, West and South Midlands. He was confident that Central would win the licence, and was capable of sustaining a high quality service to the whole Midlands Region throughout and beyond the ten-year period of the new licence.

Leslie Hill's team cheer the winning bid!
(Courtesy Roy Davis).

Central was sure that it could meet the competition from both terrestrial and satellite services, and drew attention to its record over the previous nine years. It would continue to make quality programmes, and made it clear that it applied as a producer-broadcaster, making programmes as well as broadcasting them.

It announced its intention to build and equip a 100,000 sq ft West Midlands Television Centre in Birmingham at a cost of some £18m, to join with the East Midlands Television Centre in Nottingham, at the start of the new licence period from 1st January 1993.

The Application noted that the four organisations that held more than 5% of the voting shares of the company were:

- Carlton Communications plc – 19.371 % of the ordinary shares. It provided services and products for the television industry, manufactures pre-recorded video cassettes, and processes film.
- D.C. Thomson & Co. Ltd. – 19.235% of the ordinary shares.
  It was a publisher of newspapers and also magazines for women and children.
- Nutraco Nominees Ltd. – 7.476% of the ordinary shares.
- Junction Nominees Ltd. – 5.716% of the ordinary shares.

Following the presentation of application the next phase in the process was short period of public consultation. Public and regional organisations, including local authorities, were invited by the Independent Television Commission to send in written comments on all applications.

NEW LICENCES AND THE BEGINNING OF THE END FOR REGIONAL TELEVISION

Back in 1981, the East Midlands had won its battle with ATV for better representation of their sub-region. But now a sequence of events was about to unfold that would eventually result not only the East, but also the West Midlands losing all of its major programme production.

On October 16, 1991, the ITC announced that it had awarded licences to 12 of the 15 existing regional ITV companies, but that the remaining three and the breakfast franchise would change hands. From the end of 1992, Mrs Thatcher's Broadcasting Act 1990 and the competitive tenders which were at its heart, were finally implemented; the results of the auction process were:

- Television South West lost to Westcountry Television.
- Thames Television lost to Carlton Television.
- Television South lost to Meridian Broadcasting.
- TV-am lost to Sunrise Television, who changed its name to GMTV.
- ORACLE lost to Teletext Ltd.
- All other companies, including Central, retained their licences.

Many felt that the Government had taken revenge on Thames for making the programme **Death on The Rock**, an investigation into the 1988 shooting dead by the SAS of three IRA suspects in Gibraltar. As for Carlton Television, after months of rehearsals, it went on air in London; a big mistake? Carlton Television had taken *'the jewel in the crown'* contract for London weekdays, and many believed, turned it into a *'Benny bobble hat.'* In many people's minds this was a tragedy, the 'polished, professional presentation' of Thames, which had been honed since 1956 when ABC Television began broadcasting, was rudely torn away and replaced with bulk presentation. Programmes that followed were a string of flops; it was universally recognised that Carlton had never produced a single good programme.

Central had pulled what was possibly the master stroke of this round of franchise allocation – a further split in its own region – now a triple region. The southern sub-region based at Oxford and served by the Oxford and Ridge Hill transmitters was created, with its own Regional News Service. The company was unopposed, with a tiny bid of £2,000 a year, in addition to the 11% of qualifying revenue, providing the company with a strong financial platform. But to counteract a perceived increase in costs, Chairman since 1987, Leslie Hill, cut a further 500 jobs.

The 1990 Act also relaxed the franchise ownership rules; it now allowed mergers between ITV companies, and the larger companies quickly took advantage of the situation. In addition to retaining its franchise, Central took a 20% stake in collaboration with MAI and Selec TV in the winning consortium for the South and South East franchise region, Meridian. But the Act also permitted 'publisher broadcasters' to bid for the Midlands franchise. This of course caused concern within Central and they set about reducing the production facilities in the Midlands.

The first move had come from Michael Green of Carlton in 1989 when he suggested that Ladbrookes sold their 20% share of Central to him for £29.5 million. Some six months later Central sold Zenith Productions, their independent film arm to Carlton for £8.3 million.

THE EFFECT ON THE MIDLANDS

The 1990 Broadcasting Act has been described as a disaster for the Midlands region. For until then each region worked under a programme guarantee system; consequently the Midlands region was guaranteed a particular level of production to be broadcast on the Network. Following the introduction of the Act the guaranteed level of production was removed and the Network Centre (a division of the Independent Television Association) was established. It was given the function of drawing up the schedule for the Network, to acquire and commission programming from both the licence holders and from independent producers (who were to produce 25% of the network output). Pilkington, back in 1962, had recommended a similar move, which was rejected by the Government.

The eventual result of the 'independent quota' inevitably led to it being a quota for London. The simple reason for this is that the majority of independent producers who were granted commissions to make programmes for the Network were based in that City. London 'was where the action was' and so anyone with ambition and creativity gravitated there; this resulted in a very large pool of skilled, creative and talented freelance labour being available to the independent producers.

The situation is understandable and for the independent producers perfectly reasonable. There is also no doubt that what they produce is of a high quality. But unfortunately it has resulted in a reduction in 'regionalism' in the programming;

productions from London rarely reflect any facet of the varied regions other than itself.

In recent years there have been glimmers of hope, or perhaps just gestures, **London's Burning** for a while moved to Tyneside, and **Doctor Martin** briefly moved to a strange and quirky part of Devon. Both are refreshing in that they do at least reflect something of the character and landscape of areas other than the boring, never ending suburbia that is the landscape and character of Greater London. Londoners might well recognise the difference between the East End and Sun Hill, but can the rest of the country?

DEREGULATION BEGINS

Deregulation of the ITV Network took hold after 1993. Further relaxation came, from January 1994 companies were permitted to hold two licences, providing they were not both in the London area, 20% in another, and 5% in any other. We have seen that having degraded London's television, Carlton moved on to bring its talents to other regions. Once the announcement was made in November 1993, Carlton approached D.C. Thompson and acquired their share in Central, offering 2,000% profit on their original purchase price. Michael Green of Carlton then approached Central with a bid of £758 million, which the logic of accepting was undisputed; taking what remained of the universally recognised superb standard of ATV programming. They followed this by buying the newcomer Westcountry.

Re-organisation followed to integrate the various parts of Central and Carlton. Central's production arm became Carlton UK Productions, but Central Broadcasting retained the Midlands franchise.

Take-overs were taking place up and down the network:

- Yorkshire Television and Tyne Tees Television merged.
- United News Media (MAI) bought out Anglia Television.
- Granada completed a hostile take-over of LWT; later adding Yorkshire and Tyne Tees.

So by 1994 most of the ITV Companies were in the hands of Granada and Carlton.

Central's Chairman and Chief Executive, Leslie Hill, in an article in the in-house newspaper, explained to staff why the involvement with Carlton heralded a further period of remarkable promise for the company and its staff.

He was looking forward to a successful and effective link-up with Carlton Communications. He hoped for a flourishing output of quality programmes from the Nottingham Studios, and saw the staff having the opportunity to grow, develop themselves and their careers. He said that Carlton and Central were two of the strongest and best-managed companies within the ITV system, and that together they were not far short of commanding one-third of ITV advertising revenue.

He anticipated a growing workload for Nottingham Studios, and Carlton was committed to encouraging programme makers to make full use of them. He said that it was important for the staff to remain optimistic about the future:

Many people have contributed to our outstanding success in making high quality programmes which are wanted all over the world. Our programme-making resources are among the best, our regional programmes are the best and, when it comes to distribution, we have the best international sales team in the business. It is very different from what might have happened had we attempted diversification as some ITV companies have done in recent years.

A group of personnel from the Scenes and Props Department, able to erect anything anywhere take a well earned break in the Studio Bar. (Peter Harris, 3rd from right, back row).

37. THE MIDLAND'S CONTRIBUTION
TO THE ITV NETWORK

SOLDIER, SOLDIER (Central 1991–97)
Creator: Lucy Gannon. Producers:
Chris Kelly, Christopher Neame,
Ann Tricklebank.

A programme about the King's Own Fusiliers Infantry Regiment, based in the Midlands and the effects of army service life upon personal lives. In the first episode the Regiment returns to its Midlands base from a six month tour of Northern Ireland.

Subsequent episodes follow the Regiment through their postings to Hong Kong, New Zealand, Germany, Cyprus, Australia and Africa, and into action in Bosnia. On their returns to the U.K. they are followed when on guard duty at royal palaces.

The series deals with the effects of tough army life and its routine are seen in the comradeship, the stresses and strains it puts on individuals and their families.

The characters changed throughout the series as some left or were killed and were replaced by newcomers.

PEAK PRACTICE (Central 1993)
The series was centred upon the doctors and staff of a general medical practice, called the Beeches, in Derbyshire. Dr Jack Kerruish, played by Kevin Whately, having spent three years in Africa moves into the quiet Derbyshire Dales and into partnership with the beautiful Dr Beth Glover, Amanda Burton. Sparks fly when personal and professional conflicts expose the passions and rivalries behind the façade of rural tranquillity.

Filmed on location in the Peak District, the series started in 1993.

CHANCER (Central 1990–1)

Executive Producer: Ted Childs.

Producer: Sarah D. Wilson.

Stephen Crane, played by Clive Owen, a slick, young wheeler-dealer comes to the rescue of an ailing sports-car manufacturer. He represents 'new-money' into the business. An arrogant yuppie character who lives life on the edge, he is a slick City hot-shot with a talent for making money. He is familiar with company fiddles, insider dealing and city scams and comes into the Douglas Motor Company in order to save it from decline. He succeeds through his abilities and saves the company and its owners from ruin.

Not only did he bring in 'new money' he brought his hidden past which was inevitably catching up with him. He is eventually cornered by the police who have been after him for a fraud he committed when he was only a teenager; he is charged, tried, convicted and sent to prison. Throughout the series he was sexy, devious and dangerous, which made him all the more exciting and all the more hated.

A second series picks up from his release from prison; he changes his identity to indulge in more fraud, concerning art treasures, counterfeit casino chips and a bid to save an ancestral home. Whatever viewers felt about Chancer, they certainly could not ignore him.

BOON (Central 1986–92)

Executive Producer: Ted Childs, William Smethurst. Producers: Kenny McBain, Esta Charckham, Michele Buck, Simon Lewis.

A kind hearted fireman, Ken Boon, played by Michael Elphick, becomes a freelance troubleshooter after being forced to retire from the Fire Service through ill-health. During an heroic rescue his lungs were damaged. Life was hard as he struggled to make a living, after a succession of money-making schemes fail. He places an advert in the local paper 'Ex-fireman seeks interesting work, anything legal considered' and is offered a string of strange jobs from child-minding to private detective work. But because of his kind heart and the fact that he is a soft touch, he gets involved in some not such legal work.

Ken sees himself as an 'urban cowboy' riding through the streets of the Midlands on his white horse, his prized BSA 650cc motor cycle, which he has christened 'White Lightening'. He eventually starts a courier agency, 'The Texas Rangers'. He employed a slightly dim biker called Rocky Cassidy and a teenage secretary called Debbie Yates.

His ex-fireman friend Harry Crawford becomes a hotelier, who progressively moves up from premises to premises until he finally goes bust as the owner of a country house hotel. At which time Ken and Harry form a private detective concern called Crawford Boon Security.

Filmed in many locations throughout the Midlands the series was very popular and ran from 1986 to 1992, with an unscreened episode transmitted later in 1995.

SPITTING IMAGE (Central 1984–96)

Creators: Martin Lamble-Nairn, Peter Fluck, Roger Law. Producers: Jon Blair, John Lloyd, Tony Hendra, Geoffrey Perkins, David Tyler, Bill Dare, Giles Pilbrow.

Spitting Image was a highly rated and popular cruel satire show using latex puppet images of its victims.

The show showed respect for no one, everyone was a target who could be treated without mercy. There were wicked puppets of many prominent people, the Royal Family, most politicians and in particular Mrs Margaret Thatcher, the Pope, sportsmen, entertainers and world leaders were at the mercy of its team of brilliant writers and 'voices.'

Amongst the writers of the show were Ian Hislop, Doug Naylor and Rob Grant; and voices were the country's leading impersonators and comedians: Chris Barrie, Enn Reitel, Steve Nallon, Jan Ravens, Harry Enfield, Jon Glover, Jessica Martin, Rory Bremner, Hugh Dennis, Kate Robbins, Steve Coogan, Alistair McGowan and John Sessions.

The show was always topical and at first was severely criticised but later developed a cult following and those depicted by the puppets often considered themselves to have earned some kind of honour.

OUTSIDE EDGE (Central 1994–6)
Writer: Richard Harris.
Producer: Paula Burden.
A comedy show exploring the tensions that ran high at an English Middle-class Village Cricket Club. But the show was deeper than middle-aged men who played weekend cricket for the Bret Park Village Team and their supporting wives simply providing the tea and refreshments. The real meat of the programme was to do with class divisions, sex and marital harmony. Roger Dervish, played by Robert Daws, a stuffy chauvinist, club captain with his frustrated, timid wife, Mim, played by Brenda Blethyn, were contrasted with Kevin Costello, played by Timothy Spall and his wife Maggie, Josie Lawrence. She was an ever-practical nymphomaniac who could not leave her husband alone, he enjoyed their robust relationship, but was also a bit of a slob who liked a few pints with the lads.

THE COOK REPORT (Central)

Presenter: Roger Cook

Roger was born in New Zealand but was raised in Australia, he was a fearless investigative reporter who had worked on radio before moving to television.

He exposed many fraudsters and con-men as well as attacking bungling and 'jobsworth' public utilities and companies on behalf of disgruntled consumers. He bravely tackled the most risqué of topics and frequently encountered very violent characters who hated him for exposing them. He is a big man who was never afraid to confront his often violent subjects, including child pornographers, badger baiters, many career criminals, racketeers and even terrorists.

His 'camera-in-the-face' technique of confronting his targets was both a brave approach and a television first.

TISWAS (ATV/Central 1974–82)

Presenters: Chris Tarrant, John Asher, Trevor East, Sally James, Lenny Henry, John Gorman, Sylvester McCoy, Frank Carson, Bob Carolgees, Gordon Astley, Fogwell Flax, Den Hegarty, David Rappoport, Peter Tomlinson.

Producers: Peter Harris, Glyn Edwards, Chris Tarrant.

Tiswas began as a regional programme for children on a Saturday morning in the Midlands, but became so popular that in time it gained full Network coverage. It was not only loved by the kids, their parents also loved it. It became a cult programme and there were very often dubious 'adult' jokes within it.

It was anarchic, and tore up the rule-book for children's wholesome entertainment; instead it was raucous, slapstick, custard pies in the face and buckets of water. Each Saturday morning the studio would erupt into chaos, with no attempt of control from the presenters. There were silly sketches during the show and full reign was given to Lenny Henry, Frank Carson, and Bob Carolgees with his punk dog 'Spit' to develop them as they progressed. Chris Tarrant and the other presenters often struggled to interview visiting pop stars or to introduce cartoons amongst the chaos. Lenny Henry in sketches as David Bellamy or Trevor McDonald saw him at his brilliant best.

A central feature of the show was 'The Cage' into which a selection of 'grown-ups' were detained after being captured to be treated to a shower of disgusting, foul-looking sludge, buckets of water and abuse – there was even a waiting list of adults willing to be treated in this way.

Throughout the show each week, the studio was stalked by the Phantom Flan Flinger. Dressed all in black his identity hidden behind a black face mask he would suddenly appear with his foaming pies to be thrust into some unsuspecting faces. His identity was kept a secret, and many attempts were made to try and discover who he really was, they were never successful. But after all these years his true identity needs to be revealed. The true identity of the Phantom Flan Flinger was a popular local taxi driver from Cheswick Green, Solihull, Mr Benny Mills.

Lenny Henry, Sylvester McCoy, Peter Tomlinson, Frank Carson, Sally James, Chris Tarrant and John Gorman with a few friends on the set of Tiswas.

CROSSROADS (ATV/Central 1964–1988)

Idea: Reg Watson.

Creators: Hazel Adair, Peter Ling.

Producers: Reg Watson, Pieter Rogers, Jack Barton, Phillip Bowman, Marian Nelson, William Smethurst, Michele Buck, Kay Patrick, Yvon Grace, Peter Rose.

Crossroads has certainly been one of the success stories of early British Television. The long running series was a paradox; it suffered a considerable amount of ridicule but won the hearts of millions of faithful viewers. Taunts and criticisms were constantly being made, sets were said to wobble and actors fluffed their lines, but it is often forgotten that the show was usually done in a single run through, in the early days of video tape editing was not very sophisticated and involved a razor blade and some jointing cement, so it was only done in extreme conditions. So retakes were out of the question in a gruelling five episodes every week soap. There have been many

cheap jokes about its wobbling scenery, and its quirky characters, dear Amy Turtle (Ann George), 'bobble-hatted' Benny (Paul Henry) the handy man and Carlos (Anthony Morton) the Spanish chef to name just three of so many. But the occasional rocking sets, phones answered before they rang and many fluffed lines gave it some appeal; at its peak it drew 16 million viewers to every episode. There was no electronic editing as exists today when a drama can be drawn out scene at a time over days and electronically edited into the final polished product. Today should an actor fluff his lines then another take can be done, in the early days of dramas like Crossroads there were no such things as 'Take Two' unless it was the whole programme!

Meg Richardson, played by Noel Gordon, was a widow who owned a motel in the fictional Midlands village of King's Oak. She lived with her son Sandy, and her daughter Jill.

Many celebrities appeared in the show as guests, indulging a fancy to be seen in the show; these included Bob Monkhouse, Ken Dodd and Larry Grayson. Larry appeared as the chauffeur to Meg and Hugh Mortimer on their wedding day. Many later-to-be-stars were given their break in television on the programme. Malcolm McDowell played a PR man, Diane Keen was a waitress, Elaine Paige was in the guise of Caroline Winthrop. Stephanie de Sykes played a singer Harriet Blair, she took the song she sang in the show, 'Born with a Smile on my Face' to number two in the 1974 charts. Sue Nicholls, Audrey Roberts in **Coronation Street**, made the Top Twenty with her song 'Where Will You Be' in 1968. Paul McCartney and Wings' reworking of Tony Hatch's thumpingly catchy theme tune was used on some episodes.

Noel Gordon became a household name after a long and varied career on stage and television. She first appeared in a BBC play in 1938 and shortly after assisted John Logie Baird by appearing in one of his colour Television experiments. In the 1950s, with a string of plays and musicals to her name, Noel formally studied television in the USA, returning to the UK to work for the embryonic ATV as an adviser on women's programmes. She appeared in or presented many of ATV's early programmes and in 1957 she co-presented the well remembered and respected Magazine programme **Lunch Box**.

The plug was finally pulled on the programme in 1988 after some 4,500 episodes, to a huge outcry from its faithful followers.

Crossroads was difficult to get rid of, it came back as a hotel in 2001; it lasted a year, but re-appeared yet again in 2003 to not last the year.

Reg Watson and Jack Barton went to Australia where Reg created other successes for Australian Television, **Prisoner: Cell Block H** and **Neighbours**, directed by Jack.

THE PRICE IS RIGHT (Central 1984–8)

Presenter: Leslie Crowther.

A game show imported from America and presented by Leslie Crowther was known for its catchphrase 'Come on Down', was all action, in which the contestants won prizes by knowing or guessing the price of goods when sold in the High Street shops and put on display in the studio.

Contestants were selected at random from within the audience, who were expertly hyped-up by the studio floor managers, those chosen were urged by Leslie and the audience who were always very noisy and excited, to 'Come on down' and join him in a series of games the theme of which was simply guessing the value of household items. The contestant closest to the actual value on the High Street went off with the goods as a prize.

BLOCKBUSTERS (Central 1983–94)

Presenter: Bob Holness.

A quiz show for Six Form students, where two students played against a single contestant.

An electronic display screen made up of hexagonal blocks was lit up when correct answers were given to general knowledge questions. The team of students had to answer questions to light up a line of five frames across the board to win, whilst the single player had to light up a vertical row of four. Each frame had an illuminated initial letter referring to the question to be asked. The students would choose the frames they wished to try by asking, 'Can I have an X please Bob'. The audience always roared with laughter when the contestants asked, 'Can I have a P Bob?'

Prize money was awarded for every correct answer and the block was illuminated. The winning student (or one of the pair) was then put on the 'Hot Spot' where they had to answer more questions to light up a row of five frames across the board in 60 seconds.

It was a very popular show and gained a cult following amongst teenagers and their parents. It became famous for the audience doing the 'hand-jive' to the show's rousing theme music.

FAMILY FORTUNES (Central 1980–5 & 1987–2002)

Presenters: Bob Monkhouse, Max Bygraves, Les Dennis, Andy Collins. This game show used a large computer controlled display to show the findings of a survey of 100 members of the public. The public were asked to name various items – such as 'An item you take to the beach?' Then two competing family teams, each with five members, would try to work out the answers given by the members of the public

surveyed. The most popular answers would be given the most points. For example the answer, 'A bucket and spade', might receive 50 answers. During the contest there were random cash and valuable prizes to be won.

The first two presenters Bob Monkhouse and Max Bygraves took the show to 1985. There was then a two year gap after which in 1987 the show was revived with Les Dennis as presenter. He left the show when it moved to a day time slot in 2002, when Andy Collins took over.

The show has become famous for its strange and off-beat answers given by some of the contestants, for example, 'Name something blue', answer 'Is it my cardigan?'

BULLSEYE (ATV/Central 1981–95)

Presenter: Jim Bowen.

The show was centred around the game of darts, and was divided into three segments. Three pairs of contestants had to throw darts and answer general knowledge questions to win prizes and cash.

In the first segment one member of each pair threw three darts at a standard dart board and the second won a cash prize to the darts score on answering a question correctly. After three rounds the lowest scoring team was eliminated and received a consolation prize of a 'bendy Bully', a rubber dummy of the show's mascot.

In the second segment the remaining two pairs of contestants threw darts at a 'category board', marked out with specialist subjects; again one member threw the dart and the other had to answer the question from the subject hit. They won cash for a correct answer. The lowest scoring pair were then eliminated.

The third and final segment saw the remaining pair throw at a prize board, where the numbers related to the prizes to be won, attempting to hit the number which corresponded to major prizes, TV sets, hi-fi sets, washing machines, etc. The main thrower had six throws and the non-dart player had three. Their score was totalled and they were given the opportunity to gamble their winnings for the 'star prize', hidden behind curtains. If they chose to gamble they had three darts with which to score over 101 to win the star-prize. If they scored less then they lost all the prizes they had won to that point.

The show became noted for the insensitive way in which the host treated the contestants, Jim took great delight in cruelly showing the losing contestants 'Look what you would have won!' He was very insensitive, for example he would ask a contestant what he did for a living, and on being told that he was unemployed, Jim would say, 'Super, super', and get on with the show. It became a cult show amongst students.

In addition to the main game a professional darts player was invited to throw nine darts for a charity of his choice.

CELEBRITY SQUARES (ATV/Central 1975–9 & 1993–5)
Presenter: Bob Monkhouse.
Producers: Paul Stewart Laing, Glyn Edwards, Peter Harris, Gill Stribling-Wright, Danny Greenstone.
This was a noughts and crosses quiz, which featured nine celebrities and show business personalities. The nine celebrities were seated in three tier boxes representing the squares of the noughts and crosses board. Two public contestants, representing 'X' or 'O', in turn nominated a celebrity to answer a general knowledge question and then tried to work out if they had answered correctly or not. If correct they won a point, the first to reach three points was the winner, and a line of correct answers won cash prizes.

It was a quick-fire fun show full of banter and comedy. During one part of the show the tables were turned on the presenter, Bob Monkhouse, when each celebrity fired a question at him, his correct answers won money for a charity. Kenny Everett provided the wacky voice-overs used on the show.

NEW FACES (ATV/Central 1973–8 & 1986–8)
Hosts: Derek Hobson, Nicky Martin, Marti Caine.
Producers: Les Cocks, Albert Stevenson, Richard Holloway.
This was a talent show from the Hippodrome theatre in Birmingham, between 1973 and 1978, then from 1986 to 1988.

It featured artists who had not appeared on television previously. They were judged and criticised by a panel of four 'experts' from fields such as record producers, DJs, theatrical agents and critics. Regulars on these panels were: Clifford Davis, George Elrick, Alan A. Freeman, Tony Hatch, Martin Jackson, Hilary Kingsley, Mickey Most, Peter Prichard, Ted Ray, John Smith and Ed Stewart. Each contestant was awarded marks for Presentation, Content and Star Quality.

Some panellists were very harsh and did not pull any punches often reducing contestants to tears. Each show's winner went on to a grand final show at the end of the series.

The show really did produce new artists, amongst its most successful winners were: Pati Boulaye, Jim Davidson, Les Dennis, Lenny Henry, Showaddywaddy, Gary Wilmot and Victoria Wood. Malanda Burrows (under the name Malanda Newman) sang on the show at the age of nine and became the series' youngest winner. Pati Boulaye was the winner of *New Faces, final, final*.

Presenter of the show Marti Caine, herself a New Faces champion, who presented the revived series in 1986, 7 and 8. Critics on this series included, Nina Myskow.

Music was provided by The Johnny Patrick Orchestra for the first series and Harry Rabinowitz's Orchestra for the second series.

AUF WIEDERSEHEN PET (Central 1983–6)

Creators: Dick Clement, Ian La Frenais, Franc Roddam.
Executive Producers: Allan McKeown, Laura Mackie, Franc Roddam
Producers: Martin McKeand, Joy Spink.
With the UK in a recession during the early 1980s jobs were scarce, three Geordie lads Dennis, Neville and Oz, decided to seek work abroad. They are taken on as labourers on a Dusseldorf building site where they meet up with Brummie

Cast and crew of Auf Wiedersehen Pet.
(Source: Auf Wiedersehen Pat. Courtesy Shirley Thompson).

electrician Barry, Wayne a Cockney carpenter, Bomber a wrestler from Bristol and a Scouse crook, Moxey. They all share the same accommodation hut and form a team.

As they move from job to job they share each other's joys, despairs, hopes and worries, they drink and womanize through their time abroad, getting into many a scrape and from scam to scam.

In a second series they meet up again to renovate a Derbyshire mansion owned by a gangster from Newcastle called Ally Fraser. He has forced Dennis to work for him in order to pay off his gambling debts. On completing their work on the mansion they again move abroad, to Spain where they build a swimming pool at Ally's luxury villa.

Garry Holton who played Wayne, died during the last series, but because of earlier filming on location and the subtle use of a double, he appeared in every episode.

CENTRAL WEEKEND LIVE

When the Birmingham Studio Centre closed in 1994 most of the shows produced there were moved to the Nottingham Studio Centre. One of the longest running and controversial regional shows to move to Nottingham Studio 7 was Central Weekend Live, the longest running live debate show on TV with a reputation as being the liveliest.

Those responsible for bringing Central Weekend Live from Birmingham. Their last show before the move to Nottingham. (Courtesy Roy Davis).

38. CHILDREN'S TELEVISION

The Midlands through ATV and Central Television has played an important and significant role in the development of Children's Television not only regionally but throughout the entire ITV Network.

Initially each regional company on the Network had sole responsibility for the programmes they produced and supplied to their younger viewers. These included programmes that they produced themselves and pre-made programmes from the Network and abroad.

From time to time attempts were made to standardise the presentation of children's television, but the regional set-up and independence prevented it from happening.

ATV possessed a very highly developed Promotions Department which was respected throughout the Network, so when it conceived the standardised presentation under the theme of *Watch It!*, the branding was accepted and used throughout the Network. The branding continued until 1982 with ATV designing and producing the presentation material and the regional companies, the presenters and the programmes.

Following ATV's name change to Central Television its controller of children's programmes, Lewis Rudd, introduced a new approach. The Promotions Department produced the concept of *Children's ITV*. The links between the programmes were pre-recorded and played out to the Network from Central's Studios, the programmes themselves were still inserted regionally by the supplying companies.

Children's ITV first went on-air in January 1983 and was broadcast between 1600 and 1715 each weekday afternoon. The first set used in the inter-programme links represented the command bridge of a rocket ship. Presenters rotated on a monthly basis and included Matthew Kelly from Tyne Tees TV, Isla St Clair from Central, Derek Griffith from Granada and Tommy Boyd also from Central.

As the presentation concept evolved it was obvious that with pre-recorded links from one source on the Network and programmes originating from different sources throughout the Network, problems would arise from such an inflexible system.

In 1987 *Children's ITV* went live from the original continuity studio at Central. Its presenters were Garry Terzza and Debbie Shore who presented links from a set which was designed to represent a broadcasting station. Being live there was greater flexibility and schedule changes, breakdowns, etc. could be more easily dealt with. Over time the presentation went through a number of presenters and sets.

In 1989 the contract to produce **Children's ITV** was put out to tender and was awarded to Stonewall Productions owned by Michael Jackson, who actually worked for Central. From a facilities point of view very little changed as Stonewall hired Central's facilities. Stonewall held the contract for two years and the programme came from various locations throughout Central's Birmingham Studios, with no fixed sets. It used a number of presenters and for a time introduced a large puppet dog called Scally. During the school holidays a morning edition of the programme was produced from a small studio setting with bean bags.

The contract was returned to Central in 1991 until 1993, with Tommy Boyd as the programme's presenter. The presentation studio was again used for the show.

Network arrangements changed in 1993 with the preparation of the schedule being transferred to the newly formed Network Centre. Its then controller of children's programmes sadly abandoned the in-vision links and replaced them with out-of-vision links which relied upon animations and pre-recorded promotions. Steven Ryde was used for voice-overs and fortunately he was able to adapt his voice to represent a number of different characters. Later in the year **Children's ITV** was again re-branded and became **CiTV**. But there was little change in presentation. Viewing figures had started to fall following the removal of the in-vision presenters.

1998 saw **CiTV** revert to the more viewer friendly in-vision service with Steven Ryde as programme producer. By then Central had started its downsizing exercise and had moved into its new headquarters in Central Court. With only a single studio providing Central News, a small space had to be found from which **CiTV** could present its new links. Stephen Mulhern and Dannielle Nichols were chosen as presenters for the new show.

Network arrangements again changed at this time with Central being given control of the whole CiTV service, including not only links and promotions but the programmes as well, which created even greater flexibility. A year later the **Central News** studio was also used for **CiTV** on a shared basis. The next year saw two further presenters, Andrea Green and Tom Darville being appointed.

39. CARLTON HITS THE SCREEN

GROWTH OF CARLTON

Prior to 1983 Carlton was a private company established by Michael Green and his brother David. It became a public company in 1983 and had subsidiary companies engaged in television and photographic production facilities, programming, specialist publishing, exhibition contracting and the design and sale of professional television equipment. It soon acquired a series of post–production facility houses.

It made its first move into main British broadcasting with the acquisition of a 20% stake in Central Independent Television. In 1987 the company acquired Zenith Productions from Central, which produced many high quality dramas such as *Inspector Morse*, game shows and *Wheel of Fortune*, music specials, documentaries and children's programmes.

In 1991 Carlton outbid Thames Television for the weekday London ITV licence, somehow passing the 'Quality Threshold', for a ten year period from 1993, with an option to renew for a further ten years. In November 1991 Carlton acquired a 20% share in GMTV after it deposed TV-am from the National Breakfast Television contract.

It started broadcasting in 1993 in the London area and in March of that year it acquired an 18% share in ITN. Later it made an offer for the remaining 80% of Central which became unconditional in February 1994.

Carlton and Central then made up the largest part of the ITV Network, approximately 30% of the Television net advertising revenue, 22% of the UK Television advertising revenue, and broadcast to 20 million people representing 36% of the UK population. By taking-over Central it also acquired programme production studios in Nottingham and a film and television distribution and programme library business, which distributed television programmes and film content in the UK and the international market.

A TELEVISION FORCE FOR THE FUTURE

Carlton Television, by then in control of both the London and Midlands regions, declared in its House Journal, *The Carlton UK News* of August/September 1994, itself to be a *TV force for the future*. It announced that a major new force in British television had been signalled with the creation of Carlton UK Television.

Carlton and Central staff were to be re-organised into two new powerful divisions across sites in Nottingham, Birmingham and London from 1st January 1995.

■ Carlton UK Broadcasting – to be the operator and holder of both Carlton and Central's licences, serving and transmitting to 20 million viewers across both regions.

■ Carlton UK Productions – based at The Television House in London to produce or commission all network and regional programmes required by Central and Carlton broadcasters.

■ Birmingham staff to be moved to a smaller, state-of-the-art broadcasting headquarters in the City – but with a reduction of up to 140 staff.

■ A further 40 job losses across Birmingham, Nottingham and London by the end of 1994.

■ Transferring some operations and 90 staff from Birmingham to Nottingham by the end of 1994.

■ Developing joint transmission arrangements with Granada and LWT at the new Network Transmission Centre on the London News Network (LNN) site.

■ Organising a single base for all London production staff.

Was this the right way to go, or Big Mistake? Photographs in its own House Journal told the story.

The faces of the staff said it all!

ROR, September 18, 1994 PAGE 18

'Big Brother' axes 180 jobs in video nasty

TV bosses were under fire last night for showing staff a video nasty telling them: You're sacked.

Shocked Central TV workers were even offered a FREE copy of the 18-minute film in case they'd missed the plot.

Chief executive Andy Allan appeared on a 15ft screen to announce that 180 jobs must go in a merger with Carlton TV.

One union source said: "Many felt it was callous. It was disturbing — a massive image of the chief executive, his voice booming — he looked like Big Brother."

A Carlton spokesman said: "It may seem impersonal, but we wanted everyone to get the same story at exactly the same time."

Was the Carlton Management praying?

In 1994 Carlton management closed the Birmingham Studio complex as a major programme-making facility, at the same time promising good times in Nottingham. At the time Andy Allen, the Chief Executive declared:

We are neither neglecting the city (Birmingham) nor the region. The fact is that we are enhancing the region as a programme making force. The restructuring will mean that some programmes that would have been made in London will now be made in Nottingham. We value our highly skilled workforce and we hope they will be making more programmes in the region not less.

Some hope! After saying this even Carlton productions such as **Today with Des and Mel** were made in studios at Teddington.

Jack Turner, a Birmingham Vision Engineer with many years experience on every conceivable type of production wrote a letter to the August/September 1994 edition of the *Carlton News*. Jack noted that in an address Clive Jones the then Central Managing Director, had described the Birmingham Studios as *'a very depressing building and not a very creative or satisfying environment for people to make television programmes.'* Jack wished to point out that from the time the studios were opened in 1968 until the mid-1980s they throbbed with life and programme production was at a high level. Actors and actresses, he said, enjoyed, in fact preferred to work there rather than elsewhere, because they found it a happy place to be.

The staff were happy, innovative and hard working, doing something that gave them pleasure as well as a living, but these, he said, were the days when the business

Did the flashy braces and body language portray confidence?

was run by people who had spent a lifetime in show business, the days when the show was the main thing, rather than the accountant's ledger.

Others have since noted that the London-based management that took over the business, did not have any experience or real understanding of how to effectively manage or get the best out of the business they had purchased in the Midlands. They did however have a good understanding of how to asset strip that business. Some have gone so far as to claim that Carlton never made a single decent programme. It was firstly a publisher broadcaster. They did, however, over the next few years, brand many high quality Midlands produced programmes as Carlton Productions, before it is said the asset stripping and management incompetence took over.

The Broadcasting Act 1996 relaxed the franchise ownership rules even further and ITV empires continued to expand. The Carlton Empire purchased Westcountry Television, whilst United News and Media purchased HTV. 1997 saw Granada acquire Yorkshire – Tyne Tees Television, and Scottish Media Group acquire Grampian Television. Control of the ITV network was falling into fewer and fewer companies.

ONDIGITAL – MONKEY BUSINESS

Carlton, Granada and BSkyB joined together in the digital television project ONdigital. They were awarded three digital terrestrial television licences and in November 1998 started broadcasting. BSkyB later withdrew from the project and it became a 50:50 venture between Granada and Carlton. It was the world's first multi-channel television service received through a terrestrial aerial. By 2002 it had over 50 channels, exclusive sports deals, e-mail, interactivity, pay-per-view and 1.2 million subscribers.

It entered into a costly £315m contract to show Nationwide League Football. It was a disaster and even re-launched as ITV Digital and heavily promoted with a woollen-knitted monkey, it still failed to gain sufficient audience to make it viable and it went out of business on May 1, 2002. It eventually left egg on the faces of both Granada and Carlton and many football clubs faced collapse. The woollen monkey was made redundant, but it is noted that it is back in work for PG – Tips Tea. The transmission system was later acquired by the BBC, who set up the Freeview service carrying its own digital channels as well as some from other sources including those of ITV. It has now become the UK's largest platform for the supply of digital television services.

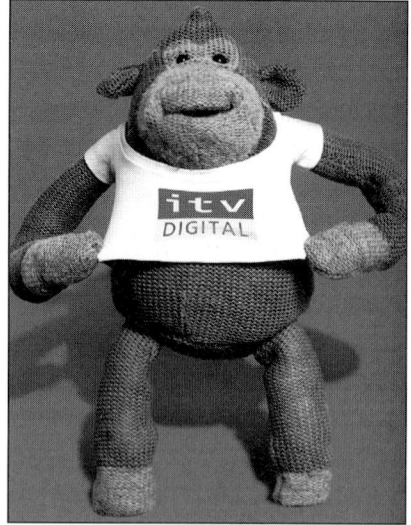

40. CENTRAL COURT – DOWNSIZING BEGINS

As promised by Leslie Hill in Central's licence application in 1991, the Birmingham operation was to be moved to a smaller, state-of-the-art broadcasting centre and headquarters in the City.

HISTORY AGAIN

Previous sites chosen to be home for Birmingham Television Centres had been those already steeped in the history of entertainment. That chosen for the new headquarters, Central Court, was different, it was the site of the original Birmingham Gas Works; this was Britain's first profitable gas works, outside of London. It ceased production around 1850 and the site became a tube works. It eventually become a monumental masons works owned by W.H. Frasely – was this an omen? Part of the original gas works canal wharf has been re-created alongside Central Court to be in keeping with the industrial heritage of this part of the City.

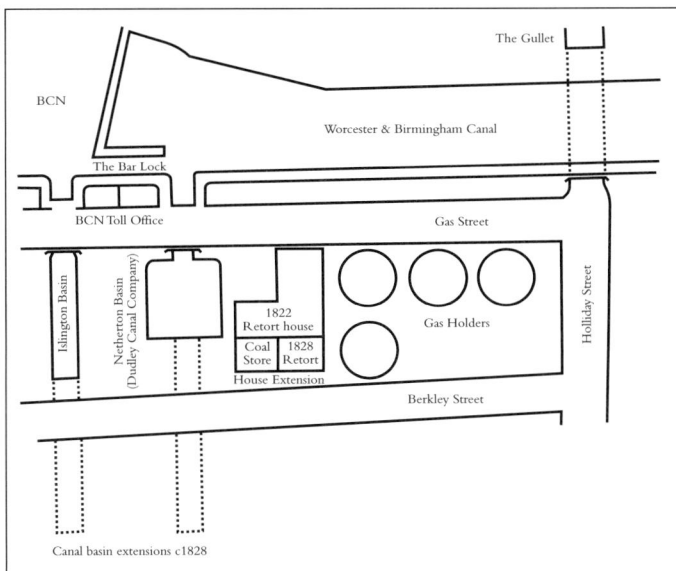

Plan of the original Birmingham Gas Works.

W. H. Fraley's stone yard Gas Street.

Carlton was committed to this project and demolition on the site commenced in May 1995 and the site was cleared. Only one building remained intact, No 35 Gas Street, a listed building, was retained and converted into a staff bistro and rest area. The foundation stone of the new building was laid on 17th November 1995 by the Lord Mayor of Birmingham, Councillor David Roy.

On 26th April 1996, Central Court celebrated the traditional building ceremony of Topping Out, on reaching the completion of the uppermost part of the building. Central News's presenters Bob Warman and Michelle Newman hosted the proceedings. Gareth Southgate of Aston Villa and England (a first class player, but known for missing a very important penalty) – another omen – performed the task of cementing the last section of roof; and Councillor Albert Bore placed a branch of a yew tree into the cement to bring good luck to the building and ward off evil spirits – perhaps in hindsight a larger branch should have been used!

The building was handed over to Central Independent Television on 9th July 1996 and the technical installation commenced on 4th November 1996. Transmission from Central Court commenced on 27th June 1997.

CENTRAL COURT – TELEVISION'S NEW AGE

Central's new headquarters, the £15million purpose built centre located in Gas Street, Birmingham, opened for business on 31st March 1997.

Although drastically reduced as a television programme producing facility, Central Court was the most advanced digitally based broadcast centre in Europe; marking the move to disc-based server technology; fully integrated facilities and systems across news, regional programmes and sport throughout transmission, editing, dubbing, graphics and studio. This meant that all commercials, news items, promotion spots, etc. were transferred onto computer disc and were immediately available throughout the station and the News Rooms at Nottingham and Oxford.

Features at Central Court included desk top editing on PCs and non-linear editing; the equivalent of a move from typewriters to word processors. The 60,000 square foot building was staffed by more than 300 staff and became the production centre for over 200 hours of Midlands regional programmes along with all the station's sports output, and the very successful CITV.

All the technical facilities were located on the same floor of the building, around the centrally positioned single studio, allowing for increased integration between areas.

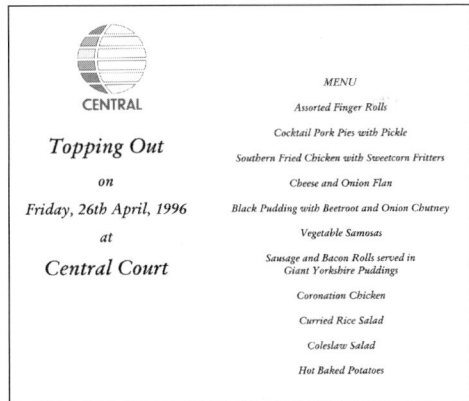

Transmission and Presentation staff at the Topping-Out Ceremony. Left to Right: Roger Quiney, Chris Carter, Anna Hill, Steve Smith, Derek Savage, Keith Horton, Steve Rehman, Rick Ives, Nick Richardson, Mike Rogers.

The studio was the heart of Central Court, principally the home of Central News West and all Central's sports, both regional and national programmes.

If the studio was the heart, then the Media Centre was the heart beat of the whole operation; packed with the latest digital storage systems and computer control mechanisms, which run the centre.

Then there were the Post Production areas, both audio and picture, where programmes were assembled and the sound tracks recorded and compiled.

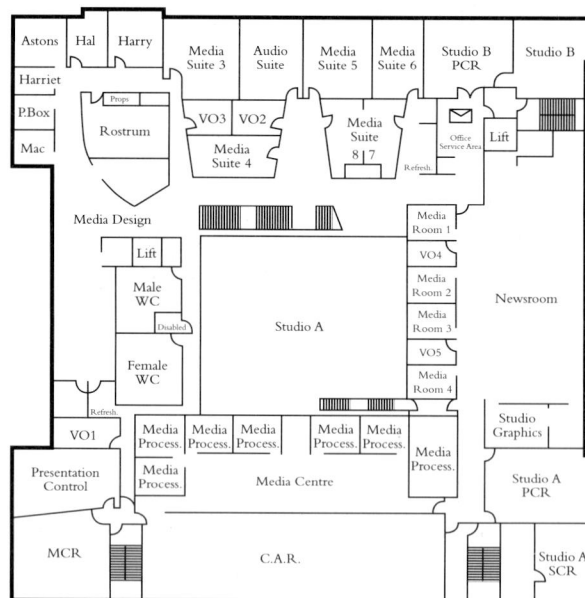

Central Court Layout of the Technical Floor.

Transmission was designed around specialist broadcast facilities, making maximum use of the emerging broadcast technology, and capable of expansion to many more channels – not limited to ITV.

The Presentation and Transmission Control Suite, the 'control bridge' of Central Court along with the Master Control Room were the final link to Central's viewers in the millions of homes throughout the Midlands area.

In the Media Design area, graphics artists created title sequences and other electronic images for all the programmes produced in the Centre. The graphics facilities at Central Court were some of the most technically advanced available from Quantel, and were the envy of the Network. In fact Central did graphics work for many other companies on the network. Besides a rostrum camera there was 'Paint Box', the industry standard graphics kit, 'Harry' the first non-linear editor which made multi-layering of live video a practicable proposition, 'Harriet' for multi-layering live graphics over video, 'Hal' the video design suite, the first dedicated graphics and compositing centre. Besides these there were the latest Aston caption generators and Macintosh computing equipment. But above all the department was staffed by some of the most adventurous and skilled and respected graphics artists in the business.

Top Left: Central News West set up in Central Court Studio. Top Right: Omnibus Transmission Profiles CAR TX Output Bays. Bottom Left: Commercial Input Suite Post Production Sound Desk. Bottom Right: Presentation Control Room Master Control Room. (All Photographs, Courtesy Roger Quiney).

Promotion making (the bits that go between the programmes and commercials to advertise other programmes) had always been big business in the Birmingham studios and continued to be at Central Court. Under the control and guidance of the industry acknowledged 'promotions guru', Jim Stokoe, promotions were made for the whole Network.

Besides being responsible for many ITV Network promotion campaigns, Jim Stokoe was one of the creators of Tiswas and also the first producer of **Children's ITV**, and became Executive Producer of the whole **CiTV** segment.

CENTRAL

A souvenir of the
Official Opening
of
Central Court

16 July 1997

The Newsroom, one of the busiest areas, was a state-of-the-art centre where journalists, on their return to Central Court from assignments throughout the Midlands, could, within moments, be editing their rushes on media P.C.s at their desktops.

In an interview four years after Central Court was opened, Ian Squires, managing director of Carlton Broadcasting's Central Region, was proud to announce:

When we moved out of our old building and into the new one in Gas Street we went from over 400,000 sq ft to 60,000 sq ft without any loss of service.

Technology has revolutionised the way we operate. We tend to make our dramas on the streets now, where 15 years ago it would all have been done in the studio.

At the time output from Birmingham, and Carlton's base in the East Midlands, was described as 'impressively high' – from network sports coverage and children's programming, to more than 17 hours a week of purely regional programmes, including drama, documentaries, entertainment and religious productions.

ANOTHER ROYAL OFFICIAL OPENING

Central Court was officially opened by HRH The Princess Royal as President of Save the Children, on 16th July, 1997.

During the Opening Ceremony The Princess was presented with a cheque for £500,000 on behalf of the Save the Children Fund raised by the Save the Children West Midlands Appeal Steering Group.

THE MIDLANDS GREAT SELL-OFF

A couple of months after the opening of the Central Court headquarters the contents of the original Birmingham Television Centre went on sale by auction in September 1997. Henry Butcher, International Asset Consultants, organised and conducted the huge sale of the contents of Central Television's Centre at Bridge Street, Birmingham. Their Catalogue listed 11,050 items for sale, to take place over three days commencing Tuesday 2nd September 1997.

Any possible television production from Birmingham, the most central and probably the most important centre was now reduced to a single studio in Central Court, a fraction of the size of the three huge studios by then standing silent and stripped of all their technical facilities. Only the ghosts of its great past and service to the Midlands communities remained to roam its dark and empty corridors.

41. THE EMERGENCE OF THE MIGHTY EMPIRES

By 1999 the ITV Network was no longer made up of 15 independent companies, although there were still separately licensed regions, most of it was being controlled by three large communications giants: Carlton, Granada and United News Media.

Carlton with new found importance took the opportunity to try and kill off the individual on-air identities of two of the regions it controlled, Central and Westcountry, which from 6th September 1999 were both re-branded as Carlton. The ITC did not intervene as it considered it as a 'marketing exercise' and outside its remit. It did however, wisely, comment:

The ITC would have thought some regional recognition attached to the Carlton title would have been a marketing advantage.

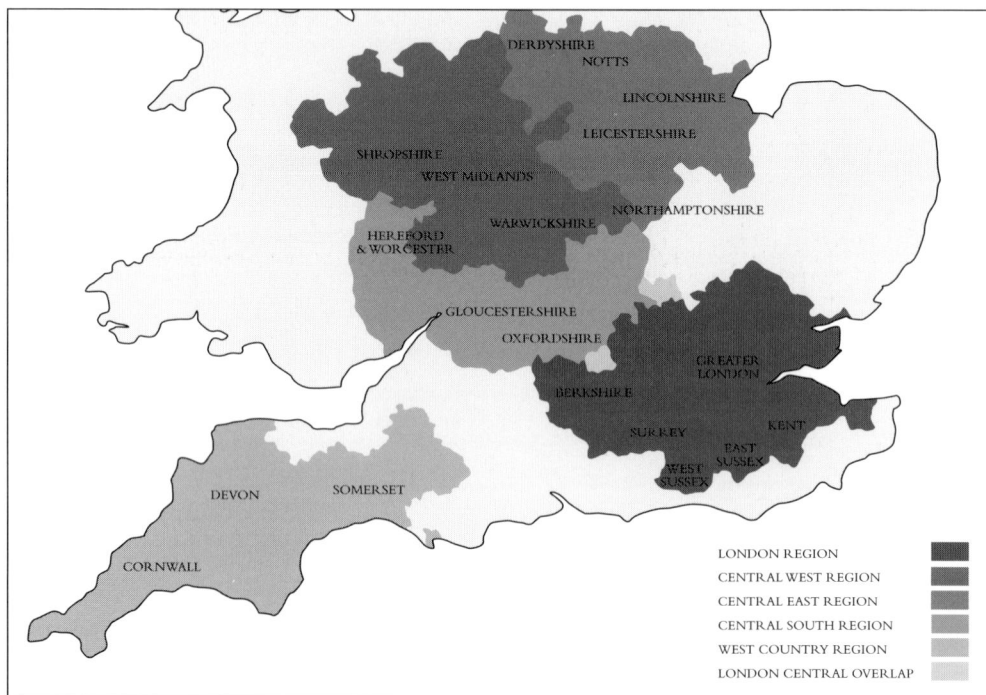

Legend:
LONDON REGION
CENTRAL WEST REGION
CENTRAL EAST REGION
CENTRAL SOUTH REGION
WEST COUNTRY REGION
LONDON CENTRAL OVERLAP

Areas covered by Carlton in 2000, before acquiring HTV.

ITV had until this time been a
federation of different companies, each
providing a service to its own region and
contributing programmes to the Network
as a whole. Carlton, it seemed, was more
concerned to please its shareholders than
its viewers.

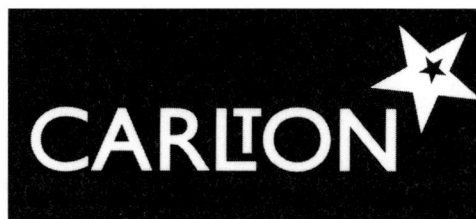

In November 1999, Carlton Communications and United News and Media
announced a £7.8bn merger, which would make them the UK's largest media
company. With a combined 37% of TV advertising revenue, but the merger was
going to breach the 25% control limit. It would reach 37 million UK viewers, 65%
of the country's households.

On 15th July 2000, the government approved the merger, but at the same time
created the biggest shake-up in commercial Television since its launch in 1955.

It radically changed the rules:

- Further consolidation of ITV ownership was deemed 'both desirable
  and inevitable.'
- The voluntary rule that any one company should not exceed 25% of total UK
  TV advertising market was rescinded.
- Any two of the three existing major players: Carlton, United and Granada could
  merge subject to conditions on premium franchises and total share of viewers.
- No ITV company could own more than two of the four premium franchises
  where the share of national advertising revenue was greater than the share of
  ITV national viewership. The four premium franchises were Carlton, Central,
  Meridian and LWT that together take 55% of ITV advertising and 40% of the
  ITV viewers.
- The Broadcasting Act that limits any ITV company to 15% of national viewing
  audience was retained.
- The Broadcasting Act rule that no company could hold both a London
  weekend and a London weekday franchise was maintained.
- Restrictions on holding multiple digital television licences were to
  be abolished.
- The 20% limit of any company's holding in ITN was maintained.
- At least two ITV advertising sales houses were to be maintained to allow small
  independent ITV franchises a choice.

Within days of the government's relaxations, Carlton Communications called off its bid for United News and Media. This decision left it open for Granada to bid for either company! By 28th July 2000, Granada had bid £1.75bn for United News and Media, acquiring in the process Anglia Television, Meridian Television and HTV (which was subsequently sold to Carlton in order to comply with the then current regulations). The bid was accepted, creating a £10bn Television Empire.

42. THE SHAPE OF ITV 2001

The shape of Independent Television can be judged from the Independent Television Commission's factfile booklet of 2001.

CHANNEL 3 (ITV)

There are 15 regional Channel 3 licensees and one licensee providing the national breakfast-time service. The licences were awarded by competitive tender in October 1991 for a ten-year term commencing 1 January 1993. The majority of Channel 3 licensees have renewed their licences for a further 10 years. The remaining have formally expressed their interest in renewing, subject to accepting the terms offered to them.

1. Anglia Television
    East England
2. Border Television
    Borders and the Isle of Man
3. Carlton Broadcasting
    London Weekday
4. Central Independent Television plc
    Broadcast name:
    Carlton Broadcasting – Central Region
    East, West and South Midlands
5. Channel Television
    Channel Islands
6. Grampian Television
    North of Scotland
7. Granada Television
    North-West England
8. HTV Group
    Wales and West of England
9. LWT
    London Weekend
10. Meridian Broadcasting
    South and South-East England
11. Scottish Television
    Central Scotland
12. Tyne Tees Television
    North-East England
13. Ulster Television
    Northern Ireland
14. Westcountry Television
    Broadcast name:
    Carlton Broadcasting – West Country Region
    South-West England
15. Yorkshire Television
    Yorkshire

Non-overlap area
Overlap area
Triple overlap area

Channel 3 coverage at the turn of the millennium.

In addition to the consumer protection requirements, which must be met by all television programme services licensed by the ITC, Channel 3 licensees have to meet significant positive requirements covering, for example, high quality, diversity, original productions/commissions, independent productions, news, regional production, networking, equal opportunities, training, provision for the deaf or hearing impaired and blind or partially sighted, national television archive and party political broadcasts. (Some of these apply only to regional licensees.) The licensees must provide services in accordance with the proposals made in their applications, unless agreed otherwise by the ITC.

The services are regulated by the ITC to check that the various requirements are met. The main instruments of ITC regulation are the ITC codes and the individual licences, copies of which can be obtained from the ITC. Performance is assessed on the basis of information derived from licensees themselves, monitoring by the ITC staff, audience research and viewers' complaints.

ITN

ITN is the organisation 'nominated' by the ITC to provide a high quality national and international news service to Channel 3 (including GMTV). The programmes supplied by ITN must be transmitted live and simultaneously by the regional Channel 3 licensees. ITN also provides news programmes to Channel 4 and 5 as well as supplying UK news and facilities to Reuters. In August 2000 ITN launched the News Channel's 24 hour service.

ITV NETWORK CENTRE

Many programmes on the services of the regional Channel 3 licensees are provided from the ITV network, which commissions and purchases programmes for the licensees collectively. Executive decisions about commissioning, acquiring and scheduling network programmes are taken on behalf of the licensees at the Network Centre. Programmes are commissioned either from independent producers or from independent production resources owned by the licensees.

DIGITAL TELEVISION

Digital television is a more efficient method of television transmission. Many television channels can be squeezed into the space used to carry a single analogue channel.

This technology also has the potential to offer other services such as high definition television and wide-screen pictures, CD quality sound and near video-on-demand (a film can be shown at different times on different channels so that the viewer can choose a convenient time to start watching), interactive services like home banking and connection to the viewers.

Digital television can be delivered through an existing television aerial (Digital Terrestrial Television – DTT), through cable (Digital Cable Television – DCT) or via a satellite dish (Digital Satellite Television – DST). A set-top box decoder is required for all types of digital delivery. The set-top box also provides the means for broadcasters to supply services for which a charge is payable. This is called conditional access. Television sets with built-in decoders are now available.

DIGITAL TERRESTRIAL TELEVISION

In 1996 the Government announced plans for the introduction of digital television based upon the use of six digital networks (multiplexers). The Government allocated the multiplex with the highest coverage to the BBC.

The Broadcasting Act 1996 enabled the ITC to licence the remaining five multiplexes. One of these was to be reserved for ITV, Channel 4 and teletext services and was awarded to Digital 3 and 4 Limited.

The licences to operate the remaining four commercial multiplexes (A to D) were advertised in October 1996. Multiplexes B,C and D were awarded in June 1997 to British Digital Broadcasting plc (BDB). Jointly owned by Carlton Communications and the Granada Group, BDB was later renamed ONdigital. ONdigital launched in November 1998 offering the free-to-air terrestrial channels and range of subscription channels.

Multiplex A was awarded in July 1997 to S4C Digital Networks Ltd (SDN). Channel 5 and S4C have guaranteed capacity on Multiplex A, which is also required to carry Gaelic programming in Scotland.

DIGITAL SATELLITE TELEVISION

Sky Digital launched its services in October 1998. It offers the free-to-air terrestrial channels (except ITV and ITV2) and a range of subscription channels.

DIGITAL CABLE TELEVISION

Services via cable delivery are available from NTL and Telewest.

43. THE FINAL CURTAIN?

With regards to 'regional identities', in a speech to BAFTA in June 2002, Tessa Jowell, the Culture Minister, said:

There has been speculation that ITV companies, on a course as they are for ever-more consolidation, will move away from their regional identities and their regional commitments… Let me take this opportunity to stress how inaccurate those views are… Regional character matters. We will look to Ofcom to defend it with vigour.

On 18th December 2003 the Communications Act 2003 came into force; the ITC ceased to exist, and its duties were assumed by The Office of Communications (Ofcom). Ofcom was created as the new communications sector regulator having wide-ranging responsibilities, inheriting the duties of five previously existing regulators. It replaced:

- The Broadcasting Standards Commission
- The Independent Television Commission
- The Office of Telecommunications
- The Radio Authority
- The Radiocommunications Agency.

As a result of the enactment of the Communications Act 2003, Ofcom varied the Licence granted to Central Independent Television plc from 29th December 2003 along with all the other licence holders.

With regards to its commitment to regional programming, the Licensee was to adhere to the following:

- Include programmes made in the UK outside the M25 area.
- To provide a suitable range of different production centres outside the M25 area.
- In both respects to be guided by Ofcom.

In particular the Licence variation referred to Regional Production (programmes made within the Licensed Region) as follows:

At least 40% of expenditure on originated network programmes in each calendar year shall be allocated to the production of programmes produced outside the M25 area and must be referable to a suitable range of production centres outside the M25 area. At least 33% of originated network programme hours must be made outside the M25 area and will constitute a range of different types of programmes.

With regards to Regional and Sub-regional Programmes (Central Television):

■ The Licensee shall ensure that the Service includes first-run regional and sub-regional programmes transmitted between 0925 and 0030, in the following amounts:
  • News 5:30
  • Current Affairs 0:26
  • Other 2:34
  A total of 8:30 hours weekly average.

■ Include in each East, West and South sub-regions a weekly average of at least 4 hours of news programmes of particular interest to the persons living in these respective sub-regions.

■ In each calendar year at least 90% of all regional programmes broadcast by time must be made within the Licensed Area.

With regards to the Regional Service, as a regional public service broadcaster, the Licensee commits to the following:

■ The regional service will include news and current affairs in the amounts shown above.

■ The service will seek to respond creatively to the evolving and wide range of tastes, interests and communities within the region and include material which is socially purposive, has educational value and reflects the cultural, artistic, sporting and spiritual life and identity of the region.

■ Diversity may be enhanced by the inclusion of both studio and location-based programmes, including coverage of major events, and a mix of one-off documentaries, magazine formats and discrete series.

■ Regional programmes shall reflect a high level of ambition no less than network programmes, and shall be appropriately researched and resourced. Some should be capable of being regarded as landmark series of particular distinction or programmes which break new ground.

Unfortunately this variation meant that Central was not committed to producing major network programmes within the Central Region, they could be produced anywhere in the UK outside the M25 area. Further, only 90% (7:45 hours per week) of its programmes for the people of the region had to be made within the region itself.

Although the 2003 Communications Act called for a suitable range of production centres, Central considered that its News facilities in the Sub-regions were adequate to fulfil its licence commitment.

At this time Granada owned the northern England licences for Tyne Tees, Yorkshire Television, and two of the southern England licences of Meridian and London Weekend Television. Carlton owned the London weekday licence, Central Independent Television, Westcountry Television and HTV.

In the light of the variations made to the Licences, Granada and Carlton entered negotiations to merge their resources. They had attempted to merge twice during the 1990s to create a new company that owned all of the Channel 3 ITV licences in both England and Wales. In October 2003 the Government agreed that the merger could take place, providing the Scottish, Ulster and Channel Island franchises remained independent.

It is perhaps worth repeating that the idea for the television series ***The Story of ITV: The People's Channel***, an ITV series, produced by Melvyn Bragg, he claims came to him while working in the House of Lords at the time when the Communications Bill about the future of broadcasting was being debated. He said, *'If you want to find the 646 most ignorant people about television then go down to Parliament and meet them. They hear about it, they complain about it, but they don't watch it.'* Yet these are the very people who make all the decisions about how it should operate.

44. THE GRANADA AND CARLTON MERGER

The Government's changing of the rules to permit such mergers appears to have been because they were trying to encourage a 'world-class' broadcaster to emerge that would effectively challenge the BBC and BSkyB in both the UK and abroad. Was it hoping to encourage foreign interest in the UK media industry? Had it in mind the possibility of USA media giants like Viacom and Disney as likely contenders to take-over ITV, if the price was right? It has been said that there is very little 'world class' about the current ITV. Unfortunately it could soon become one of the many non-descript channels instead of being the prime commercial channel it should be.

But the merger was going to produce a system that would be a far cry from the network's origins as a group of tightly-knit regional companies. Before Commercial Television started critics feared that it would be a vulgar influence on British life and Sir Winston Churchill feared that it would become a 'peep-show.' So to ensure that this did not happen the original regulator set up by the Government, the ITA, was given huge powers to control the quality of the output of the companies. This model held the ITV Network together and tightly controlled for at least forty years. The success was largely due to tight regulation but also to the responsible attitudes of the individuals who owned and ran the companies. The companies worked together in a responsible manner. The Regional structure was a guard against any drift into mediocrity, as each franchise holder could be replaced by the regulator should it perform badly; what sanctions has the regulator left should a single ITV be deemed to be performing badly?

With regards to the merger, Granada and Carlton saw it as a means to free up money to plough into the schedules, because it realised that better programmes would bring in more viewers, which in turn would bring in more money from advertisers. The new company needed to produce shows of sufficiently high quality to be watched by as many people as possible. The ITV Network had, since the two companies had been in control of the Regional broadcasters, and after being weakened financially by the poorly judged venture into ONdigital, been losing its market share of viewers to the other channels in particular to cable and satellite. The ONdigital collapse had caused huge losses, and it was believed that a merger would save the new company some £50million a year by cutting out duplication in management and facilities.

But by closing its major facilities around the regions it has weakened its base, particularly in the regions and most of all has lost what Howard Thomas had once described as its 'battle hardened' programme producers at all levels. The huge numbers of redundant staff have either left the business or been snatched up by the Independent Companies.

CONTRACTS RIGHTS RENEWAL AND OTHER SAFEGUARDS

The Government in allowing the merger between Granada and Carlton did insist on safeguards to protect the advertising industry from being overcharged. Recognising the concerns of the advertising community about the vast market power ITV plc was likely to have following the merger the Government put in place the Contracts Rights Renewal remedy, a formula devised by Charles Allen. This was intended to protect the advertising market:

- By guaranteeing that advertisers and media buyers were no worse off following the merger.
- By putting in place an automatic 'ratchet' which reduced the amount advertisers had to commit if ITV's audience shrank.
- In particular it gave advertisers and media buyers the right to renew their contracts on a rolling annual basis, adjusted for changes in ITV's audiences, with no reduction in discounts.

It also safeguarded the Scottish (STV), Northern Ireland (UTV) and the Channel Islands Regional broadcasters; but it did not specifically make any conditions regarding the other regions within England and Wales. It appears that they saw no need, as they did not expect that those Regional broadcasters would cease to provide regional news and regional programmes. The new company had assured the Government that it wished to develop strong local and regional news programmes.

WE'RE ALL IN GRANADALAND NOW

After a long regulatory struggle the merger of Granada and Carlton finally occurred at the end of January 2004. Charles Allen of Granada emerged as proposed chief

executive of a single ITV, with Michael Green, former boss of Carlton as the designated chairman; described in the press as two 'lame-ducks' in television production terms. The future had begun to look a little dark for those working in the industry. But Green was ousted by the shareholders, who had not forgiven him for the failure of ITV Digital, whilst 'Teflon Allen' as he was called, remained immune from any blame, and found himself in sole charge of the new company.

On 26th February, 2004, a new company came into being: ITV plc. The choice of name is considered to be controversial as it implies that the company runs the whole network, which of course it does not, yet! It was launched on the Stock Market, valued at £6.5bn.

It proceeded to announce a major restructuring of the television operations in the Midlands. The new company, in a document entitled *Looking Forward*, announced:

The production arm of ITV plc, now called Granada, incorporates the combined talent, creativity and heritage of the Granada, Central, LWT, Carlton, Anglia, Tyne Tees and Yorkshire production companies. For almost 50 years these companies have produced programmes that are the envy of the world and have enjoyed unparalleled commercial and creative success. These programmes cover all genres from soaps to arts, children's, documentaries, costume drama and factual, from across the regions of the UK. This talent has now been aggregated into one world class production company within ITV plc.

MIDLANDS TELEVISION PROGRAMME PRODUCTION CEASES

With control of all this accumulated talent and production capacity, Charles Allen realised that he could make considerable savings by cutting back on production across the Regions. The Midlands-based production facilities committed to the Midlands Region by ATV in 1980, and opened in 1984; when as a condition of its Licence it was required to build a state-of-the-art studio complex in Nottingham, and close its successful studios at Elstree, were amongst the first to be removed.

At the end of June 2004, the management of ITV plc. closed the Nottingham Studio complex, resulting in some 200 job losses, and to the detriment of the area. The Lenton Lane studio complex, initially employing 700 people, had made such hit shows as **The Price is Right**, with Leslie Crowther, **Celebrity Squares**, with Bob Monkhouse,

Family Fortunes, presented by Les Dennis, ***Supermarket Sweep***, establishing the television career of Dale Winton, and ***Bullseye*** with Jim Bowen. Also made there were programmes for the BBC including ***Kiss Me Kate***, ***Doctors and Nurses*** and occasionally ***Question Time***, hosted by David Dimbleby. By 1990 the complex was running at a loss and cuts began. The re-vitalised ***Crossroads***, was an unexpected flop, viewers were unimpressed. It was not surprising that UK studio centres were running at a loss when 'top-rated' shows were being made in the Australian rain forest.

Following the Nottingham closure, the remaining staff from Lenton Lane, those who worked on ***Central News East***, were moved to Birmingham.

Then, at the end of September 2004, all transmission output ceased from the Birmingham Studios at Central Court. Transmission was moved to the Northern Transmission Centre at Leeds. All programmes were routed through Central Court to Leeds for presentation and distribution back to the Midlands transmitters. Also lost from Birmingham were ***CiTV*** and ***ITV Sport***.

It has been argued that this was a big mistake, technically the Birmingham set up was the way ITV should have been run, in order to cut costs effectively the Birmingham operation was the one that should have been retained. It clearly had the most professional presentation within the ITV Network; it had state-of-the-art technology and techniques. But this, all new digital, server-based, set-up was scrapped and transmission transferred to YTV in Leeds which was poorly equipped and clearly outdated.

The competitive and economic structure of Management, Engineers and Technical Operators, along with a lively training programme for Technical Operators – ideal starting point for youngsters starting out in television – that made other ITV Companies look archaic and expensive, was destroyed.

This left some 270 people employed in the whole of the Midlands region to produce programmes purely for that regional audience. In Birmingham those involved contracted onto a single floor of the Central Court complex, the other floors were to be let-out as offices. The small single studio in Birmingham was physically divided into two, to provide downsized studios for ***East Midlands*** and ***West Midlands News***. The Nottingham News operation closed down and its journalists transferred to Birmingham. Only the Oxford operation remained intact. The whole region was reduced to the production of the minimum requirement of 8.5 hours of regional programming per week, most of it local news.

ITV plc. proposed to have three major production centres for network programmes in London, Leeds and Manchester. Back to London for the same reason as ABC

The Midlands – Reduced to this! Equipment taking the television signal to Leeds and back to the Midlands Transmitters. In the picture: Transmission Co-ordinator Steve Smith with the RPOC Bays. (Courtesy: Roger Quiney).

Television found in the 1950s, much of the fashionable creative talent believe that they can only work in that City. Leeds and Manchester, of course produce long running soaps of **Coronation Street** and **Emmerdale**. Yorkshire is also the centre for a number of other ITV drama productions, **A Touch of Frost**, **Where the Heart is**, **Heartbeat**, **The Royal** and **Fat Friends**.

Production of major television programming has become polarised with large facilities remaining in London and the rest clustered around West Yorkshire with a small overspill around Manchester (presumably because it still produces the ever popular regionally significant back-street image of **Coronation Street**).

One is left to consider what current television programme production, other than limited local news and current affairs programmes, reflect the cultural, artistic, sporting and spiritual life and identity of the Midlands region of the country, Derbyshire, Worcestershire, Warwickshire, Gloucestershire, Leicestershire,

Nottinghamshire, Oxfordshire, Northamptonshire, Staffordshire, Shropshire, Herefordshire and the extensive fringe areas beyond.

Is the Midlands and its diverse communities to become 'The Forgotten Region' with regards to television programming and recognition?

Currently Ofcom is conducting a major review of public service broadcasting, and as part of that review has issued a report that the regional programme commitment by Licence holders in England be reduced to 1.5 hours per week. The report goes even further in proposing that even local news programmes should only remain if 'financially sustainable.' Who, we wonder, will decide that question?

In the past it has been recognised that regional television is vital to local democracy and regional identity, and that in its absence regional voices will be stifled both within the regions and from a UK perspective. The situation is an attack on democracy, are we to return to the days when the only voice to be heard was that of London and the South-east? It did seem that the main ITV channel was being seen as not the place to show regional programmes.

THE RULE OF CHARLES ALLEN

In August 2005 Charles Allen, Chief Executive of ITV plc announced that the Granada-Carlton merger was then complete, and that the management ethos and strategy was in place to take the company forward.

Charles Allen was born on January 4th 1957, in Lanarkshire, Scotland. At seventeen he was a management trainee working in finance department of British Steel. In 1979 he became deputy audit manager for Galaghers and three years later he was director of management services at Grandmet International.

Compass Catering Group was created from a buyout from Grandmet and Charles Allen worked there between 1985 and 1991, rising to managing director. In 1991 he moved to Granada's Leisure Division as chief executive, following his Compass colleague Gerry Robinson, who became Granada's chief executive. Robinson and Allen went on to form a strong double act.

Robinson put Allen as chief executive of Granada Television, telling him to sort out the financial performance of Granada, which was then losing £4m. Charles Allen caused an outrage with a round of job cuts, the well loved Granada producer David Plowright was fired, and the number of executives was reduced to five from 13. The howls of protest were loud, and have never gone away. But Allen saw himself as a new broom sweeping away egos and stale thinking. It is reported that John Cleese was so incensed by this episode that he sent a telegram reading: 'F**k off, you jumped-up caterers.'

Charles Allen began to dream of creating a single ITV company. He clearly disliked the Network – full of grandiose fiefdoms – a club that made him feel uncomfortable and which he obviously did not see himself fitting into. He became obsessed with the idea of a single ITV.

In 1994 Granada began its series of takeovers; in that year LWT was acquired for £765m, following a long battle in the City, Greg Dyke the boss of LWT angrily resigned and Charles Allen took over his job. This hostile bid enhanced Allen's reputation as ITV's boot boy.

Gerry Robinson was promoted to Granada's executive chairman in 1996, and Charles Allen followed him up to become chief executive of Granada. A year later Granada purchased Yorkshire Television and Tyne-Tees Television.

The start of the new millennium saw another move by the company when they took over the ITV broadcast licences of United News & Media (Meridian, Anglia and HTV). This followed the failed attempt of United News & Media to merge with Carlton. Because of the then licence restrictions Granada sold HTV to Carlton, and Granada bought Border Television.

Also in 2000 Gerry Robinson retired as Granada's executive chairman, and following what was becoming a pattern, Charles Allen moved up into his chair.

Following the completion of the Granada-Carlton merger, Charles Allen set about his streamlining of the ITV Network into a single entity. In April 2005 he purchased SDN, which held a 38% stake in Freeview, in order to bring in rental income, as well as providing space for ITV's emerging digital channels; Allen saw it as a great deal.

He began pressing Ofcom for a 'level playing field' for all broadcasters; ITV he claimed, were paying a £200 million super-tax, not required from any of its competitors. In June 2005 he finally secured a £135m reduction in licence fees from the new regulator Ofcom.

At the same time the new regulator, Ofcom was commencing its first-ever review of Public Service Broadcasting. Charles Allen said that ITV was working hard to ensure that the reviews being undertaken by Ofcom produce an outcome that safeguards commercial public service broadcasting for future generations and underwrites ITV's ability to continue investing in public service television and transmit ever-improving programmes for its viewers.

During the year ITV were clearing the decks following the Carlton-Granada merger, in the hope of raising £500 million. Charles Allen sold ITV's shares in French electronics company Thompson for £172m, and offloaded publisher

Carlton Books for £3m, followed by the sale of its 18% stake in Australian movie producer Village Roadshow for £36m. The special-effects firm Moving Picture Company was then expected to go for about £53m, and Carlton Screen Advertising, the cinema advertiser. ITV had 75% of the breakfast broadcaster GMTV after buying out SMG, but the remaining investor Disney had refused an offer for its stake.

By the end of the year there were strong rumours that ITV was *'a tasty takeover story waiting to happen.'* In November its turnover had swelled to almost £48m and the price of its shares were increasing amid speculation that its days of independence were numbered. Fund Manager, Anthony Bolton, 'the quiet assassin' at investor Fidelity, who was instrumental in ousting Carlton's Michael Green as future chairman, owns 11.3 % of ITV. It was rumoured that he was losing patience with the ITV management and in private was suggesting to his friends and clients that a 'cash-rich' predator should pounce.

Meanwhile ITV's market share had been slowly eroding by sheer volume of the other channels despite launches of such popular programmes as ***I'm A Celebrity, Get Me Out Of Here***.

By February 2005, Charles Allen's 'pressure' on Ofcom appeared to have succeeded in that he won consent from the media regulator to make substantial and controversial cuts to ITV's £250million public service obligations. Religious programmes, children's television, documentaries and regional programming were most likely to be affected.

The reduction of public service requirements, expected to be hailed as a great victory by Charles Allen, was expected to improve ITV's share price and allow it to gain more revenue by screening programmes that are more attractive to advertisers as they attract more viewers. The regulator has been convinced by ITV's arguments that it needs more freedom to compete against the growth of multi-channel television. The press speculated that ITV was also likely to cut costs by reducing staff levels on regional programming even further. The move was condemned by unions and politicians, 100 MPs backed calls last year protesting against any cuts, which would produce job losses as well as further eroding the amount of locally made programmes.

The decline in the television industry at regional level continued; at Anglia, the mothballing of the studio meant more job losses. Rather than fighting to keep the studio open and obtain further work, the company preferred to rely on its US-made ***Animal Precinct*** - type of programmes and its back catalogue of shows. It would continue for a while transferring its old tapes of the ***Survival*** programme onto an up-to-date format for showing on ITV3. Further job losses were to take place at YTV and at Tyne Tees due to redundancies in the regional programme department of YTV and due to relocation and new technology at TTT.

Tony Lennon of BECTU, saw attacks on his members on all fronts:

Conservative prime ministers don't get much coverage in this magazine, but a quote from Harold Macmillan, Tory leader in the late 1950s, deserves an airing. When asked what most worried him about the future, he famously replied: "Events dear boy, events."

As we begin 2005, nothing more aptly sums up the position of many BECTU members. Boy, have we got some events coming up.

In almost every section we face change and upheaval on an unprecedented scale. ITV's retrenchment following the Carlton-Granada merger, and the insistence of industry regulator Ofcom that 'a light touch' is appropriate, have allowed the network to mount a full-scale retreat from public service broadcasting, particularly regional programming, and jobs are still being closed as a result.

The press reported that ITV was now looking to buy new TV channels to prove that it could return to growth after several difficult years. They wanted to launch new pay-TV channels, to start a new gambling channel, hoping to use celebrities to tempt housewives to have a flutter through interactive TV sets.

It was reported that Charles Allen was in a confident mood at the annual brainstorming session for 120 ITV managers, who spent two days in the lavish Landmark Hotel plotting their future strategy and drinking until 2am. Now that Ofcom had said that ITV could halve its output of regional programmes to 1.5 hours a week. This giving the company more cash for current audience pleasers like ***Get Me Out of Here....*** as it struggles to hang on to advertisers.

Ofcom boss Stephen Carter denied that he was taking pity on the £5bn broadcaster; Mr Allen and many viewers in the country must believe a different story! Mr Carter said: *'ITV has billions of revenues and last time I looked a pretty healthy profit line. (Taking Pity) is not our job."*

It was not long before Charles Allen was back at Ofcom's (perhaps now being seen as a soft touch) door begging again for more favours. This time ITV wanted to squeeze more advertising into its schedule as its audience share continued to fall because of increased competition. He was asking Ofcom to let the company increase the time for adverts per hour from seven to nine minutes (equivalent to an extra commercial break). Although Ofcom had already let ITV cut its religious and children's programme output so that it could plough more money into ratings-winning dramas and soaps, ITV were now considering getting the rules changed on product placement and advertiser funded shows; the company would also like its viewers to spend more on premium rate telephone calls and text messages for voting, as they were encouraged to participate in shows.

Charles Allen's 'night of the long knives' came in September 2005, when Granada's broadcast chief Mick Desmond and finance director Henry Staunton were sacked and Simon Sharp was appointed director of television.

In his continual struggle to get 'a level playing field' Charles Allen returned yet again to Ofcom's door, this time in an attempt to overturn the complicated formula (the Contracts Rights Renewal devised by him) it imposed following the Granada-Carlton merger that puts a cap on the amount it can charge for ITV-1 advertising spots.

In the meantime ITV continued to sell-off assets. In September 2005 it put the outside broadcast arm 021 up for sale with the expectation of completing the disposal within two months. 021 regarded as one of Europe's leading outside broadcast operations, has provided extensive coverage of sporting events, including the Olympics, the Rugby World Cup and the Premier League matches. Its sale was expected to provide ITV an extra £10 million, to add to the £270 million already raised by selling-off 'non-core' businesses, to plough-back into improved programming. In fact in January 2006 ITV announced the sale of 021 to Gravity Media Group Ltd. for £4.5 million, far less than expected. ITV stated that the sale represented a continuation of the successful disposal of non-core assets which has generated £281 million in an eighteen month period since July 2004.

It is strange to think that a television company the size of ITV should consider 021; one of the UK's largest outside broadcast facility companies as a non-core asset!

In December 2005 he paid £175m for the Internet Website Friends United, the largest community site in the U.K.; a step towards his new vision. He saw home entertainment becoming a single centre in the home, providing television programmes, computer games, internet and communications – screens in the home will, he envisaged, do everything. He saw the company becoming 'convergence' in its operations – different types of media coming together and working for each other – ITV was not going to be reliant on Television Advertising.

ITV fought off a private equity approach, in March 2006, by a group backed by Greg Dyke, which was offering 130p per share, valuing the company at £5.3bn.

In June of that year ITV set out a fresh strategy including more merger savings and promising a £500m cashback for ITV shareholders.

But a month later pressure was mounting on Charles Allen to go, as the share price fell below 100p, 30p lower than the Dyke offer in March, and down from 149p some eighteen months earlier, advertising revenue melting away, as were the viewers (less than 17%). The value of ITV fell to £3.9bn. Although Charles Allen did not accept that the programme schedule was poor or that it had declined during his reign, something clearly was not working – the wheels were coming off!

Reports from Granada's heartland in the Manchester Evening News read:

Tom Gill, Salford University's head of journalism and media expert has said: 'I think ITV has lost its way. It is not producing programmes that people want to watch and has not been able to keep up with the multi-channel companies. Charles Allen has been very good in dealing with the City and advertisers but I think his days are numbered. ITV needs a complete overhaul and take a look at the share price – its languishing at around 100p.'

Professor Tudor Rickards, of Manchester Business School, said: 'There is turmoil as ITV is being squeezed by the new multi-media companies. The whole industry is changing and I think ITV is going to bring in new people to deal with it.'

Constraints on advertising pricing under a complex contract rights renewal scheme, devised by and negotiated with the regulators by Charles Allen, as a means of getting the Granada-Carlton merger accepted, had also put him under considerable pressure. The deal limits the amount of money ITV can demand from advertisers, making it even more difficult for ITV to make money.

Some analysts claimed that ITV's decline from being a dominant broadcaster to just a part of the multi-channel world with its ruthless competition and fragmenting viewing audiences was simply a fact of life. Whilst others blamed Charles Allen and his programme making team for not innovating enough and for failing to engage in the hostile market in the way that Channel 4 had done.

The BAFTA 2006 Awards highlighted the disastrous effect of his reliance on cheap, mind numbing reality television and aging soaps, which moved in the opposite direction, from reality to fantasy – there were twenty awards, only one of which went to ITV.

As August arrived ITV announced that Charles Allen was to step down from the company.

Amongst the first to comment upon the end of his rule was BECTU the television technicians union, who welcomed the announcement.

They commented that during his reign, he had presided over mass redundancies (approximately 4000 since the ITV merger), of highly skilled television production staff and technicians, cost cutting and a consequent dumbing down of programme content. He had made significant cuts in the regional programming, and the closing down of television production facilities throughout the regions (destroying the basis upon which the ITV Network was originally founded).

Charles Allen had come to Television with a reputation of being a cost–cutter and that during his time in charge he had lived up to and enhanced that reputation. Unfortunately for television, the viewers and ultimately himself, he had failed to invest the savings he had made in the production of programmes of quality, instead making it available as dividends for shareholders.

The union believed that he had not known when to stop cutting costs, and that his complete lack of programme making background had resulted in a significant drop in ITV audiences.

He has left a demoralised workforce, who have been ground down by his successive rounds of facilities closures, redundancies and cuts in programme budgets.

The union hoped that his replacement would be able to reverse some of his destructive policies and recognise that to improve ITV had to invest in programmes of quality, and in the staff capable of making them.

Richard Simpson, showbusiness reporter for the Daily Mail summed up the general feeling in his article of the 9th August 2006, with the headline:

ITV's £10m Failure – *Broadcasting boss forced out as ratings and profits slump, but he still picks up a bumper package.*

A City source said:

He's a terrific cost-cutter; he's a great negotiator with Government and the regulators, but he's a very cautious man at the helm of a company that is crying out for boldness, vision and inspired leadership. ITV has been like watching a slow car crash for two years.

It is quite clear that Charles Allen will not be remembered as one of the giants of television, during the two and a half years he headed ITV, he will be remembered for such dross as **Celebrity Wrestling**, **Love Island** and **Its Now or Never**.

But he will not leave a poor man, his payoff is very handsome, but will he retire to put his feet up, sit back and watch television at his London home or his home by the sea in Cape Town?

HEADING FOR THE 50TH ANNIVERSARY

During the time that Charles Allen was in control of ITV, the Network was heading for its 50th Anniversary, and the media press began to reflect on how well it had done since 1955 and to where it was moving on.

Stephen Glover writing in the Daily Mail in May 2005:

When ITV was launched in September 1955, many feared it would debase standards of public decency. Of course, no one could conceive in those days of anything as low as **Celebrity Love Island** *being broadcast on national television. Nevertheless, dire warnings were issued from editorial columns and pulpits that commercial television would burst the bounds of propriety which the BBC then observed. Lord Reith, who had virtually created the BBC, thought that ITV was a 'potential social menace of the first magnitude.'*

In fact none of these prophecies was borne out. Although ITV was looked down on in some households, the new channel made up of 15 regional contractors, not only observed the same standards of decency as the BBC, but began to produce programmes which were equal, and sometimes superior, in quality to the output of its established rival.

Looking back, it is, of course, only too easy to wax lyrical about old ITV programmes.......

So what went wrong?... ITV's viewing figures have fallen even quicker than BBC1's, and the channel which could once attract eight viewers in ten to **Sunday Night at the London Palladium** *now accounts for only about a quarter of the television audience. Once it dominated Saturday evenings. Now it struggles to be noticed.*

As he went on to say ITV has attributed this decline to the rise in digital television, the launch of Channel Five, the lowering of programme quality from the BBC, which, in a fight for viewers, had copied much of the worst offerings from ITV.

All these factors, no doubt, have had an effect but it is easy to blame outside influences as though that was all there was to it. It is too easy to forget why ITV programmes produced by companies like ATV were so successful. The Press believed that the decline began when the ITV companies ceased to be controlled by people who understood the entertainment business and its customer's wants and desires, and who employed creative people to make programmes to fulfil them. They became broadcasting companies bent on cutting costs to a minimum and letting others produce the programmes they would then buy in. The creative people were replaced by a mass of 'Media Studies' graduates, producing some very good programmes amongst a much larger proportion of 'dross.' Unfortunately they do not possess the huge resources and show business 'clout' once possessed by companies like ATV, ABC and Granada. ITV of course now owns it all but has over time disposed of, or mothballed most of the resources around the original network. ATV's legendary, world renowned, programme making facilities in Elstree, studio centres in Birmingham and Nottingham for example all closed down and the vast depth of professional and highly skilled staff dispersed.

The Press complained that programme quality had consequently declined at an alarming rate to a point where the dwindling number of viewers are now treated to a schedule of programmes featuring garden make-overs, house make-overs, cooking, antique auctions, car-boot sales, the world's worst this and that programmes; besides the ***Get me out of...***, ***Celebrity*** this that and the other, ***Big Brother*** type of peep shows, where we are treated to people degrading themselves, and insulting others whilst we peep at them, giggle and mutter 'How shocking!'

Governments and their 'regulators' have not helped. The auctioning of the ITV franchises to the highest bidders in 1990 had been a step in the wrong direction; and resulted in replacing an established and well-respected programme making company, Thames Television (itself grown out of ABC Television) by Carlton a company commercially driven and without any programme making experience and with little interest in being one. Then in 1993 the government announced that takeovers within ITV would from then, be allowed. This made it possible for Carlton and Granada, itself by then in the hands of bean-counters to begin to swallow all the smaller individual ITV companies of the network. The important regional service, reflecting the regional characteristics of the areas they served, that these companies had provided since the start of the ITV Network was severely curtailed.

Although the number of viewers continued to decline, programme quality dropped and costs within ITV were slashed, assets were being sold off, the company was still able to announce a 49% increase in pre-tax profits to £325 million in 2004; as Stephen Glover said, '*The bean counters know how to milk mediocrity and decline.*' The company announced its annual results in March 2006; pre-tax profits were again up 36% to £452 million.

It seemed that no one cared! Where were all those Labour MPs and media critics who back in the early 1980s orchestrated the campaign to get the East Midlands its rightful share of representation on the screen? Now very little of the Midlands is represented and even the ***East Midlands News*** has returned to Birmingham to share a single small studio with the ***West Midlands News***.

A NEW IDENTITY AND THE STRUGGLE TO RETAIN VIEWERS

It has been argued that the loss of the Regional Identities along with many Regional production facilities across the country is unacceptable and should not have been permitted to have taken place. But on the other hand it has been argued that the federation of Regional Companies, each providing a main service and a regional service could not survive the move to a digital multi-channel service; that ITV as a whole needed to consolidate and become a single, streamlined entity in order to compete in that new environment.

Having renamed its main channel '**ITV-1**' in 2000, and set about shedding its original many regional identities across the country; deciding what programmes to show through a single scheduler at the newly set-up Network Centre and selling-off its 'non-core' assets Independent Television was able to work as a single unit.

ITV appeared to believe that eventually it would lose its place as one of only five established channels on the analogue service and that it would have to fight for viewers from amongst the competing mass of companies offering themselves on the multi-channel digital service.

Others believed that although ITV faced a tough battle to retain a reasonable share of the viewing audience, it was not too late and that the company, by improving its quality of programming, needed to establish its new identity amongst its existing viewers and build up a base of loyal viewers which it would take with it following the change over to digital.

Whilst its programme quality continued to fall and ITV-1 audience base continued to erode, it seemed that the company decided that it should first establish itself on the existing multi-channel digital service by opening up a family of ITV branded digital channels. First came **ITV-2**, launched as long ago as 1998, which shows a mixture of imported and homemade programmes as well as extended coverage of ITV's reality television programmes; the next was the **ITV News Channel**, showing ITN news bulletins for 24 hours a day; then in 2004 came a further general entertainment channel, **ITV-3**. The **ITV News Channel** has already bitten the dust! But the family continues to grow. **ITV-4** has recently been launched, **CiTV** a Kid's channel went on air in March 2006 and **ITV Play** followed in April 2006. **ITV Play** is a participation television channel; two of its main features being *The Mint* and a *Rovers Return Pub Quiz*. *The Mint* is described as a high-energy late-night compendium of live participation studio games, call games, puzzles, stunts and events. It is set in a stylish and opulent house type of set with a cash vault (the mint) at its core. Viewers will be able to call or text to participate in individual games for smaller prizes or the chance to win The Mint Jackpot. The Rovers Return Pub Quiz has cash prizes and *Coronation Street* star appearances.

Another new channel ITV Consumer (**ITVC**) is also about to be launched – '*to build businesses which create and monetise direct consumer relationships for ITV.*'

Charles Allen believed that **ITV Play** would make a £20 million profit in its first year from viewer interaction by paying for text messages and phone calls.

Over the last few years the Press has constantly reported that ITV appears to be losing the current struggle to retain its audience share; it is true that recent figures show that ITV's share is continuing to fall alarmingly. On 28th August 2005 the Daily Mail had the headline, **Shadow over ITV as viewers slump**. The following article by Jon Rees had the following to say:

ITV will record the worst-ever audience share for its main channel this month, piling on the misery of a run of damaging falls in viewing figures.

Unless ITV's audience picks up soon, the broadcaster could face a loss of advertising revenue of up to £150 million, (due to the current cap on what advertisers can be charged) *according to industry estimates......*

ITV is set to record an audience share of less than 20% for August – the third month in a row that the channel's share has dipped below that figure. The longer term trend clearly shows the pressure ITV is under. Its flagship channel has seen its share decline every month this year since February and it has fallen more than 12% since then.

Director of Programmes, Nigel Pickard, described two of its high-profile shows **Celebrity Wrestling** *and* **Celebrity Love Island**, *as 'poxy.'* (He has since been ousted, in January 2006 after being blamed for these high-profile flops).

While ITV1's audience share has fallen by almost 10% in the past three months, its commercial rivals have thrived.

ITV can take limited comfort from the success of its own digital channels ITV2 and ITV3 – but even so the combined audience share for all three channels for the past quarter is still down by nearly 9%.

ITV is promising a strong 2005 autumn schedule of programmes to revive its main channel.

Mr Lovelace of the media consultancy Lovelacemedia has said that:

The days when ITV was able to market itself as: **Channel 3 Britain's most popular button**, *seem a distant memory – its total audience has halved since the early 1980s, as first Channel 4 and then Five started to erode its lead.'*

Big hitting soaps like **Coronation Street**, recently judged number one, by the viewers, of ITV's best fifty programmes, and **Emmerdale**, along with the BBC's **Eastenders** still constantly hold the evening audience, with each bringing in around 9 to 10 million viewers. It appears that these viewers watch these three programmes in succession. The ITV1 audience drops to around 3 million whilst **Eastenders** or **Holby City** is showing.

Around this time muddled messages were coming from ITV as it struggled to adjust its strategy; one ITV spokesman said:

We will be investing more in programmes. Viewers will get better programmes – they will get more special events and more dramas. The recent merger will create a stronger ITV which will deliver for viewers.

Then a spokeswoman was reported as saying:

The unique role ITV plays in bringing together the regions of Britain in our programming will be sustained. ITV programmes are mainly made outside of London and ITV will be able to invest in the richness of regional culture. We will see more seamless news programming – divisions between regional, national and international news will go and there will be more coherence.

But the constant closing of regional facilities over the last few years does not give much credence to this and is 'seamless news' (whatever that means) what viewers really want from their regional news programmes?

Time is short, the Government has recently announced that it will commence switching off the analogue television broadcasting signals within the next three years, and completely by 2012; forcing viewers to switch to the digital channels, Terrestrial Freeview, Cable or Satellite. It is estimated that 70%, 18.8 million of the population has already done so, Freeview currently has over 8 million subscribers, BSkyB a little less and Cable Television has some 3.3 million. Currently 3 out of 4 new digital homes purchase Freeview and by 2007 it has already become the largest UK television platform.

There are warnings that the remaining 30% of viewers who have not yet switched to digital may cause a problem. Findings from research by Mediaedgercia, the advertising agency, indicate that some 29% of the viewing population say they '*never will*' make the switch to digital television. Reasons given were confusion over using the new technology, unhappiness at the cost and distrust at the need for so many extra channels. They seem to be content with the five 'main' channels on analogue television and see no reason to go to digital. With regards to cost, the Government recently spent more than £1 million converting 475 homes to digital during a trial in Wales – more than £2,100 per house. Government Ministers say they have no idea how much the change-over is likely to cost viewers, who will be required to purchase new equipment such as set-top boxes, improved aerials or satellite dishes.

But the situation is likely to be very different when the switch-over actually takes place, and all viewers have access to the whole range of digital channels available. Those viewers who at present show a reluctance to go-digital will suddenly find that they can watch their existing channels, but are also presented with much more choice in available programmes and realise what they have been missing! Will ITV-1 then lose its special place as being on-a-par with the BBC, and become just another channel amongst all the other digital channels vying for the viewer's attention or will it have made the right moves, in the direction of good quality programming to remain prominent amongst them?

ITV has accepted that the decline in its viewing figures is inevitable as people move across to greater choice on digital television. Not a month goes by without newspapers reporting 'the worst ever' decline in ITV or BBC viewers. These viewers are switching to digital and become dispersed amongst the many channels available. The BBC have already decided to change, it has been told not to continue in a race for viewers with ITV-1 by following it into a downward spiral of cheap, mind numbing programming. By the end of 2006 the BBC annual percentage share of the audience was levelling out whilst ITV-1 continued to fall.

But it has to be recognised that the next couple of years will be a transient period and ITV needs this time to re-establish its main channel as the real alternative to the BBC. Even so, for ITV in particular, it is the rate of decline, which this year has been the worst of any terrestrial channel that is worrying. Unlike the BBC whose income is guaranteed, ITV's income is almost entirely dependent on the audiences it can present to the advertisers. The competition means that ITV must fight harder for its viewers. This of course can only be achieved by producing high quality programmes in order to attract the viewers and consequently the advertisers. Producing low quality programmes which appeal to the lowest common denominator, with howling hyped-up audiences, and participants degrading themselves is not likely to work. It only worked for a time in the Roman Coliseum, and ITV needs to rise above the cheaply produced dross already available on the digital channels, not join it. It is important that it builds up a loyal audience to carry over to digital when the analogue signal is finally switched off; it only has a few years left to achieve this. ITV could end up with the 29% of viewers who do not want to switch over to digital, are these the same viewers who make up the audience for the evenings 'soaps'? Keeping them is a good thing but attracting the young and high-spending audience (that advertisers love) that seems to have moved to Channel Four should be a priority.

In its early years the ITV companies clearly recognised that their viewers were their most important asset and that every effort made in order to involve them was essential. They achieved this by making the viewers feel that they were part of the company, that it was their television station, by involving them in the shows it produced, and by making programmes that reflected the people in their region, and so on.

Not, as has recently been the case, by treating their viewers as a mass of dim-wits who were there to be 'fleeced', by encouraging them to participate at a cost, by using the 'premium-rate' phone lines for voting, entering competitions and texting messages. Thank goodness this outrageous scandalous way of boosting profits has been exposed. But the fact that ITV could stoop so low indicates how in recent years they have come to de-value the importance of their viewers.

45. A NEW DAWN?

A CHIP OFF THE OLD BLOCK – A RETURN TO THE TOP GRADE

Following the resignation of Charles Allen in August 2006, ITV spent the next few months searching for a replacement; many names were put forward and considered, but it seemed none was quite right. ITV was in deep trouble following a drop in advertising revenues and audience figures, and was still sinking, the future looked bleak. Who could restore it to its former glory and help it return to a grade one television station. Now there's a name….Grade!

Michael Grade resigned as Chairman of the BBC and took over from Sir Peter Burt at ITV to become Executive Chairman in January 2007.

As ITV continues to battle a weak advertising market Sir Peter Burt the outgoing Executive Chairman said:

ITV's challenges particularly on the programming and advertising side are considerable and Michael's particular blend of skills will provide both the continuity of experienced media management and the creative leadership which ITV needs to move forward rapidly.

After months of searching for a new Chief Executive had it now found its man? The company expects Michael Grade to remain as executive chairman for up to three years; during which time they expect to appoint a chief executive so that he can step back from day-to-day management and become non-executive chairman.

Mr Grade said that it had been a tough decision to leave the BBC, who described him as an inspirational leader, but that the move was an opportunity he could not resist, given his family's history in the founding of ITV and his own background at London Weekend Television.

He said that his first priority at ITV would be to support the team in accelerating the improvement in programming performance for the viewers and advertisers alike. He was very excited to be joining ITV, but denied that he had a grand turnaround plan in place just yet. He was prepared to stop the rot by wielding the axe:

We have to cull the stuff that has been on too long to make room for new stuff.

Michael Grade will always be in the shadow of his father and his uncles, but that is a very good place to be; as a young man he will have lived the life and seen how they operated at first hand, they were extremely successful and between them produced many, many hours of entertainment not only for every home in the country but across the world. Their experience and knowledge enabled them to judge the audience and instinctively know what satisfied them. If Michael Grade can now draw upon that knowledge and experience that is inbred in him then maybe ITV will recover, be rescued from the accountants and be restored to its show business roots, to blossom once more.

THE DIGITAL REVOLUTION AND REGIONAL PROGRAMMING

Although Lew Grade never backed away from new technology, in fact he embraced it; a side of the business that he never had to consider was the digital revolution and its relationship to regional programming, which is advancing at an ever faster rate. It is reported to be attracting more than 250,000 new households every month. Viewers who enter the digital world have far greater choice, a wider choice of the best from the past and high quality new ones from across the world, providing that they can be bothered to search for the programmes that they enjoy watching. But where is the programming that relates to the different regions of the U.K?

People can now watch television on their computers over the internet and are able to download programmes that they might have missed. Thousands more are even able to watch on their mobile phones. This is fine: the possibilities seem to be limitless, but the question that has to be asked is:

Now that the ITV service has all but ceased to be regional in nature, is it the right medium for broadcasting regional programmes?

Although ITV-1 is now virtually a National Channel it still holds the individual licenses for each of the Regions created by the ITA. These licenses still require that the holder produces a significant amount of regional programming, although this has been reduced considerably over recent years. Regional news gathering and transmission facilities still remain in those regions.

In the digital age might it be possible to remove the regional programming requirements for the Regions from the main ITV-1 channel and develop the regional news gathering facilities into facilities for providing those requirements?

ITV-1 is still clearly the right medium for Public Service Broadcasting at a national level and should continue to do so; but at regional level this might be more efficiently and practically achieved by some other medium.

OFCOM AND THE REVIEW OF PUBLIC SERVICE BROADCASTING

Ofcom is required by the Communications Act to carry out a review of public service broadcasting at least once every five years. The public service broadcasters are

BBC, ITV, Channel 4, Five, S4C and Teletext – their purposes being set out in the Communications Act. The first review recently completed asked:

- How are they meeting the purposes set out for them?
- How can the quality of PSB be maintained and strengthened in the future?

The review was carried out in three phases:

- Phase 1 consisted of a detailed programme of research and analysis to assess the current performance. Ofcom concluded that the PSB were performing well in delivering impartial and independent news, and high quality programming originating in the UK. They proposed a new definition of PSB, and set out the provision of PSB should be delivered in the evolving digital world.
- Phase 2 concluded that the old PSB model would not be sustainable in the run up to the switchover to digital and beyond.
- Phase 3 sets out in more detail Ofcom's proposed framework for the future. And the steps to be taken to maintain and strengthen the quality of public service broadcasting for some years to come.

Ofcom recognised that the established model was already breaking down in commercial television due to increased competition for advertising revenues. They predict that at some stage in the future that their existing licences will not be worth retaining, given the other transmission options available to broadcasters. They conclude that after switchover to digital they will no longer be able to ensure that commercial PSBs will deliver the existing wide range of obligations, such as regional programming.

A new model was needed to be put in place to secure PSB for the future. Ofcom, first set out a new definition of public service broadcasting, which it described in terms of purposes and characteristics:

- PSB PURPOSES
  - To inform ourselves and others and to increase our understanding of the world through news, information and analysis of current events and ideas.
  - To stimulate our interest in and knowledge of arts, science, history and other topics through content that is accessible and can encourage informal learning.

- To reflect and strengthen our cultural identity through original programming at UK, national and regional level, on occasion bringing audiences together for shared experiences.
- To make us aware of different cultures and alternative viewpoints, through programmes that reflect the lives of other people and other communities, both within the UK and elsewhere.

■ PSB CHARACTERISTICS
  - High quality – well funded and well produced.
  - Original – new UK content, rather than repeats or acquisitions.
  - Innovative – breaking new ideas or re-inventing exciting approaches, rather than copying old ones.
  - Challenging – making viewers think.
  - Engaging – remaining accessible and enjoyed by viewers.
  - Widely available – if content is publicly funded, a large majority of citizens need to be given the chance to watch it.

Ofcom proposed a new model, which would secure that PSB would continue to be provided from a range of providers, that had different remits, and access to different funding sources, and with different institutional approaches. With regards to ITV-1 it proposed that it should focus on its strengths of news and high production value origination from around the UK. They believed that it was better for ITV-1 to prepare for its future role as soon as possible, rather than to be asked to preserve in full a range of commitments designed originally for a very different analogue world.

ITV has, in Ofcom's view, an important but evolving role to play as part of the overall UK broadcasting mix. Its aim was to ensure that ITV reflected fully the lives of people from around the UK, and provide independent and impartial news and current affairs, similar to those available on the main networks. Further it has a special responsibility for providing regional news, current affairs and other regional programming.

Ofcom's specific proposals to achieve ITV's role, focused on regional news and high-quality original production for the main network are:

Channel 3 licensees will be required to provide regional news and current affairs.

ITV's quotas for out-of-London production for the network to be increased to 50% (by value and volume), which represents more than £40 million additional spend per annum outside London in 2006 and beyond.

Ofcom will work with ITV to secure improvements in the range of production centres around the UK represented on the ITV-1 network, including introduction of a new production partnership fund, to help build capacity outside London.

Ofcom will work with the Government and other parties to explore the options for digital local television.

PUBLIC SERVICE PUBLISHER

Ofcom has proposed the creation of a new Public Service Publisher, which would be explicitly charged with developing services and content which take full advantage of new distribution technologies. Part of its remit would be to provide local and community services.

Research carried out by Ofcom confirms that the public values local news, information and other content which is focused on their own particular locality – digital television and broadband provide new opportunities to serve such local needs more effectively.

THE FUTURE FOR THE VIEWER

Ofcom recognises that the emergence of mass-market digital technologies opens up new opportunities for the provision of services that would have been technically impossible as little as ten years ago.

These new technologies they say will have a profound impact on the way viewers will watch television, they list some as:

- Within the next decade, the achievement of digital switchover will mean that everyone in the country has access to at least thirty television channels.
- People are increasingly likely to want to watch television at a time, place and pace of their own choosing.
- Personal video recorders (PVRs) will become increasingly commonplace and high speed broadband internet (greater than 2 Megabits per second) will allow different on-demand services and interactivity.
- Improving digital compression technology could provide the capacity to carry at least double the current number of channels in the future.
- Wireless networking will distribute media throughout the household.
- Mobile devices will increasingly be used for viewing television services.
- Sophisticated flat LCD and plasma screens will enhance viewing, and high definition television will create new opportunities in the medium term.

- Home multimedia servers will personalise content and allow efficient storage and access.

LOCAL TELEVISION

Research suggests that local services continue to matter to people. Digital local content could deliver a range of benefits in future, including more relevant local news, improved access to local services, better consumer information and advice, stronger involvement in community affairs, enhanced democratic participation, greater capacity for individuals and local organisations to make and distribute their own content, support for local production and training, and advertisers access to local markets.

So a new tier of local television stations could be one of the benefits of digital technology. Following the recent Ofcom reports local television within the UK is undergoing a major and exciting rethink.

Experiments are already underway by the major broadcasters:

- ITV is experimenting with a broadband delivered service, based on Brighton and Hastings (www.itvlocal.tv).
- BBC is using a mixture of satellite television and broadband for a trial in the West Midlands (www.bbc.co.uk/localtv).

In both experiments viewers are encouraged to participate and contribute to the development of future services.

For ITV local-tv at this level opens up new advertising markets. ITV of course has always made its money from advertising but mostly from national advertisers. In the past there were a considerable number of local advertisers but these have fallen to just a few. Remember the 'slide and voice over adverts' for Allied Carpets that sold many rolls for that company? Local-tv would again enable local High Street (and Back Street) businesses to once more use television advertising to its local markets at reasonable cost.

Delivered by broadband local-tv on the ITV model would mean that ITV would not be tied to a regional network of transmitters. In theory all local-tv for whatever region or locality, town or community could originate at a single source. Regional Newsrooms already exist throughout the ITV Network and are well placed to provide content for such local services.

What could this mean for the Midlands viewers? Local stations could be based upon a Region, with a selection of more local news, services, advertising, etc. from different parts of that region, at City, Town or even community level.

Besides this the station could produce information that would not only be of interest to the whole of the Midlands Region but other regions, as examples:

Features on Historical Houses, many National Trust and British Heritage properties exist in the region and could form the basis of an interesting series.

The National Exhibition Centre has a vast range of interesting exhibitions, shows and events which could be given coverage in order to attract more visitors from within and outside the region.

Other exhibition centres within the region would benefit from similar coverage.

Local Authority consultations prior to decision making could be aired more fully by being discussed on the channel; other regions might gain some value by understanding this regions problems and how they are overcome (or not).

The region's sporting activities, news and achievements could be covered in greater depth than at present.

National television only covers the top sporting events; the top of the pyramid, there is so much, in all sports, going on at a lower level that needs covering and nurturing that regional coverage would benefit. Local motor racing, horse shows, even Sunday League football, all could be covered.

The various Shows in the region, Malvern Spring Fair and Three Counties, The Royal Show, etc. could be covered in some depth, encouraging people to attend.

Research projects of public interest being carried out at the regions many universities could be reported.

Stories of success (or otherwise) from within the business and industry of the region could also feature.

The region's tourist attractions could be featured from Robin Hood of Nottingham, Shakespeare of Stratford-upon-Avon, the canals of Birmingham.

Many more items of interest to the Midlands region and to the other regions are available and their coverage could be of great benefit to the economy and pride of the Midlands. ITV could be where anything of importance is taking place. ATV and ABC television knew this very well, and ITV could so easily do the same now. Not only would it attract national advertisers but many local advertisers, rarely seen on television nowadays. ITV needs to be everywhere anything of importance is taking place, to be associated with local events and local people, at local level.

So, finally the actual future form local-tv output takes in our Midlands region will largely be in the hands of us all, the viewers. We first need to come to grips with the switchover to digital multi-channel television. But view the experiments taking place and have your say! For us viewers, and for ITV, exciting times lie ahead.

To re-quote Tessa Jowell, the then Culture Minister, in a speech to BAFTA in June 2002:

There has been speculation that ITV companies, on a course as they are for ever-more consolidation, will move away from their regional identities and their regional commitments..... *Let me take this opportunity to stress how inaccurate those views are.... Regional character matters. We will look to Ofcom to defend it with vigour.*

APPENDIX 1

GROWTH IN TELEVISION SET OWNERSHIP 1956–2007

The total number of homes in the UK grew steadily between from just over 15 million in 1956 to just over 25 million in 2004.

The number of those homes with televisions was just over a third, 5 million in 1956 and grew quite quickly until about 1976 from which time it grew at about the same rate as the number of total homes. That is from around five million homes or 37% in 1956 to over 18 million or 97% in 1976.

From the introduction of ITV in 1956 the number of homes with television capable of receiving ITV increased rapidly until around 1968 and from then at about the same rate as television ownership in general. That is from around 3% in 1956 to 97% in 1977.

The homes with colour television sets grew very rapidly from its introduction to around 1984 and then more slowly until around 1998 when again its growth has followed the number of total homes.

Homes that are capable of receiving multi-channel television stood at 2.3 million in 1992 and has risen quickly to reach 18.6 million in 2006.

Television Ownership in Private Domestic – Households: 1956–2007

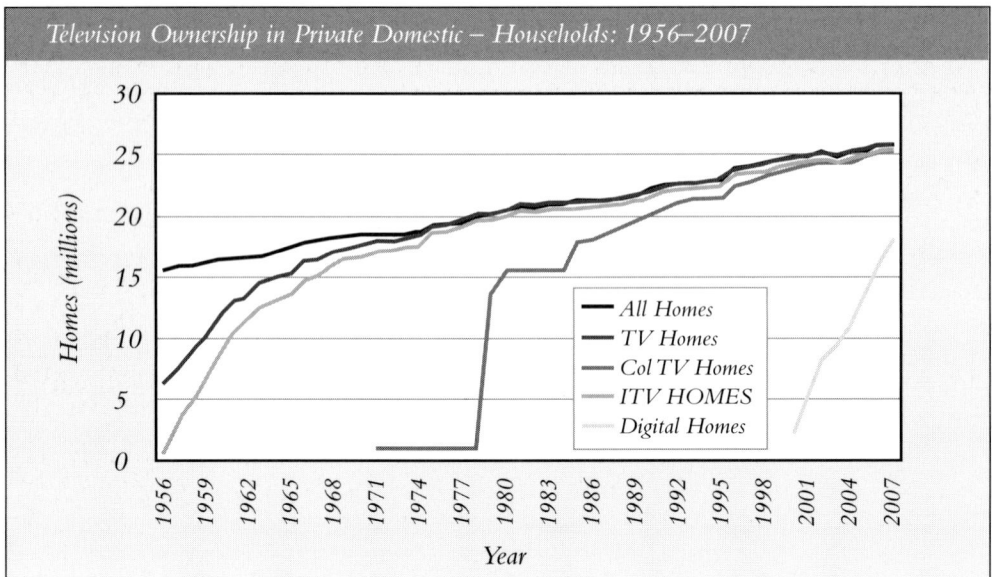

ANNUAL SHARE OF VIEWERS 1981–2006

In 1981 ITV1's share of viewers stood at just under 50%, exceeded that of the BBC1 by 10%; BBC2 took just 12%. With the introduction of Channel 4 all three dropped marginally and C4 attracted just 4% of viewers.

By 1991 things had not changed greatly, ITV1 stood at 42%, BBC1 at 34%, BBC2 at 10% with C4 up to 10%, Channel Five had just been introduced and took 4% of the viewers.

By 2006 the picture was very different, ITV1 had dropped to 19.6%, BBC1 had also fallen but not so fast to 22.3%, BBC2 and C4 each still attracted a little under 10%, Channel Five had risen to just under 6%, but the biggest gainers were Cable, Satellite and Freeview, which between them held 33.3% of the viewers.

ITV was clearly not able to hold its share of viewers. Early in 2005 the Press were reporting *Viewers are turning off ITV in droves*; Laura Benjamin of the Daily Mail reported that:

Viewers have abandoned ITV1 in record numbers over the past few months. One in ten has switched to another channel, along with a quarter of the highly-prized 16 to 34 age group.

In March 2006 Matt Born, the paper's Media Editor was reporting *Why a million viewers a week turn off ITV1*:

A million viewers a week have deserted ITV1 as the biggest commercial channel faces mounting pressure from digital and satellite rivals.

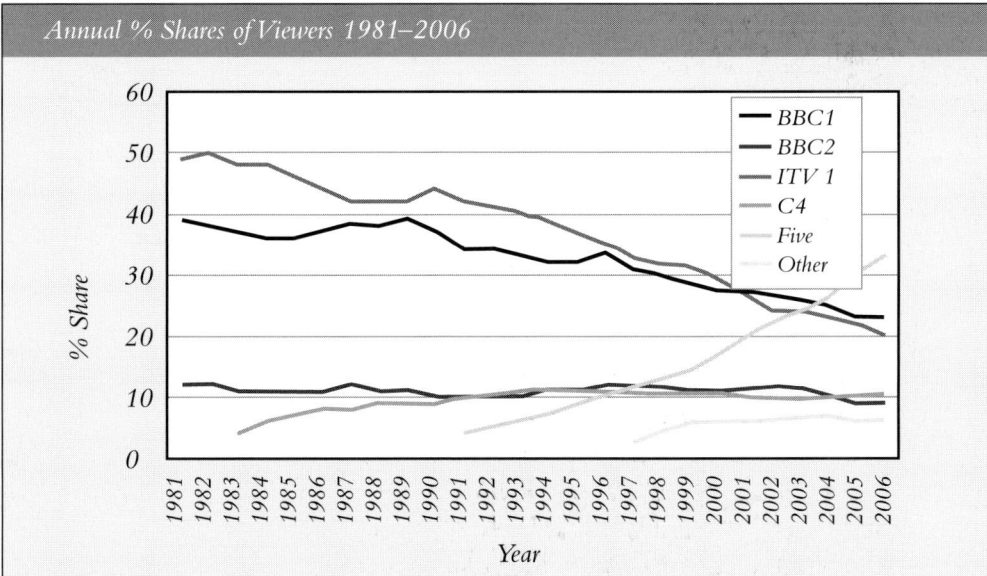

Annual % Shares of Viewers 1981–2006

275

ITV revealed yesterday that advertising revenue on its flagship channel fell by £50 million last year, as new figures showed that its audience share has slumped by 8% in 2006.

At the same time the Government was warning the BBC to stop chasing ratings by copying ITV's style of programming, but to beef up its public service output. All BBC services will have to meet targets over quality and range of output. This is clearly designed to ensure that the BBC remains the prime channel in the UK and is not dragged down in a race chasing viewers with low-cost makeover shows and copycat programming. In fact BBC1 appears to have halted its drift down by the end of 2006.

THE DEVELOPMENT OF MULTI-CHANNEL DIGITAL TELEVISION 1992–2007

Homes able to receive multi-channel digital television initially were either satellite or cable subscribers. Both grew steadily from 1992 until about 2000 when they had some 4 million subscribers each. From then cable subscriptions have remained fairly constant whilst satellite subscriptions have doubled to 8 million.

But the real take-off has occurred with the introduction of DTT (Digital Terrestrial Television) that is received through a normal aerial without subscription. From a start in 2000 its take-up has risen sharply to nearly 9 million. Its rate of rise has been nearly four times as fast as satellite, and has by January 2007 overtaken it.

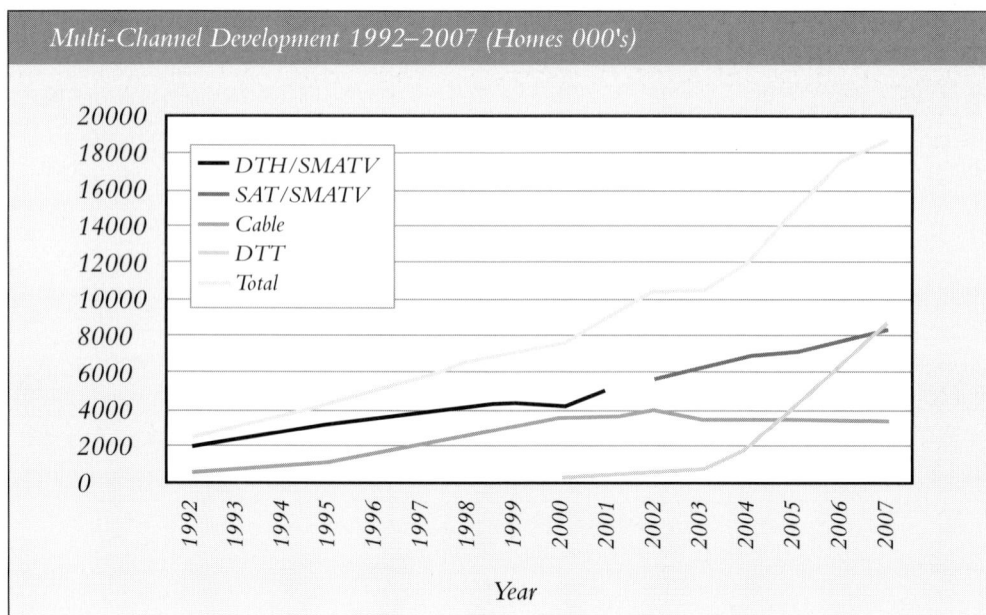

Multi-Channel Development 1992–2007 (Homes 000's)

But none of this takes into account the other reception possibilities of digital television, broadband reception on computers and reception on mobile phones and iPods.

Figures used in this Appendix are published by BARB – The Broadcasters' Audience Research Board Ltd.

BARB (Broadcasters' Audience Research Board), is the organisation that provides in-home TV viewing measurement for the UK. It uses a panel of around 11,500 viewers, representative of the whole UK, recruited from all sectors of the population, distributed across 5,100 homes; recording viewing by residents (and their visitors) on a minute-by-minute basis, including PVR (digital Personal Video Recorders) and VCR (Video Cassette Recorders) playback. All viewing environments in the house are represented, including multiple TV sets, covering both analogue and digital delivery by cable, satellite and terrestrial distribution.

BARB recognises that television distribution platforms in the UK are in a period of modification and in order to be able to accurately measure and report on all future broadcasting platforms and methods of viewing, it has commenced a consultation survey of the TV Industry. It needs to understand and measure the uptake by viewers of various methods of distributing television programmes and the methods available for viewing them, as they develop and become available, so that broadcasters can respond accordingly.

Their very interesting and informative report on the survey, **A View into the Future,** can be viewed from their website, www.barb.co.uk

APPENDIX 2 – THE PURPOSES OF BROADCASTING

From its earliest days, broadcasting was deemed to have a particular quality of character which required it to be dealt with in a different manner to other information communication outlets such as newspapers. Are the public interest in national culture and the integrity of the home as centre of family life and the need to protect and nurture that life in a way quite different to that considered appropriate for the press or other media?

It has been said that the people can choose their governments but they cannot choose their media moguls.

SYKES COMMITTEE

The financial difficulties of the newly set up BBC were considered by the Sykes Committee in 1923. In its conclusions it said:

Broadcasting holds social and political possibilities as great as any attainment of our generation. We consider that the control of such a potential power over public opinion and the life of a nation ought to remain with the State, and that the operation of so important a national service ought not to be allowed to become an unrestricted commercial monopoly.

But it did recommend that the BBC should be independent of government.

HERBERT HOOVER

On 11th March 1924, Herbert Hoover, as Secretary for Commerce addressed the US House of Representatives Hearing before the Committee on the Merchant Marine and Fisheries on the theme 'To Regulate Radio Communication, and for other Purposes' said:

It is not conceivable that the American people will allow this newborn system of communication to fall exclusively into the power of any individual group or combination. We cannot allow any single person or group to place themselves in a position where they can censor the material which shall be broadcast to the public, nor do I believe that the Government should ever be placed in a position of censoring this material.

Radio communication is not to be considered as merely a business carried on for private gain, for private advertisement or for entertainment of the curious. It is a public concern impressed with the public trust and to be considered primarily from the standpoint of public interest to the same extent and upon the basis of the same general principles as our other public utilities.

CRAWFORD COMMITTEE

The recommendations of this committee in 1925 led to the Charter and Licence which created the BBC. It noted that the public property in the airwaves was a valuable national asset which should be used in the general public interest and not for the benefit of powerful or rich interest groups.

LORD REITH

The Crawford Committee recommended that the BBC should:

Act as Trustee for the national interest and that its status and duties should correspond with those of a public service, and the purposes of such a service was not simply to entertain but also to inform and educate. The subjects covered were to be wide, the standards of presentation high, and controversial matters were to be treated impartially. The programmes were to be made available to a vast majority of the population.

John Reith became the BBC's first director-general in 1926. In this position he was adamant that the BBC should become a national broadcaster, allowing news and events that had previously been accessible only to a minority of people, to become an everyday part of British life. He called it 'making the nation as one man.' He also sought to use the BBC for education and improvement, forming strong links with adult education services and firmly inculcating the BBC with its public service ethic.

Lord Reith said that the purposes of broadcasting were to inform, educate and entertain. Broadcasting was to be a service to the public. John Reith was undoubtedly determined to use broadcasting as a means for making a better society. It was under him that the BBC inaugurated the first regular schedule of public television broadcasts in the world, in 1936.

ITV 1955

The BBC, the national broadcaster, as a monopoly, financed by annual fees on receiving equipment, had been both broadcaster and the regulator of its own affairs under its Royal Charter.

The Television Act 1954 was the law which permitted the creation of the first commercial television network in the UK. It created the Independent Television Authority which was to closely regulate the new commercial channel in the interests of 'good taste.' During the extensive debate that took place before the Act came into being, Tory MP John Rogers said that he did not believe that the only people who have good taste resided in Broadcasting House.

So, when ITV started in 1955, its aims were clearly in accord with the Reithian tradition, and basically this is the way things stayed until the late 1980s.

PILKINGTON 1962

In July 1960 the Government set up a Committee under Sir Harry Pilkington to consider the future of broadcasting services in the UK. As commercial television had only been operating for a few years it was an opportunity to review its success or otherwise and put forward ways in which the system could be modified if necessary. It was highly critical of the Independent Television Authority for not being *'in effective control of Independent Television'*, in that it was not keeping itself sufficiently informed of public reaction to commercial television programming. This led to changes that required the ITA to ascertain the state of public opinion concerning the programmes as well as the advertisements.

Chapter III of the Pilkington Committee Report of 1962 discussed the purposes of broadcasting. Its main concern was – what makes good broadcasting? From the evidence and representations submitted to the Committee, it considered the product, then judged the producers, considered as organisations constituted to provide a public service, by reference to it. What it did or did not do was to formulate principles of constitution and organisation first and then apply them to the BBC and independent television.

The Committee recorded that the submissions entered by viewers showed much disquiet and dissatisfaction. The disquiet derived from the view that the power of television to influence and persuade is immense, and that there was a lack of awareness of, or concern about, the consequences. The dissatisfaction sprang from the conviction that many of the best potentialities of television were not being realised.

In discussing the disquiet about television, the Report asked first what the effects of broadcasting were likely to be; it recorded the view of those who gave evidence to the Committee that they were likely to be profound; but it observed that this was opinion and not proven fact – if, indeed, proof was possible. It strongly refuted the argument that, failing proof, the broadcasters could ignore the issue; and concluded that, unless and until there was unmistakable proof to the contrary, the working assumption must be that television in particular would be a potent factor in influencing the values and moral standards of our society.

LORD ANNAN 1977

Lord Annan's Committee on the Future of Broadcasting reported in March 1977. It received submissions from many sources regarding the purposes of broadcasting, amongst which were:

The Standing Conference on Broadcasting suggested that the purpose of broadcasting should be to improve and maintain intellectual, moral, political and cultural health of society.

The Church of England General Synod said that the mainstream of opinion surely holds that the standards reflected in the programmes transmitted by a publicly controlled broadcasting service which is received in people's homes should be higher than the average of those found in contemporary society.

The Nationwide Festival of Light believed that the role of broadcasting was to inform, entertain and yes to give a positive lead to reinforce or set a standard of morality and social behaviour which would uplift and strengthen, not debase and corrupt.

The Committee said that much of what people consider today (1977) as good broadcasting would have been rejected by Lord Reith's definition of that term.

It went on to say that those who advocated a policy of control of broadcasting to make a better society seemed to suppose that social and moral objectives could be formulated, agreed, and then imposed on broadcasters and the population. No doubt they could be in a totalitarian country, but could they, in this democratic country?

They asked, was it part of the broadcasters function to act as arbiters of morals and manners, or to set themselves up as social engineers? In politics, for instance, the broadcasters should not elbow Parliament aside. Parliament was the place where issues were finally decided and political parties the forum where national policies were devised and advocated. The broadcasters' duty is to see that the different policies which purported to solve our problems were given an airing without showing bias to either side.

The Annan Report to some extent endorsed the views of the Pilkington Report of 1962 in that the effect of broadcasting on society could be compared to that of water dripping on a stone, and concluded that, until there was unmistakable proof to the contrary, there must be a presumption that television would have a considerable influence on the moral standards of our society.

The Report noted that:

It seems to us that Governments and Broadcasting Authorities are bound to take note of the facts that many people assume that because broadcasting services are seen and heard in nearly every home, broadcasting is an all-pervading and powerful medium of communication having a direct effect on people's attitudes and behaviour.

It endorsed the objectives for broadcasters of providing entertainment, information and education for large audiences, but proposed an additional one, that of enrichment; to enlarge people's interests, to convey to them new choices and possibilities in life, this is what broadcasting ought to try to achieve.

In conclusion:

In the end someone has to have the responsibility for deciding which aspects of public interest should prevail and what can be broadcast in particular circumstances at any given time. In our view, the ultimate responsibility should rest with the broadcasting authorities, as the mediators between the professional broadcasters and the public. The Authorities are themselves accountable to Parliament for their decisions, and the services they provide, and Parliament itself is accountable to the electorate. This pragmatic solution to a complex problem has stood the test of fifty years of operation, and we consider should be maintained in its essentials. We therefore recommend that broadcasting authorities should continue to be responsible for all broadcasting services and that they should be independent of Government in the day to day conduct of their business.

BROADCASTING ACT 1990

In 1987 the Conservative Party's election Manifesto included proposals to enable broadcasters to take full advantage of the opportunities presented by technological advances and to broaden the choice of viewing and listening. It also promised that there would be stronger and more effective arrangements to reflect perceived public concern over the portrayal of sex and violence in television and radio programmes. The new Conservative Government took the first step by setting up the Broadcasting Standards Council in 1988, to draw up a code on standards of taste, decency and the portrayal of sex and violence in programmes; to monitor programme standards in these areas, to consider complaints from the public and to initiate research into public attitudes.

The Conservative Government's stated objects for the new independent broadcasting regime were the introduction of a fifth channel, and statutory programme requirements to include regional programming, high quality national and international news and current affairs programming, a minimum of 25% of original programming to come from independent producers and a proportion of programmes from the European Community. With regards to regulation, this was to be provided by a new Independent Television Commission which would replace the IBA to licence and supervise all parts of a liberalised commercial television sector. The ITC would have the power to impose tough sanctions, but was intended to operate with a much lighter touch than the IBA.

Mrs Thatcher's government changed things with the Broadcasting Act of 1990. It appeared to be totally and ideologically opposed to the whole notion of public service broadcasting. This was clear from its attitude to the **Death on The Rock** programme produced by Thames Television. The fact that television could presume to question Government actions and find them at fault seemed an affront.

COMMUNICATIONS ACT 2003

The Communications Act of 2003 replaced the ITC with a new regulator, Ofcom, the Office of Communications. Its 'touch' was to be even softer than that of the ITC and its principal duty is to further the interests of citizens in relation to communication matters, and to further the interests of consumers by promoting competition. In doing this it is required to secure the protection to members of the public from:

- The intrusion of offensive and harmful material
- Unfair treatment in programmes
- Unwarranted infringements of privacy

Ofcom also must have regard to:

- The desirability of promoting competition
- The appropriate level of freedom of expression
- The vulnerability of children and others in need of special protection
- The desirability of preventing crime and disorder
- The opinions of consumers
- The different interests in the different parts of the UK, of the different ethnic communities and of persons living in rural and in urban areas

It is required to set standards that:

- Protect persons under the age of eighteen
- Material, likely to encourage or to incite crime or lead to disorder is not included

- News is presented with due impartiality
- News is reported accurately
- The proper degree of responsibility is exercised with respect to the content of religious programmes
- Protect the public from offensive and harmful material
- The prohibition of political advertising
- Prevent misleading, harmful or offensive advertising
- Prevent unsuitable sponsorship
- Prevent undue discrimination between advertisers
- Prevent the use of 'subliminal' advertising

OFCOM – REVIEW OF PUBLIC SERVICE BROADCASTING

Ofcom is determined to go 'back to basics' and to take a fresh look at the underlying rationales for public intervention in the UK communications sector. This exercise provides industry players, and of course the public, with an unusual opportunity to contribute to the regulatory debate.

In the case of the Public Service Broadcasting Review, Ofcom is in effect asking itself and everyone else:

- Why should the public sector intervene in the broadcasting market at all?
- Assuming that intervention is necessary, what form should public intervention take?
- How should the effectiveness of public intervention be measured?

The public purposes of broadcasting are set out in the Communications Act 2003, and comprise 'range and balance', 'diversity', 'quality', and 'social values' (informed democracy; educated citizens; cultural identity). Ofcom is charged with considering how broadcasting can best advance and deliver these purposes.

Ofcom, for the benefit of those in the industry and users alike, wishes to establish the grounds for public intervention in any given market place, as well as the means for assessing the effectiveness of intervention. It wants to engage with those it regulates in order to develop a common understanding and agreement on these issues.

All should welcome this desire for consistency of regulation and transparency. It is an opportunity for people to influence the framework of a new regulatory settlement and the future development of the UK communications industry.

A PUBLIC SERVICE FOR ALL – MARCH 2006

In March 2006 Culture Secretary, Tessa Jowell, published a White Paper on the future of the BBC. The Paper throws light on the current Government's thinking on the purposes of public service broadcasting.

The Culture Secretary said that entertainment should lie at the heart of the BBC, and laid out six new aims for the corporation. These are:

- Sustaining citizenship and civil society
- Promoting education and learning
- Stimulating creativity and cultural excellence, including film
- Reflecting the UK's nations, regions and communities
- Bringing the world to the UK and the UK to the world
- Acting as a 'trusted guide' in building a digital Britain

The BBC's purpose was to offer services that are entertaining and popular, whilst not being derivative or merely chasing ratings, or making programmes solely to tried and tested formulae. All BBC programmes should be at least one of the following things:

- High quality
- Challenging
- Original
- Innovative
- Engaging

Its mainstream programmes should portray and celebrate the diversity of cultures and communities across the UK.

Is this seen to be a return to Lord Reith's vision of using broadcasting as a means of making a better society?

APPENDIX 3 – DIGITAL TELEVISION

CHANGE OVER TO DIGITAL

The Government has announced that it will commence switching off the analogue television broadcasting signals within the next three years, and that the switch over to digital will be completed by 2012. This means that the signals which have provided viewers with a choice of the main five channels BBC1, BBC2, ITV1, CH4 and Five will no longer exist. They will be replaced by digital signals which will provide the same channels and much more besides.

Currently around 70% of households can already receive the digital signals. The satellite subscription service BSkyB has around 8 million subscribers, the Cable subscription providers have around 3 million and the fastest growing provider Freeview has some 9 million. Before the final switch off of the analogue signals all households will have to make arrangements to receive their television signals from one of the above alternative sources.

A recent study has found that some viewers, around 29% would not switch over. Their reasons for not doing so are said to be based upon the following reasons:

- The high cost of necessary equipment, new television sets, set-top boxes and aerials, especially to homes that use more than one television receiver.
- High subscription charges for satellite or cable connections.
- Content with the existing service.
- Too much complication – excess of choice – not interested in interactive television.
- Lack of knowledge about the advantages of digital television.

WHAT IS DIGITAL TELEVISION?

Digital television is a new form of broadcasting, instead of transmitting pictures and sound as analogue signals it turns them into digital signals, similar to computer language. There is no need for the viewer to understand the technical differences between analogue and digital to appreciate and use the advantages it gives. It is likely that not many viewers understand the technology involved in the existing system, but they are quite capable of using it.

Digital Television is good for the viewer, probably better than the changeover from the 405 line system to 625 or the change from black and white to colour. It gives the viewer far greater choice of channels to view and better quality of sound and picture. Because it is a more efficient way of delivering the television signal it enables the same services to be delivered in less space (on the spectrum), several television channels can be carried in the space used by the current analogue system to carry one channel, and with greater clarity.

Not only does the viewer get a greater choice of channels it also means that the television receiver, instead of being a stand alone device is turned into a form of computer so that viewers can interact directly with the programmes in a way not possible before. The system allows much more information to be transmitted giving viewers many benefits, if they wish to use it. For instance a football match, where usually the viewer sees the game through the eyes of the director by his choice of camera shots, can transmit a number of different camera outputs and the viewer can select his own way of viewing the game. BBC Wimbledon coverage already allows a number of different tennis matches to be transmitted at the same time allowing the viewer a choice of matches to watch.

The system does not force these benefits on to the viewer, they are there to use if wanted. The less adventurous viewers, who simply wish to relax in front of the TV and choose between their 'trusty normal' five channels, can still do just that.

HOW TO RECEIVE DIGITAL TELEVISION

The viewer has a choice of ways in which to receive Digital Television:

- Through a normal (or improved) television aerial and a set-top box which converts the digital signals back to analogue to be viewed on an existing television receiver. Twenty five free channels and some 12 pay to view channels. Only initial cost of set-top box and possibly an updated aerial necessary.
- By buying a new updated television receiver with a built in digital tuner.
- By subscribing to a Satellite Digital service. Many different packages available with up to 200 channels – around 80 free to view. Need to buy a package of channels before any channels can be viewed.
- By subscribing to a Cable Digital service. Different packages available with up to 100 channels.
- By viewing on a computer over a broadband connection.

THE BENEFITS OF DIGITAL TELEVISION

The Government says that completing the switch to digital television will bring significant benefits to consumers, to broadcasters and to the UK economy as a whole:

- It will bring digital terrestrial television signals to 25% of the population who live in areas that cannot currently receive them because of spectrum limitations.
- It will give increased quality and choice for viewers.
- Broadcasters will no longer have to incur the costs of transmitting signals in both formats, releasing resources for investment in programming and other services for consumers.
- Spectrum will be released to allow the development of more television and other services for consumers.

INFORMATION LEAFLET

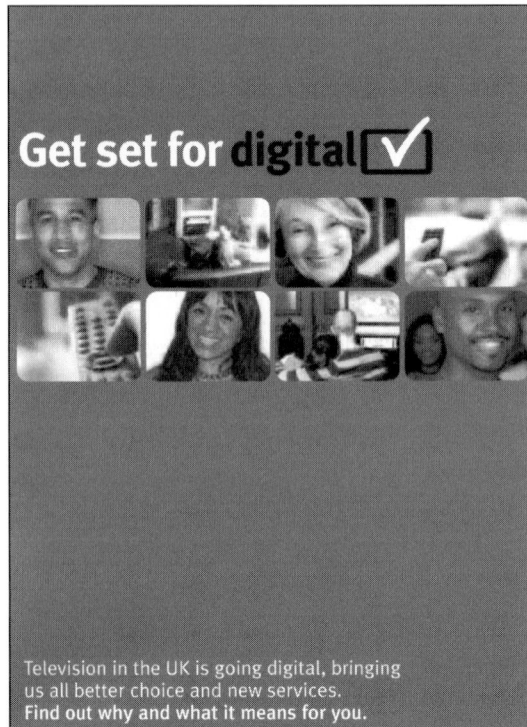

An information leaflet can be downloaded from: www.digitaltelevision.gov.uk

SOURCES AND FURTHER READING

Commercial Television, Wallace S. Sharpe, Fountain Press 1958

Five Years at Your Fireside, ATV 1961.

The Future of Sound Radio & Television Broadcasting, Pilkington Report, 1966 HMSO.

ITV2 – ITA submission to Minister of Posts & Telecomms, ITA, 1971.

Independent Broadcasting Authority – formerly ITA, 1973 HMSO.

Independent Broadcasting Authority Act, 1974, HMSO.

1955–1976 Twenty-one Years of Independent Television, Broadcast, Sept 1976

This is ATV, 1980 ATV.

A Double Eye for a Double Region, 1980 ATV.

ACTION! – Fifty Years in the Life of a Union, 1983 ACTT.

Broadcasting in the 90s, Competition, Choice & Quality, Home Office, 1988 HMSO.

Time to stop playing Monopoly – edited speech, Charles Allen, 2003 RTS.

ITV: The People's Channel Granada Ventures – Reynolds & Hearn Ltd, Simon Cherry, 2005.

Charles Allen, Management Today, 2006.

Make TV Local, Philip Reevell, 2006 RTS.

WEB SITES

- ATV Centre
  http:/www.sub-tv.co.uk
- Band II Convertors
  http:/www.thevalvepage.com/tv
- BARB
  http:/www.barb.co.uk
- Deregulation, Franchises, The Future – 1980s Perspective
  http:/website.lineone.net/~tv-research
- Digital Television
  http:/en.wikpedia.org/wiki/Digital_television
- Getting Digital Television
  http:/www.digitaltelevision.gov.uk

- Guide to Carlton – History
  http:/production.investis.com/carltoncomms/ccomm_history1
- History of UK Television
  http:/freespace.virgin.net/peter.cullen/history.htm
- ITV at Fifty – The Network that Trashed Itself
  http:/www.transdiffusion.org/emc/itv50
- ITV plc
  http:/www.itvplc.com
- Ofcom – Review of Public Service Television Broadcasting
  http:/www.ofcom.org.uk

There are many sites on the internet dealing with all aspects of Television Broadcasting. Searching for a particular topic can be daunting, a search on the single word 'Television' will provide over 43 million sites; 'Television Broadcasting' will give about 1.5 million and 'Television Broadcasting History' some 350,000.

A good place to start is a site called Answers.com, described as the world's greatest encyclodictionaimanacapedia™.

NAME INDEX

INDEX